Understanding organized notes is the prototype of learning.

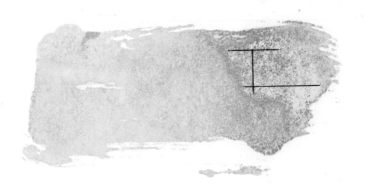

ORGANIZING
AND MEMORIZING

ORGANIZING
AND MEMORIZING

Studies in the
Psychology of Learning
and Teaching

By GEORGE KATONA

(Facsimile of 1940 Edition)

HAFNER PUBLISHING COMPANY
New York and London
1967

Originally published 1940
Reprinted 1967

Printed and published by
HAFNER PUBLISHING COMPANY, INC.
31 East 10th Street
New York, N.Y. 10003

Library of Congress Catalog Card No.: 67-20563

© Copyright 1940, Columbia University Press, New York

Printed in U.S.A. by
NOBLE OFFSET PRINTERS, INC.
NEW YORK 3, N. Y.

FOREWORD

WHAT ARE the essentials of learning?

Every good teacher enjoys teaching and learning when really sensible learning takes place: when eyes are opened, when real grasping, real understanding occurs, when the transition takes place from blindness or inaptness to orientation, understanding, mastery; and when, in the course of such happenings, mind develops.

Experimental psychological investigations of learning have for the most part taken a direction foreign to these issues. Repetition, drill, has become the focus of investigations; the very concept of learning—the idea of what learning is—seems now for many psychologists to be centered essentially in the feature of repetition, of memorizing. Teachers are often seriously puzzled when they realize that memorizing series of nonsense syllables is taken, broadly, as the appropriate material for establishing *the* laws of learning.

Historically various factors have brought this about. I mention some. First: Drill is used in school teaching. Although the range of its use has changed through the centuries, it is emphasized that after all we have to learn such things as the alphabet, have to memorize not-understood or not-understandable aggregations, so-called "memory-stuff." Second: In certain developments of philosophy and psychology the assumption has been made that forming connections of this kind (connections between arbitrarily aggregated items or data) is *the* essential issue for learning; there is the belief—or the hope—that learning of sensible material is nothing but a complication of such connections. Third: Another important factor developed with the aim to make psychology scientific in terms of quantitative, exact investigations in experiments in which all the elements were controllable. To this end the use of nonsense syllables, mazes, and similar material, that is, of arbitrary aggregates of items, seemed technically ideal in contrast to the much more difficult problems involved in other kinds of learning. The possibility of reaching clear-cut, exact, quantitative laws in a comparatively easy way, added weight to the general assumption.

The very first idea of gestalt psychology involved the confrontation of sensible structures with senseless aggregations. Scientifically, by studying structural features, it put the problem whether or not it is appropriate to view sensible structures as sheer products of and-summative aggregations. Contrasting the senseless and the sensible, gestalt psychology envisaged senseless aggregations as a special rather than the general case—the case in which inner-correlatedness, sensible structural whole-qualities, approach zero (and which, psychologically, may be not nearly so simple as supposed).

Methods were developed, tools of scientific approach, which opened the way to structural features, features other than and-summation and repetition. They led to a reunderstanding of what grasping is, what understanding is, and what it requires—in perception, in learning, in other fields of psychology.

Dr. George Katona who was for years connected with G. E. Mueller, a master of associationism, in the psychological institute of Goettingen, and who continued his research at the universities of Frankfort and Berlin, and the New School for Social Research, New York, has taken up some of the problems involved, studying learning in quantitative experimentation with regard to differences in retention and application, employing gestalt methods and the technique of transfer as developed by American psychologists.

Dr. Katona makes use of the fact that there are not only senseless and sensible materials to be learned but that sensible material may be learned with or without real structural understanding, which makes direct quantitative comparison possible in measurements of results of learning.

Although for reasons of experimental technique Dr. Katona chose for his main quantitative experiments certain topics which are outside the realm of school teaching and which do not in themselves represent the ideal of sensible material, I have no doubt that his results and discussions will be of vital interest to the psychologist and to the educator. The goal of the psychology of learning is not only to clarify theoretical issues but also to find ways of improving teaching and learning. This book will be of help in this task.

MAX WERTHEIMER

New School for Social Research
New York, February 26, 1940

ACKNOWLEDGMENTS

THE RESEARCHES reported in this book were made possible by a grant from the Carnegie Corporation of New York, for which I hereby express my gratitude.

This investigation into the theory of learning could not have been carried out without making use of the approach to psychology developed by Wertheimer, Köhler, and Koffka, which is called gestalt psychology. The critical reader will be able to discern for himself to what extent the author is indebted to the investigations published and the theories formulated by gestalt psychologists during the past twenty years. However, because of extraneous circumstances Professor M. Wertheimer's psychological lectures and his researches on "productive thinking" have not yet been brought before the public. The theory of thinking and the theory of learning are intimately connected. I have been able to use Wertheimer's basic concepts in my research, especially those concerning the nature and the role of sensible processes in contrast to senseless processes and those concerning the role of structure in understanding, and I want to express here my deeply felt thanks to Professor Wertheimer.

I owe also sincere thanks to several professors and instructors in the College of the City of New York (uptown and downtown branches), Brooklyn College, New School for Social Research, and Newark University, who kindly permitted the use of their classes for experiments, and to several hundred college students, colleagues, and friends who served as subjects in the experiments. My most pleasant duty is to thank my wife for her valuable assistance in the experiments and in preparing the manuscript.

In these times I cannot lay down my pen without expressing my gratitude to the country in which this work was done and in which scientific research flourishes in the atmosphere of freedom and democracy. The development that is this book is due not least to the spiritual stimulation I have encountered here.

GEORGE KATONA

New York
December 28, 1939

CONTENTS

ORGANIZING
AND MEMORIZING

Chapter I

THE FIELD OF RESEARCH

THE TOPIC of this investigation is human learning. Since learning is a process that leads to definite results, it may be investigated from two different angles. We may investigate it by taking the results or by taking the processes involved as our point of departure. There is a greater measure of agreement about the results or effects of learning than about the nature of the processes. The result of learning is that past experience can be put to subsequent use. Learning enables us to utilize experience—to profit from experience. If a performance is better than a previous performance —that it is merely different is not sufficient—and if, moreover, the improvement is due to the effects of the previous process, then we call the previous process "learning."

The formulation just set forth has the advantage of being so general that it does not exclude any important instance of learning, which is often done when certain qualities of the learning process rather than its results are taken as the essential criteria of learning. But reference to the utilization of past experience does not help to answer the most important questions. How do we learn? Is the learning process always the same, or does it differ according to the nature of the material learned and the ability of the learner, or are there fundamentally different kinds of learning?

The most commonly accepted theory of learning identifies the learning process with forming and strengthening connections. This leads to the question: what do we connect when we learn? The answer has undergone changes in the development of psychology. Today it is more usual to speak of an association between stimuli and responses than of an association between ideas or between contents. Learning is assumed to consist of forming and strengthening connections or bonds between stimuli and responses—no matter whether it is learning a list of words in a foreign language, learning to dance, or learning a new theory in physics. The learning process is often said to be fundamentally the same whether the learner is an animal, a child, or an adult; whether the task is attempted by an inmate of an insane asylum or a student of mathematics.

Certain differences in learning have, of course, always been recognized, namely, those between learning nonsense material and "logical learning." At this point it is sufficient to state that the differences are usually held to be quantitative. It has not been generally admitted that a basic qualitative difference exists between slow accretion by repetition and acquisition of knowledge by a flash of insight, or between mechanical fixation of habits and the understanding of a complicated matter. It is held to be true that in all these instances two contents previously unconnected become connected in such a way that the reappearance of one content tends to evoke the second. The number of connections and the number of contents connected may differ, but not the quality of the connection itself. The word "connect" would thus describe the same physiological, psychophysical, and psychological processes regardless of whether we speak of connecting the nonsense syllables "kem" and "fap" (by saying three times "kem-fap") or of connecting two consecutive steps of a dance (by performing them according to the example of a teacher). Connection is said to become more complicated in order to acquire knowledge of Einstein's theory, but its character would not change fundamentally.

Undoubtedly the theory just described is not the only possible theory of learning. Without discussing for the moment the various theories which have been proposed to explain the learning process, we may say simply that it is logically possible to assume that there are two different kinds of learning, or five, or many more. It is also possible to assume that there is a unitary learning process, but that it differs from the association bond between two nonsense syllables. Our first task, however, is not to decide whether or not there are different kinds of learning or to decide which theory of the basic forms of learning is correct. The main objection to the prevailing theory, which makes one kind of connection the basis of all learning, is not that it may be incorrect, but that in the course of psychological research it has prevented an unbiased study of other possible kinds of learning. Our first objective, therefore, is to know more about the nature of what we may call the complicated learning process, which according to common sense and judging by educational practice appears to be described rather poorly as the establishment of a connection or a bond between a stimulus and a response.

Distinction between Meaningful and Senseless Learning

A procedure that has often proved fruitful for scientific progress is to assume that a given general and fundamental proposition is incorrect. What would be the consequences of starting anew by asserting that there are different processes of learning? Suppose we dare to forget for a moment the theory that to learn is to form and to strengthen connections. Let us ignore all its achievements in understanding animal and human learning and in giving a unified and consistent picture of the working of the mind. Let us not search for this or that flaw in the structure of the old theory or weigh the empirical and logical arguments in favor of or against its principles, and let us abstain from criticism. Instead, in order to clarify our line of thinking, we shall proceed from a positive assumption of a different kind. Let us say: there are two kinds of learning. Connections established by the conditioned-reflex technique or by repeating the same contents or responses over and over again, as in all forms of drill, are characteristic of one kind of learning. Then we draw a thick dividing line. On the other side of the barrier we find processes of learning that are described by expressions such as "apprehension of relations," "understanding of a procedure," "insight into a situation." In order to complete this as-yet-unproved differentiation we may go one step further and affix on both sides of the barrier undefined but at least unmistakable labels. "Senseless" may be written on one side of the line where there is the depository of connections, and "meaningful" on the other side, where the achievement brought about by learning may be called understanding. Our assumption then is that the processes described by these labels differ from each other in the sense that the laws and rules of one do not apply to the other. Is there a way to prove or to disprove this assumption?

The first step from our new point of departure is this: if the two kinds of learning differ from each other they must yield different results. Empirical evidence of significant differences in a few, in many, or in all results of the two different ways of learning would make it probable that different fundamental laws of learning exist. We shall thus start our investigation of learning by examining the results and shall expect later to characterize the processes involved.

How can we compare the results of different learning processes? The first possible approach, the application of the well-known distinction between various materials of learning, is not satisfactory. Memorization of nonsense syllables, verbatim learning of lists of words and of poems, acquisition of skills, logical learning of a meaningful text, understanding of a principle—to name but a few of the many topics of investigation into learning—all yield different results. But can we compare the results of memorizing a a list of words with the results of understanding a mathematical principle? The difficulty is that we can hardly expect comparable results from the learning of different materials. What we must do, therefore, is to apply the different methods of learning to the *same* materials. Suppose we achieve our aim. Suppose we can learn A in a senseless way by forming the connection a-b-c, without understanding why and how a, b, and c are connected. Suppose, too, that we can learn the same A in a meaningful way by understanding A. Then it would be important to decide whether the effects of the two learning methods are the same or not and to determine the causes of any difference.

We may state the conditions for comparing the results of the two learning methods by devising the following experimental set-up:

Stage I	*Stage II*	*Stage III*
Not knowing A or being unable to perform A	Application of learning method I Application of learning method II	Knowing A or being able to perform A

Both methods, the senseless and the meaningful, ought to be methods of learning; therefore, by definition they should enable the learner to profit from the experience represented in the above scheme by Stage II. One might believe that different learning effects cannot occur under such circumstances, since both methods should lead to the same Stage III. Fortunately this conclusion is unwarranted, inasmuch as it is due to a concealed and incorrect assumption. There is not just one learning effect, but there are recognizable many different learning effects. Suppose Stage II follows immediately after Stage I, and Stage III immediately after Stage II. Then we may perform our experiment by making Stage I and Stage III identical for both methods. That means that the two different learning methods should be applied to the same material in such a way as to ensure immediately after the learning period the same degree of knowledge or the same ability to perform a task. Thus the comparability of the two learning methods is assured. But what happens if we distinguish between a Stage III*a* and a Stage III*b* by testing the knowledge of A immediately after Stage II and again four weeks later? Will the results remain the same, or will they differ on the two occasions? This must be determined by experiment, and the results will be discussed later. At present it should suffice that we have found one field in which we can compare the effects of two different learning methods, the field of *retention,* especially of long-span remembering.

Notwithstanding our requirement that the results of both learning methods must be comparable, they may differ in some respects other than amount and quality of retention. Learning effects vary greatly. It is possible that practicing A will result in some ability to perform B, C, and D (letters which represent tasks more or less related to A). Then we may compare the effect of the different learning methods on B, C, and D, asking whether or not there are differences in amount and quality of transfer of training. Such a comparison can be made immediately after the learning period, as well as on later occasions. *Applicability* of what has been learned may thus serve as the second field of investigation.

Ability to remember or to perform a task after the passage of some time and ability to apply the knowledge under different circumstances are two effects of the various learning methods which we propose to compare. Our selection of these topics is not due simply to the requirement that we need comparable experimental sets. Learning, or at least learning worthy of the name, should not only be measured by the achievement immediately after the practice period and under the same conditions. For example, I learn a short poem by reading it a few times and can recite it immediately after the fifth reading. Or I learn to find the square root of 157 on a slide rule by being shown three times where to place the indicator and which scales to compare, and I am then able to find the square root of 157 without any assistance. These tests do not suffice to determine the real learning effects. Retention appears to be a good test of my first learning process: can I recite the poem a week or four weeks later? Applicability appears to be an adequate test of the second learning process: can I find the square roots or the squares of numbers other than those which I have practiced? The tests applicability and retention may be combined: can I find the square root of numbers other than 157 four weeks later? Thus the two criteria of learning which will be primarily investigated are apparently of great practical as well as theoretical importance. By establishing the fact that in these two respects the results differ we may hope to arrive at the fundamental theoretical implications of the various learning processes.

These considerations will serve as the general background for the experimental investigations to be reported in this book. But at first we must proceed more cautiously by considering a few questions about the hypothetical assumptions which formed our starting point. Is it possible to apply various kinds of learning to the same materials, and do those learning processes which we have allocated to opposite sides of a barrier really differ from each other? For it is possible that in spite of different learning effects obtained by different kinds of learning the dividing line is not insurmountable and we have investigated only two of a large number of learning processes, between which there is a continuous transition.

A Preliminary Experiment

An experimental study of the nature of the learning process should begin with a description of an experiment. We shall start with a simple experiment, not intended to prove the point, but only to present a preliminary survey of the field which is to be studied later.

In order to show how different learning methods may be applied to the same learning material we begin by investigating the memorizing process of a material frequently used in psychological experiments. Let us not refer now to "higher mental processes," but let us ask the simple question: is it possible to learn a list of digits by different methods? If so, are the learning effects the same in all cases?

Three classes, each consisting of ten adults, were asked to learn a series of twelve digits.

Members of the first class were instructed as follows: "I will show you a list of digits. Read it slowly three times so that you can recite it afterward. For example: if the numbers are 390714 628, then you read 'three hundred and ninety, seven hundred and fourteen,' and so forth." After this introduction the subjects were presented with a card on which the following figures were typed: 581215192226. The subjects read as if 581 215 192 226 had been typed. Immediately after the learning period nine out of ten adult subjects were able to recall the series without a mistake.

Subjects belonging to the second class were instructed as follows: "I will show you a list of digits. Read it slowly three times in order to know it completely and precisely." The subjects were first presented with a card on which was typed: "The Federal expenditures in the last year amounted to $ . . . " Then followed the presentation of a second card containing the figures. This time the card differed from that presented to Class 1, in that a decimal point [1] was added between the tenth and eleventh figures: 5812151922.26.

Subjects who were permitted to use a pencil immediately made three small signs and read: 5 billion, 812 million, 151 thousand, 922 dollars, and 26 cents. Those who were not permitted to use a pencil read the figure in the same way, but more slowly. Their immediate reproduction was slightly worse than that of Class 1 (which also was not allowed to use a pencil). Mistakes were too few, however, to establish the differences in the results in a reliable way.[2]

As emphasized before, learning cannot and must not be measured by the results of immediate recall alone. One week after the learning period five members of each class, who had made no mistakes in immediate recall, were asked, "Do you still remember the numbers learned a week ago?" Members of Class 1 considered this question unfair. The typical objection was that they were not told they would be asked to recite the figures after a lapse of time. When a reconstruction test was made, by asking the subjects to write one figure in each of twelve empty squares, the best result was five correct figures (not consecutive) and seven errors.

Members of the second class showed no resentment. "I learned that the expenditures of the government were 5.8 billions," was the prompt answer of the first subject. Two others gave the same answer, referring, however, to the deficit instead of the expenditures of the government. But when I asked them to recall the exact amount of the expenditures, they, too, were indignant, and they made many mistakes. Yet, even if the mistakes were calculated in the way described above (which makes a mistake of one dollar

---

[1] The point is a slight blemish on the experiment, but it is reasonable to assume that it does not affect the comparability of the classes.

[2] Quantitative results of such an experiment will be given in Chapter VII. Here it should suffice to point out that the experiments would have to be made in a different way if the intention were to study the question of immediate recall. Then the learning period might consist of one single reading, or the series might be longer. In the cases described here the difference in the results is qualitative rather than quantitative: the kind of mistake made differs in the two classes.

as important as a mistake of one billion dollars), the members of Class 2 made a somewhat better performance than those of Class 1. Measuring the results of the second test in a different way, we find that four of the five subjects recalled that the expenditures exceeded 5 billion, 810 million. This performance was obviously far superior to that of the subjects in Class 1.[3]

Subjects belonging to the third class were instructed simply to "try to learn the following series." Then the same card was presented as to the first class. Some of the subjects began to read 58 12 15, and so forth, hesitated for a moment, and then showed signs of understanding, of surprise, and of pleasure. They noticed a certain regularity embracing the groups 12 15 19, and so forth. Two subjects went further; they divided the first group (58) into two parts, and now the regularity embraced the entire series:

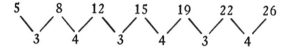

The difference between 5 and 8 is 3; the difference between the following two groups is 4; the next, 3; then, again, 4; and so forth. Once that was discovered, the card was returned to the experimenter. No repetition was required; having discovered the principle, the subjects were able to recite the series without error. The recitation was somewhat slower than it had been by subjects of the first two classes. But the greatest variation of results was obtained when retention was tested a week later. With very few exceptions all members of the third class who found the principle during the learning period were able to recite the series without a single mistake—an achievement exceeding by far that of any members of the other classes.[4]

In order to learn about the nature of the mistakes, five subjects

---

[3] Recollection of the fact that the amount of Federal expenditures was learned was assisted by experience gained outside the learning period of our experiment. But the knowledge "5 billions" cannot be attributed to previous or outside experience, because in reality the Federal expenditures in the fiscal year prior to the experiment were somewhat more than 8 billions, and the deficit more than 4 billions.

[4] For quantitative results see p. 189.

who had a perfect record in the first test were asked four weeks later whether they could recall the series. Three subjects remembered correctly that there were gaps of 3 and 4 alternately between the groups but found it difficult to remember how the series started and with which figure it ended. At last, one subject decided that the first figure was 5, another that it was 8; the continuation was correct in both cases. The third subject began with 7 and continued 10 14 17 . . . Most of the figures given by this subject were "incorrect," that is, they were not the figures in the original series, which the subject professed to recall. Nevertheless, we cannot say that the subject forgot "everything," that he no longer showed any effect of the learning period. We must distinguish between him and an imaginary subject, who after starting with 7 would write 890123 or any other random combination of figures. The comparison of each figure in the "remembered" series with the corresponding figure in the original series is unfair, because it does not reveal whether or not the principle is remembered. The third subject retained the principle perfectly, but transposed the individual numbers.[5] A fourth subject showed an example of recollection of a somewhat lower order. Four weeks after the learning period he began correctly with 5 and proceeded 7 10 12 15, saying that there were gaps of 2 and 3. Here, again, is a performance of memory. The subject knew several important characteristics of the principle: that the numbers which separated the groups were alternating; that the gaps were of two sizes (not one or three); that the number representing the second gap was one higher than the first; and so forth. Thus we have an example of transposition—this time not of figures, but of certain moments of the principle. At this point, however, we are not interested in the qualities of transposition. We have to note only that the mistakes made by members

---

[5] The concept of transposition as used in the text is a fundamental concept in gestalt theory, one of the characteristics of a gestalt (or of most gestalts) being that it can be (and often is) transposed. We recognize a melody if it is played in a key other than that in which we originally heard it (and in reproducing a melody we often use a different key), which means that the melody is remembered, not the specific notes or the original key. It is similar in our number series: the reproduced series may begin with a number other than 5, but the series, based on the new starting point, remains structurally the same as the original series.

of Class 3 differed entirely from those made by members of the other classes.

Heretofore we have dealt only with subjects who found the principle of the series without assistance. Discovering a principle is a very important part of learning, and we shall discuss its role later. But for the achievement just described, finding the principle without assistance is only a special case. If on presentation of the series the principle is explained to a subject (that is, if he is told of the alternating gaps of 3 and 4 between the groups), the same results may be obtained. Five subjects who were told of the principle were able to recall the series perfectly a week after the learning period.

Is the learning process of Class 3 the same as that of the other classes? Even a superficial examination will reveal significant differences. We shall state summarily the characteristics of the learning process of Class 3, disregarding the fact that they are derived from only a single experiment. What characterizes the learning results which are due to finding a principle embracing the entire subject matter?

1. *Retention* lasts for a long period of time. Forgetting does not begin immediately after the memorizing period and does not accelerate within a few hours as is commonly asserted; the curve of retention seems to run quite differently.

2. Learning is possible without *repetition* of the series. No repetition of the series was necessary when the principle was discovered by the subject (or when it was told to the subject), although without knowledge of the principle repetition was necessary.

3. The answers of Class 3 were given with greater *certainty* than those of Classes 1 and 2. When the experimenter, in later tests, suggested that the fifth number should be 3 instead of 1, members of Class 3, sure that he was wrong, refused to modify their statement.

4. "Reproduction" is not necessarily the exact repetition of all the items; transpositions and altered order may also reveal effects of the learning period. The *variability* and flexibility of reproduction, however, are not unlimited. Their range, which is

dependent on the principle, will have to be studied. This characteristic leads us to two other qualities inherent in the series of numbers as learned by Class 3 in contradistinction to the two other classes.

a) An altered series can be *corrected*. Experiments made by changing the series and asking the subjects to correct it showed that those who knew the principle could readily do so, while members of Classes 1 and 2 were able to correct only a few individual items (which they happened to remember). If a subject of Class 3 should reproduce 5 8 13 15, it would indicate not only that he had forgotten the fourth group but also that the fourth group was not in agreement with the other groups and with the principle of the series.

b) The series can be *continued*. To ask the subjects to continue the series has different meanings in the various classes. In Class 1 it means to ask for arbitrary additions, whereas in Class 3 it means a reasonable demand to which the subjects conform by applying a consistent principle (by saying 29 33, and so forth).

Later we shall study the qualities which seem to distinguish the learning process of the third class from other forms of learning. For the moment we ask: what would be the most common explanation of the differences in the learning processes of our three classes? We usually think of "relations" when the question arises as to causes of long retention, quick learning, great certainty, and variability of reproduction. But reference to relations alone is not a sufficient explanation. Not all aggregrates of relation between various parts of the learning material change the learning process in the manner described. Let us suppose that our list of digits is learned by a telephone operator who has had much practice in learning groups of four figures. She grasps first the number 5812, in which the difference between the first two figures is the same as the sum of the last two figures. Then 1519, which is an easy telephone number, the second half being larger by four than the first. Then 2226 (three times two are six). By learning in this way the telephone operator uses relations, but these relations are not of quite the same order as the relations we have in mind. By relating some of the digits to each other, the telephone operator may be able to reproduce the numbers after a long time, to correct the numbers if they are stated incorrectly, and to do so with great assurance; but by remembering the relation of the digits in one group of numbers to one another (for example, the first four numbers) she cannot recall the whole series. Moreover, she will not be able to continue the series.

The interrelations discovered by Class 3 are distinguished from other possible relations as follows: (*a*) the relations comprise consistently the entire series, and (*b*) the whole or its principle determines its parts. The second quality indicates the main difference between the grouping by Class 3 and the other forms of grouping. If one part is missing, it can be *derived* from the other parts on the basis of the principle of the whole. Knowledge of the principle enables one to construct the individual items. There is no arbitrary connection between two neighbors, but they complement each other by inner necessity.[6]

We began by reporting the results of a simple experiment in learning a list of digits in several ways. We then abandoned the cautious experimental attitude and attempted to describe as a preliminary step the main features of a learning process having characteristics unlike those disclosed by the usual conditions of drill. This description will be referred to in later endeavors to determine the nature of "meaningful learning." At present we shall inquire whether the number experiment enables us to answer our specific question: is it possible to apply different learning methods to the same series of figures?

[6] The concept of inner necessity or "requiredness," in contrast to arbitrariness, is used here as it has been developed by Wertheimer (104, p. 57 f., also 103, p. 181 ff.). Inner necessity is connected in these publications with the concept "meaningful," and the distinction between sensible and senseless processes. (Wertheimer's definition of "meaningfulness" will be described in Chapter X.) A more detailed description is given in Wertheimer's paper on ethics (108, p. 360 ff.), where determination in a blind way is contrasted with determination by the demands of the situation. What the situation requires, what is appropriate to the structure (cf. p. 19, below) is again connected with the concepts "sensible," "logical," and "ethical." "Requiredness" is the central concept of Köhler's *The Place of Value in a World of Facts* (46). The numbers in citations to publications refer to the numbered Bibliography, p. 307.

Apparently we can, for we found different methods of learning, which brought about different results. We compared the learning of a series of figures by rote with the learning of the series based on the understanding of a principle. Retention of the figures after the lapse of one week or more appeared to be the most suitable field for comparison, and in this field vastly different learning effects were noticeable.

The methods of learning applied in the various classes differed. The subjects behaved differently; they did one thing in one class and something else in another. But may we still speak of one series if in the first case the series consists of figures, in the second case of an amount in dollars, both having been repeated several times with the intention of learning, while in the third case the series was comprehended as being governed by a principle? It may be maintained that doing different things with the same material makes the material different. In what respect methods of learning and materials of learning are interdependent is an interesting question which will be studied in further experiments. In some of these experiments instead of dealing with the same materials, we shall set the same tasks for different groups of subjects, who will be taught to solve them by several methods. In other experiments the instructions concerning the learning material or its "environment" will differ. In all these experimental approaches we shall attempt to find out how different learning processes influence and change the materials to be learned and the effects of the learning.

A further question asked before describing the foregoing experiment was whether the differences between the learning methods were insurmountable. Is it apparent that we must still distinguish sharply between forming arbitrary connections on the one hand and apprehending inherent interrelations on the other? By emphasizing the qualities of the learning process of the third class we have presented arguments in favor of such a distinction. Yet there were similarities as well as differences in the learning processes of the three classes. It is significant that *grouping* was used in every learning process. As shown on the following page, three kinds of grouping occurred; but there was no learning without grouping.

Class 1: 581 215 192 226
Class 2: 5 812 151 922 26
Class 3: 5 8 12 15 19 22 26

Is the method of grouping irrelevant, or does it essentially affect the learning process? We found that the learning effect varies according to the grouping. The grouping by Class 2 facilitated the retention of number 5 (5 billions), whereas the grouping by Class 3 facilitated the retention of the fact that there are alternating differences. These examples suggest that the groups exert influence on their components. We may then proceed to the generalization that grouping influences learning. This will have to be re-examined later.

How is grouping determined? We can answer this question by referring to the foregoing experiment. Grouping was determined in Class 1 by an arrangement suggested by the experimenter; in Class 2 by habit; in Class 3 by qualities inherent in the material itself.

The grouping resorted to may be caused by any one of a number of factors. A certain kind of grouping may be arrived at by chance alone. Such grouping is similar to that used in Class 1, because whether the grouping is accidental or whether it is arranged by the experimenter or the teacher, the manner in which the material is grouped remains arbitrary. The way in which the material is presented will appear as a further cause of grouping: a series containing three numbers in red, three numbers in black, three numbers in yellow, and so forth, is "automatically" grouped according to the arrangement of these colors, just as habit leads us to group an amount of money in thousands, millions, and billions.

Is grouping for purposes of memorizing elicited only by special circumstances or will it arise in all cases because of chance, habit, suggestion, or superficial arrangement? In order to answer this question we shall undertake to study in Chapter VII the literature dealing with the traditional memory experiments. We shall find that grouping has laws which are operative even in case of rote learning of nonsense syllables.

At this point we are not yet ready to analyze in detail the processes for which our first two classes served as examples, and which may be described as the forming and the strengthening of connections. Yet the possibility that the same mechanism operates in all methods of learning must be recognized, since it was found that grouping is an essential part of learning in all phases of our experiment. Instead of assuming that there are two entirely different kinds of learning we may therefore form the hypothesis that there may be a continuous series of many different methods of learning. At one extreme we may find rudimentary grouping, where the grouping is arbitrary and artificial and the influence exerted by the whole on the parts relatively weak. No one form of grouping chosen because of external influences (chance, command, and so forth) is more adequate than any other. We may then find other methods of learning in which the grouping becomes less arbitrary. In such cases grouping may be due to the arrangement of the material, and in yet other instances to a principle. We shall find reason to speak of *adequate* and of *inadequate* grouping, because the groups may or may not correspond to the requirements of the material. Judging by Class 2, certain parts may be emphasized and others neglected by the grouping process. At the other extreme the parts may be not only influenced by but determined by the whole: in Class 3 the parts could be derived from the principle. Should this description be found appropriate, our task would be to compare the results of learning by a learning method near to one extreme of the series with another near the mid-point and a third near the other extreme.

In addition to the quantitative measurement of the learning effects, with special regard to the curve of retention and the possibility of applying the knowledge gained, the investigation thus obtains a further objective—the qualitative analysis of the different methods of learning. We have found that grouping is a part of the learning process in many different cases. It follows that grouping in itself does not suffice to explain the special kind of learning described in Class 3. Where else may we look for a principle explaining the course taken by that learning? Memorizing the following series of figures may help us to find the way: 14916253649

. . . This series can be grouped (*a*) arbitrarily as 14 91 62 53 64 . . . or (*b*) according to a principle (the square of the consecutive numerals) 1 4 9 16 25 36 49 . . .

The square series may help us to understand the concept of adequate grouping. In the first alternative the grouping is inadequate; in the second it is adequate. Why? The preliminary answer is that a simple structural principle is apparent in the second case, while in the first it is not. In the first case grouping proceeds in violation of that structural principle, while in the second case grouping is appropriate to it. The learning effects differ, just as they differed when the series 5812 . . . was grouped in various ways. Therefore, not grouping as such, but a special kind of grouping forms the explanation for the learning process which is to be distinguished from drill and memorizing. Learning may take place by organizing or grouping the material adequately. This is possible if there exists an intrinsic relationship of the parts to the whole and if the organization of the material serves to make that relationship apparent.

This formula must be taken as provisional. One of the main tasks of the investigation to follow will be to clarify the role of organization in the learning process. The example of the "square numbers" was, moreover, introduced in order to point to a second problem. With regard to the difference between learning a series of digits by rote and a series arranged according to a principle, the latter example may suggest an explanation which runs counter to our whole line of argument. It suggests that past experience is the cause of adequate organization. This counterargument may be presented as follows:

It has been shown—an opponent may argue—that there is a difference between senseless and meaningful materials of learning. This is not new. Many well-known experiments tend to show that nonsense syllables are more difficult to learn than a series of unconnected words; the latter in turn causes greater difficulty than words in a context; while it is much less difficult to learn a meaningful text. Researchers did not stop with describing the differences between materials, but proceeded to explain them.

They were traced to differences in the subjects with regard to the amount of prior learning, knowledge, and experience. The series 1 4 9 16 25 36 . . . is much easier to learn than a series of random figures. This is due to our prior knowledge. We have learned that $1 \times 1 = 1$; $2 \times 2 = 4$; $3 \times 3 = 9$; and so forth, and in learning the new series we are able to utilize that previous learning. When we first learned $2 \times 2 = 4$ we used the same type of connection as in learning a senseless series. The differences between senseless and meaningful material are differences of complexity due to various degrees of generalization.

The main question to be investigated in the next few chapters is: what are the essential differences between meaningful methods of learning and the formation of senseless connections? In attempting to find these differences we shall inquire also into the problem raised by the counterargument: is it true that it is easier to learn in a meaningful way than to pile up connections, because in meaningful learning we are able to utilize previously acquired knowledge? It will appear that, not learning more or learning less, but learning in a different way is required in order to achieve lasting retention, great certainty, and that flexibility of knowledge which permits its application under varying circumstances.

In this way we shall proceed gradually, devising experiments intended to throw light on the role of past experience. But not until the end of this inquiry will we be able to attempt to refute in a specific way the argument that meaningful methods of learning differ from senseless methods only in that the former make use of a great number of connections piled up by habit. First we must arrive at a better understanding of what meaningful learning is.

Historical Background

The starting point of this study has been described in the foregoing pages without reference to specific investigators and their theories. We proceeded in that way in order to present the possible extreme approaches and to differentiate between them sharply. In fact, the actual theories of many scholars are modified to some extent by concessions to other viewpoints. But the lack of reference to other authors in the preceding pages should not imply that the views to be developed in this book are uninfluenced by previous investigations. Science is a coöperative undertaking. Each new research merely adds another small building block to the edifice that constitutes the entire knowledge in a scientific field. Some blocks, of course, serve an "ornamental" purpose only or go into outlying wings, while others replace outworn blocks in the main building or its foundation. Whatever is the goal of an individual research worker, he is helped in his endeavors by using most of the other blocks in the edifice, even the outworn stones he attempts to replace as well as the solid and serviceable ones.

A sketch of the historical background of an investigation can hardly be made complete. The enumeration of a great number of similar or only slightly differing studies and theories would serve no useful purpose and perhaps would mar the clearness of the final picture. Moreover, the researches relating to several specific problems in this investigation will be reviewed in their proper places in the following chapters. This applies above all to our two main problems, transfer of training and forgetting. At this point, therefore, only a few representative theories will be outlined in order to show the position of the present research among the established systems of the psychology of learning.

A classification of the various attempts to treat the problems of learning in a systematic way may facilitate our task. We follow a rather usual distinction by reviewing separately associationism, behaviorism, and the gestalt theory.[7]

Associationism.—By restricting ourselves to the description of

[7] This threefold division was made by Tolman (among others), who says: "There are, it seems to us, some three other [namely, in addition to his own theory which he calls a subvariety of the gestalt doctrine] main theories of learning, the Conditioned Reflex Theory, the Trial and Error Theory, and the Gestalt Theory" (96, p. 319). The same division is given by Dashiell, according to whom the manifold theories of learning naturally group themselves into three general types, trial and error, conditioned response, and gestalt (14, p. 261). In one of the newer textbooks of psychology we read: "We shall review three of the major views concerning the nature of learning: learning as conditioned response, the association theories, and the gestalt theories" (63, pp. 328–30). In a short textbook on educational psychology is a chapter entitled "Psychology of Learning: Three Theories"—namely, behaviorism, Thorndike's theory of learning, and the gestalt school (83, p. 53).

the theories which influence contemporary research, we may dispense with references to the age-old history of association as well as to the beginnings of nonsense syllable investigations. It suffices to say that the association school has to its credit the first experimental researches on the phenomena of memory. This school may be represented by two newer systematic studies of learning, undertaken by G. E. Mueller, in Germany, and E. L. Thorndike, in the United States. These two scholars applied their fundamental conviction, the theory of the basic nature of the associative connections, to the extensive empirical data assembled in the past few decades.

Reproduction of ideas is the basis from which the study of the higher mental functions should start [Mueller, 72, p. 3].

Connection-forming . . . is obviously the primary fact [in learning] [Thorndike, 90, p. 20].

Our present psychology finds that mind is ruled by habit throughout [Thorndike, 92, p. 458].

The theories of both Mueller and Thorndike, who repeatedly incorporated new experimental data into their systems, were developed during a lifetime of research. Consequently, the final forms of these theories consisted of the enumeration of a great number of principles and rules.

Mueller's fundamental thesis can be outlined as follows. Laws of association determine the train of thought (*Vorstellungsverlauf*) in reasoning (*Verstandestaetigkeit*) as they do in remembering. In order to understand how nonsense syllables are reproduced and how a task (*Aufgabe*) is executed, we need not assume that different principles are functioning—"associative and perseverative tendencies . . . suffice" (73, p. 476).

What will actually be reproduced depends on two factors; first on the relative strength of the competing associations contingent upon the number and distribution of the repetitions which formed them, and secondly on the degree of readiness (*Bereitschaft*) to which the ideas corresponding to the reproductive tendencies have been raised by the preceding mental processes [73, p. 488].

Thus the mechanism of reproduction is more complicated than is apparent from the traditional laws of association. The strength and effectiveness of an association are dependent on many factors, of which Mueller enumerates twelve (75, pp. 20–24). Frequency of repetition is the first, but it is not emphasized more than the following ten, among which are attention, the age of the connections, their temporal and spatial distribution, the effects of environment and of inhibitions. The twelfth principle is dealt with in most detail because of its paramount importance for "economical learning." We learn "by uniting the members of a series into solid groups through collective apperception" (75, p. 25).[8] Grouping is a factor determining the strength of the resulting associations (72, pp. 253–403). In Chapter VII the conception of groups and Mueller's experimental evidence for the facts and effects of grouping is dealt with at length. Therefore only his final conclusion is quoted here:

Association of two ideas is not always due to the formation of an associative path (or the improvement of its conductivity) connecting the trace centers of the ideas, but dispositional fixation (*Einpraegung*) also occurs . . . It is to be assumed that the learning of a unitary group of successive impressions is dispositional: a trace center acquires the disposition to respond to certain stimuli by the activation (*Ablauf*) of the entire process [75, p. 54].

We shall begin the description of Thorndike's system by quoting what he calls the "first approximate description of learning":

Certain responses become connected with certain situations because of sequence in time, provided the response is treated by the mind (or brain) as "belonging" to the situation . . . The repetition or frequency or use of a connection means sequence in time *plus* belonging. Other things being equal, such use strengthens connections. The chief other thing is the sequel or after-effect or consequence of the connection. This works back upon the connection, satisfiers strengthening it and annoyers often strengthening some alternative connection [93, p. 101].

There are still other factors instrumental in bringing about the learning effect, such as readiness, identifiability of the situation,

---

[8] We shall not here answer the question whether Mueller's explanation of the formation of groups is in accordance with the latest facts. "Collective apperception" is in Mueller's theory an associative principle and different from gestalt principles (cf. Köhler, 44a).

and availability of the response. The emphasis is again placed on the relative strength of several coexistent factors which determine jointly whether a connection will be formed and whether it will survive. The quotation shows that, in his more recent work, Thorndike takes into account a greater diversity of learning than is indicated by the older short Thorndikian laws of use and effect, even though the definition of learning remains unchanged, namely, the acquiring of new connections and the changing of old connections.

We shall discuss some of Thorndike's concepts in greater detail during the course of our investigation. His theory of identical elements will be studied in Chapter V, and his evidence for belonging in Chapter VII, where we shall try to clarify the similarities and differences of "belonging" and certain gestalt concepts. At this point we want to show only that Thorndike's former description of trial-and-error learning as a form of associative learning fits into the newer development of his concepts. The process involved in acts of learning is, according to Thorndike, a process of selection. An act is selected because it brings satisfaction to the animal which chooses it (93, p. 164).

We learn by the gradual selection of the appropriate act or judgment and its association with the circumstances or situation requiring it, in just the way that the animals do . . . If we follow the course of animal evolution, we find the associations thus made between situation and act growing in number, being formed more quickly and becoming more complex and more delicate [93, p. 166].

We may make the essential point of this view still clearer by quoting an early formulation by Thorndike: The "simple semimechanical phenomena . . . which animal learning discloses, are the fundamentals of human learning also. They are, of course, much more complicated in the advanced stages of human learning" (90, p. 16).

Behaviorism.—In studying the present-day behavioristic approach to human learning we can refrain from discussing Pavlov's original technique of conditioning, the slow transition from unconditioned to conditioned reflexes. On the basis of the experiments of Pavlov and his successors, the behaviorists formulated that learning consists in attaching a response to a stimulus which did not originally call forth that response. J. B. Watson's thesis that "the conditioned reflex is the unit out of which the whole habit is formed" (100, p. 166) may be cited as the extreme formulation of this school. Statements such as "all learning is fundamentally of the conditioned reflex type" (Hunter, 34, p. 622) have been frequently made by other authors.

For human learning the most important theoretical implication of the studies of conditioning is expressed as follows: "The conditioned response is in principle the same as association" (McGeoch, 63, p. 329). It should be emphasized that conditioned response and association are *basically* the same, because the details of the regularities assumed in the case of the conditioned response do not appear to be the same as those of the complex processes discussed by associationists. In stressing the role of belonging and of the after-effect Thorndike points out one of these differences: "Mere sequence which is weak in ordinary learning is very powerful in conditioned reflex learning" (94, p. 409). But the conditioned response and the so-called "law of associative shifting" have many identical features. C. L. Hull incorporates evidence supplied by Ebbinghaus, the founder of the experimental research on association, and Pavlov, the discoverer of the conditioned reflex, as postulates in his own theoretical system (31, p. 503). Hull concludes that "the Pavlovian conditioned reaction and the Thorndikian associative reaction are special cases of the operation of the same principle of learning" (32, p. 17).

A further similarity between the behavioristic and the associative approach is shown by the following quotations from the *Psychology of Learning* by E. R. Guthrie, who declares that conditioning is the "fundamental principle of learning."

The most certain and dependable information concerning what a man will do in any situation is information concerning what he did in that situation on its last occurrence [27, p. 228, also p. 18].

The greater part of all that we can predict of the individual man is predicted in terms of the association of specific features of response with specific features of a situation. And the only form in which such information has been offered or can be offered is some form of association theory [p. 19].

The feature in this behavioristic associationism which will prove most important for the present study is the emphasis put on the specific nature of that which has been learned. G. W. Allport gives the following definition of a "specificist": "A specificist contends that the essential element in the structure of psychology is habit and no organization of a higher level exists" (5, p. 248). In this sense Thorndike's system appears to deal with specific processes; we quoted above his statement that "mind is ruled by habit throughout." Hull's theory also appears to be a theory of specific processes, since his starting point is the assumption of excitatory and inhibitory tendencies which are initiated by an individual nonsense syllable as stimulus (31, p. 501–2).

By studying the accounts of learning in textbooks of psychology, we find that the type of textbook based on behavioristic or associative principles is much more common than the textbook which does not assume that the formation of specific connections reveals the fundamental features of the psychology of learning. Special mention must be made, however, of *Experimental Psychology* by R. S. Woodworth (112), who concludes his discussion of the conditioned-reflex research by stating: "The conditioned response . . . is perhaps no more simple than other types of learned responses, and we cannot regard it as an element out of which behavior is built" (p. 123). Woodworth's own viewpoint, more hinted at than expounded, cannot easily be classified as emphasizing either specific or nonspecific processes. The essential quality attributed to the learning effect appears to be that it is a "concrete performance." We shall discuss in Chapter V Woodworth's application of this basic idea to the questions of transfer of training. But his concluding remark on transfer must be quoted here, since it applies to the learning process generally. "Perhaps anything that can be learned can be transferred. But does not everything that can be learned have the concrete character of an act or way of acting?" (p. 207).

In recent literature criticism is often directed against the assumption of specific processes in learning. In demanding a new type of educational psychology C. H. Judd contrasts a "psychology of the higher mental processes" with the "psychology of particular experiences" (38, p. 201). He pleads for a "clear recognition of the difference between the lower and the higher forms of mental activity" (p. 165). The lower form is characterized as the "acquisition of specific items of experience," the higher form as the "level of abstract generalization."

Animals below man live in mental worlds which are made up of meager, circumscribed experiences . . . Fortunately, there are in human mental life other and far broader experiences . . . At the higher levels transfer is typical, not exceptional. Indeed, the function of the higher mental processes is to release the mind from particulars and to create a world of general ideas [38, p. 200].

It is the distinguishing characteristic of the human mind that it rises at times to the high levels of abstraction and generalization [37, p. 78].

Abstract thought and generalization are not possible until the mind has passed out of the early and immature stages of learning [37, p. 344].

As the quotations indicate, Judd is in the front rank of those who object to the approach of the "specificist" in psychology (that is, in human psychology). The positive implications of his theory, which may be called a two-stage theory, will be discussed later.

The gestalt theory.—Gestalt theory as applied to the problem of learning rejects the assumption of associationism that the basis of all learning is the establishment of neutral bonds. In 1921 M. Wertheimer characterized the thesis that mere existential simultaneity or successivity has the tendency to bring about associative connections as one of the most important examples for the assumed effectiveness of "and sums" in mental life (104, pp. 49–50).[9] In contradistinction to that thesis gestalt theory asserts that "data have to be understood in most instances as parts of whole-

---

[9] "And sums" are the sums of pieces which are connected in an arbitrary manner. If we have first a_1 b_1 c_1 and if b_2 c_2 is substituted for b_1 c_1, then, according to certain schools of thought, the result is supposed to be a_1 b_2 c_2, because it is assumed that pieces are interchangeable, their connection does not affect them, and their properties do not determine the nature of the connection (104, p. 49).

processes" (p. 52). From qualities and conditions of the whole the road is open to the understanding of the function of the parts (p. 54). In memory processes the whole-qualities and the structural context play an important role. The essence of memory processes is not adequately grasped in terms of pieces and their sum (or of piecemeal generalization); "association, habit in the sense of arbitrary existential connections, and mechanical memory in general are merely limiting cases" (p. 56). "Thought processes, processes occurring in solving problems, processes at grasping and understanding, are different . . . In their essential feature they are concrete and definite gestalt processes" (p. 56).

Wertheimer asks: "Is experience merely the repeated coexistence of pieces and relations, or is it not something fundamentally different?" The answer to this question is provided by the following example:

One can repeat often a mathematical proof, one can learn it by heart, one can even see the stringent logical relation between every two consecutive statements of the proof, and yet one may completely lack understanding, may make the most senseless mistakes—if one has learned (because of a certain kind of school drill, etc.) the statements only in their individual relation to their neighbors and has not understood the individual steps as parts with a definite function and role in the whole, determined by the whole [106, p. 51].

K. Koffka denies that association operates as an external bond between individual parts, and therefore he reformulates the law of association:

If the phenomena A, B, and C . . . have been present once or oftener as members of a configuration, and if one of them reappears while still possessed of its membership-character, it will have a tendency to supplement itself more or less definitely and completely with the remainder of the total configuration [49, pp. 260–61].

When a new configuration arises under fixed objective conditions, this behavior of the organism is somehow preserved. Upon repeating the objective conditions, the configuration will accordingly arise much more easily and swiftly than it did the first time [49, p. 263].

K. Lewin (58) has shown that the laws of association as hitherto conceived are not sufficient to bind together two contents, but instruction, attitude, and readiness to act in a certain direction are fundamental in determining the reproduction.

W. Köhler discusses the difference between the laws of association and the laws in physics or chemistry: "Wherever an A and B have anything to do with each other in physics, the effect is found to depend upon the properties of A and B in their relations to each other." But the concept of association states: Any A and any B may acquire that neutral bond if only they occur together a number of times (45, p. 280). The positive formulation arrived at by Köhler is: "Neighborhood in space and time influences association only insofar as it determines organization" (p. 290). "Association depends on organization because association is just an after-effect of an organized process" (p. 299). Koffka adds: "To explain reproduction we do not need an assumption of special associative bonds; rather the possibility of reproduction follows from the fact of organization and the general principle of the interaction between trace and process" (50, p. 567). "A gestalt is . . . a product of organization, organization the process that leads to a gestalt" (p. 682). Gestalt psychology attempts to discover "concrete gestalt laws," that is, regularities, tendencies, and determinations of whole-processes and their parts (Wertheimer, 104, pp. 52–53).

In Chapters VIII and IX we shall discuss Köhler's investigations, in which he applied these principles to the process of reproduction, and the theories of traces developed by Köhler and Koffka.

B. H. Wheeler has made one of the most detailed applications of gestalt principles, especially of the concepts of "maturation" and "insight," to the learning process. Repetition of response, he formulates, is an untenable assumption; "repetition of stimulation is a condition of learning . . . because it induces maturation" (109, p. 299). Since learning involves growth of insight, its "very essence is not repeating a performance, but making a new one"

(110, p. 351). Because a later response to the same situation is not a repetition of the previous response, Wheeler denies that there is a revival of past experience (110, p. 391). This leads him to the expression of extreme views. He believes that there is no justification to assume traces.[10]

Among the systematic studies of learning which are related to gestalt principles is E. C. Tolman's *Purposive Behaviorism* (96). Tolman starts his system with "pre-gestalt laws of learning," which are "stimulus laws concerning conditions of presentation" (p. 389). But learning is "an affair of sign-gestalt formation, refinement, selection, or invention" (p. 372); therefore we need laws which deal with the relationship in the material itself. Lastly, we need "capacity laws" relating to individual differences in the capacities involved in learning (p. 389). We have no space to discuss the rich content of Tolman's book.

G. Humphrey (33) found that the theory of the conditioned reflex is too great a simplification because it "considers a situation as an aggregate of isolated stimuli" (p. 232). His main objection is directed against the assumption that "any stimulus can come to act as a substitute for certain other stimuli" (p. 231). We should not "consider the neural responses to successive presentations of the combined stimulus as separate. . . . If the successive presentations are regarded as aspects of one total situation . . . and not as discrete, disconnected stimuli" (p. 119), then Humphrey believes that we can account for the plasticity of the learned response. Habit is not a rigid chain of specific responses (p. 244).

Since the physiology and the pathology of the learning processes will not be dealt with in this book, all references to the history of these disciplines are omitted. It suffices to state that in the development of modern brain physiology and pathology more and more evidence has been accumulated that the processes in the brain, especially those relating to learning and conditioning, must not necessarily be thought of as the functioning of specific, stereotyped conduction paths. We are learning from the work of several

[10] This view is not shared by other gestalt psychologists, cf. Koffka, 50, pp. 457 ff.

outstanding investigators not to deal with the learning effects in terms of activation of specific neurons.[11]

The application of gestalt principles to the psychology of learning will lead to a fuller characterization of the learning process. We shall endeavor to accomplish this by analyzing the results, qualities, and laws of that kind of learning which consists of understanding organized wholes.

[11] Cf. Gelb and Goldstein (23, 25), and Lashley (54, 55). In view of the role played by the "specificist" (as defined by Allport) in the psychology of learning, it is interesting to note that Lashley entitles an important section of his book "Non-specificity of Cerebral Structures for Learning" (54, p. 122).

Chapter II

EXPERIMENTS ON TWO PROCESSES OF LEARNING

IN THE PRECEDING CHAPTER an experiment was described in which different groups of subjects learned the same list of digits in different ways. The results differed greatly, and this was attributed to the fact that the methods of learning differed. In order to confirm this assumption and to investigate in greater detail the effects of applying different methods of learning to the same learning material, we must look for another field suitable for our experimental research. The following objectives guided the author in his search for appropriate materials:

1. Learning material should be chosen which can be learned in different ways, such as by mechanical repetition and by apprehending a principle.

2. It should be possible to vary and to apply the learning material extensively.

3. The learning material should present a novel situation.

How can material be found which may be learned in different ways, is easily varied, and constitutes a novel situation? Experiments on problem solving furnished a clue. In those experiments the material is usually new and strange, and the subjects are in a novel situation. If we should use the "square series" or subject matter belonging to a school discipline as the material of our experiment, the subjects might be aided in their learning by past experience concerning the specific problem in question. This difficulty we attempt to eliminate by working with problems that belong to a field in which our subjects have not accumulated a great amount of readily usable knowledge. Unfamiliar problems may thus help us to attain our third objective. The second objective can easily be attained by using such problems, since tasks which are suitable for problem-solving experiments can often be varied extensively.

When the goal of an experiment is the study of the subjects' ability to solve certain new problems or the analysis of the process leading to the solution of new tasks, the experimenter usually observes the subjects until they are able to solve the tasks or have reached the time limit. Such problem-solving experiments can be changed into experiments on learning. It is possible to *teach* the subjects how to solve the problems and how to master the tasks. Different methods of teaching can be applied: the solution can be taught once in a senseless way and at another time in a, let us say, more intelligent way. Therefore problem-solving experiments can help us to arrive at an understanding of different ways of learning. We will attempt to find out how the results of the various methods by which the same task is taught differ with respect to the curve of retention and to applicability.

In the usual problem-solving experiments in which the process of arriving at a new solution is studied, the same subject cannot be used twice. This holds true also for our experimental set-up. If a subject were taught the solution of a task by one method today and by another method a few weeks later, the results of the two learning processes would not be comparable. The second time the subject would not face a novel situation, and our investigation would be complicated by the after effects of the previous learning process. We have overcome this difficulty in the experiment on "Federal expenditures" by comparing the results of groups of subjects. Of course, the groups must be comparable, because it would not serve to use groups which vary greatly in age range or with vastly different schooling. We shall therefore divide students belonging to the same college class into groups. Should the results of one such group which has learned by Method I greatly differ from another which has learned by Method II, then we would suppose that the differences in the results cannot be explained by the fact that different subjects were used.[1]

---

[1] In later quantitative experiments the author introduced, in addition to the use of a large number of subjects and the avoidance of sampling errors, another method of checking the comparability of the subjects (cf. pp. 280 ff.).

This chapter will be devoted to experiments dealing with an arithmetic problem, a certain arrangement of playing cards. We shall refer to these experiments in short as card-trick experiments. But no "trick" in the sense of fraud or deception of the subjects was used. A purely rational solution of the problem was possible. These experiments will not show logical learning of a high degree; they were chosen because the tricks can be learned both in a senseless way and by a method involving a principle. Furthermore, the tasks can be varied extensively, and they were "new" to our subjects, who had had no experience with such card arrangements.

These experiments with card tricks were exploratory experiments. We had to try out a large number of tentative experimental set-ups before appropriate materials and appropriate methods of learning were found. These exploratory experiments indicate, first, the actual development of the investigation. Second, although the results of these experiments are open to certain criticisms, they permitted a thorough qualitative analysis of the different learning processes. For that purpose various methods have been used: observation and complete description of the subjects' procedure, reports given by the subjects after the experiment has been finished, introspection (that is, the subjects in some experiments were encouraged to give a verbal account of all the steps and ideas used), and analysis of the written results. Individual experiments and experiments with small groups, even though not fit for statistical treatment, suited these purposes better than extensive experiments with a large number of subjects.

A Card-Trick Experiment

At the beginning of every experiment the experimenter showed the subjects a trick with ordinary playing cards. He held in his hand ten or twelve cards, arranged in an order which was not known to the audience, and addressed the subjects as follows:

I take the top card and place it on the table. It is a red card. Then I take the next card and put it at the bottom of the deck without determining what it is. I place the third card on the table. It is a black card. The following card I put undetermined below the others; while the next card, which is red, I put on the table.

The procedure of alternately placing one card on the table and one at the bottom of the deck was continued until all the cards of the deck were placed on the table; the cards appeared on the table in this order: red, black, red, black, and so forth. Then said the experimenter, "it is a nice trick, I suppose you would like to learn how to do it. I will teach you."

The card trick, the learning object of our experiment, is sufficiently absorbing to awaken the interest of the subjects and the wish to learn it. This is an important point, because thus we are assured of the subjects' willingness to undergo the procedure. Learning took place because of interest in the matter rather than by request or because money or some other inducement was offered. The subjects, of course, did not know in advance whether they would learn the trick in a senseless or in a meaningful way.

The card trick is sufficiently difficult to be used as an object of a learning experiment. To discover the solution of the problem without any instruction took much longer than to follow the procedure in the learning period. In order to prove this point problem-solving experiments were made with comparable subjects who did not take part in the learning experiments. They attempted to learn the trick without assistance. With a deck of thirteen red and thirteen black cards a correct solution was never obtained in less than five minutes. For most adult subjects even ten minutes was insufficient.

The card trick described above can be presented with many variations. First, it is possible to vary the number of cards; the trick can be performed with 4, 21, 52, or any number of cards. Second, one can use an order other than the simple order of alternating red and black cards. To place thirteen spades on the table in the order Ace, 2, 3, 4, and so forth, is one alternative which was frequently used. Third, the trick can be varied by putting two or three cards instead of one card at the bottom of the deck each time after a card was placed on the table. A fourth simple variation consists in beginning the trick by placing under the deck one or two undetermined cards.

Teaching and learning were performed, not with actual cards, but with paper and pencil. The papers of the subjects thus contained a record of trials and mistakes.

Mastery of the card trick was taught in two different ways. To one group of subjects was given the concrete arrangement of the cards required for the solution of a specific trick. They read the sequence several times: for example, "two red cards, one black card, two red cards, three black cards." To the other group of subjects was explained the way in which one could derive the solution of the trick. The experimenter showed a scheme of construction which brought about the required result.[2]

In this way the procedure during the learning period differed in the two cases. In the first type of learning repetitions were used. No explanation was given, and the subjects were not told why the order in which the cards were presented was the correct order. The active participation of the subjects, their learning, consisted of repeating the material. They memorized a certain series presented to them. Learning by *memorizing* is thus the most appropriate name for their performance.[3]

The second procedure seems to have consisted of attentive listening only. The right way to arrange the cards was explained, and the learners merely watched the demonstration, which was given once. There was no repetition, the learning process was over when the experimenter achieved the proper arrangement. Of what did learning consist under these circumstances? At present we are only able to use a rather general expression and assert that the subjects learned by *understanding*. One of our main tasks will be the search for a more complete description of the process of understanding. Is that process the same as or similar to the process of memorizing? And does learning by understanding yield the same results as learning by memorizing? We now turn to the discussion of the experiments which were made in order to answer these questions.

Experiment 1.—A trick with alternating four red and four

---

[2] In Appendix 1 the actual contents of both instruction periods are stated.

[3] Cf. McGeoch, "The repetition of verbal material is called memorizing" (63, p. 304).

black cards by constantly omitting one card.[4] Two subjects obtain one type of instruction, and two the other type. The learning process requires one minute for memorizing and four minutes for understanding. Immediately after the learning process the subjects were tested for retention; those who learned by memorizing arrived at the correct result much quicker than did the other learners. Two weeks later another test was given, in which the two "meaningful learners" solved the task in less than two minutes. One of the memorizers was unable to recall the order; the other wrote, after some hesitation, the correct order, but changed it after a few seconds, thus proving at the end that there had been no correct retention.

Experiment 2.—A trick with thirteen spades by omitting one card each time. Two subjects memorized and two "understood" the arrangement. The learning process required four minutes for the first and five minutes for the second group. The tests were made in the same way as in Experiment 1. In the test immediately following the learning process none of the four subjects made a mistake, and the memorizers were ready in shorter time. After eight days both memorizers were unable to recall the order while both subjects of the second group succeeded in producing the correct result.

Experiment 3.—Same material as in Experiment 2. Again there were two subjects in each group. In the first test immediately following the learning process, the problem was solved by all four subjects. Then a different task was given; the experimenter asked how the cards should be arranged for the trick with four red and four black cards alternating after the omission of one card each time. Those who learned by the understanding method produced the correct result after two and one-half and three minutes, respectively, while the memorizers were unable to achieve a satisfactory result within five minutes.

---

[4] This short designation of the trick should indicate that the subjects were taught how to arrange eight cards (four red and four black ones) in such a way that they were able to put first a red card on the table, then one card at the bottom of the pack, then a black card on the table, then one card at the bottom, and so forth.

After these experiments, in which each subject was treated individually, a small group experiment was made. All the subjects were graduate students of psychology in the New School for Social Research, New York. None knew the trick or had ever heard of similar tricks with cards. The subjects were divided by lot into three groups. *Memorizing Group* consisted of nine subjects who learned by memorizing, *Understanding Group* consisted of nine subjects who learned by understanding, and *Control Group* consisted of four subjects who were not subject to any training process at all. In the training period the groups were separated. The Memorizing Group learned first the order of Trick A (four red and four black cards) and then of Trick B (eight spades). The members of the group repeated five times aloud the arrangements required to solve these tricks. The total learning period lasted four minutes. The Understanding Group also learned for four minutes by listening attentively to the explanation of Trick A given by the experimenter. Trick B was not shown to this group. The test which began a few minutes after the completion of the training period consisted of six tasks given at the same time to the three groups. The subjects had four minutes to work on each task. All papers were collected after each task.[5]

The following table shows the quantitative results of the experiment. "Correct" means that the correct result was found by the subject; "false" means that the correct result was not found. Thus "false" comprises a large number of different cases: incorrect results, no result at all, solution not completed because of lack of time, and so forth.

[5] Task 1: Four red and four black cards, omit one card each time; learned by both groups. Task 2: Three red and three black cards, omit one card. Task 3: Four red and four black cards, omit two cards. Task 4: Eight spades to be arranged so that cards with even and uneven numbers should alternate (by omitting one card after each card placed on the table). If we identify "even-uneven" with "red-black," Task 4 has the form of Trick A, although the material of Trick B is used in this task. Task 5: Eight spades, omit one; learned by the Memorizing Group, easy application for the Understanding Group. Task 6: Four red and four black cards, omit one. First all four red cards should be placed on the table, and then all four black cards. This task can be solved almost immediately by most intelligent persons even though they have never seen the trick before and have not received any instruction.

TABLE 1. RESULTS OF THE FIRST CARD-TRICK EXPERIMENTS

Number of Subjects

	UNDERSTANDING GROUP		MEMORIZING GROUP		CONTROL GROUP	
	Correct	*False*	*Correct*	*False*	*Correct*	*False*
Task 1: Trick A	6	3	8	1	0	4
Task 2: Easy variation of Trick A	6	3	1	8	1	3
Task 3: Difficult variation of Trick A	5	4	2	7	0	4
Task 4: Trick A with material B	6	3	5	4	1	3
Task 5: Trick B	6	3	7	2	0	4
Task 6: New easy task	9	0	7	2	3	1

This general summary of the results reveals that the Memorizing Group had a slight advantage in the pure memory tests, but that the Understanding Group had considerable advantage in the tests in which variations of the learning materials were presented. Trick A, which was included in the learning period of both groups, was solved somewhat better by the Memorizing Group than by the Understanding Group, and the same holds true of Trick B, which was taught to the Memorizing Group, but not to the Understanding Group. On the other hand, the results obtained with Task 2 and Task 3 indicate that the Understanding Group as a whole was able to apply its knowledge to variations of the practiced task, while the Memorizing Group was not. The results of the Control Group indicate the degree of difficulty in solving the tasks without any instruction.

The analysis of the test papers of the Understanding Group [6]

[6] In order to understand the results more fully we may differentiate between two kinds of false solutions. A false result may have been reached by a member of the Understanding Group either because the subject did not understand the explanation given or because he was too careless or too hasty in executing a task which he fully understood. Mistakes due to carelessness occurred seldom when the experiment was performed individually. In the group experiment, however, subjects arrived at incorrect results in nine cases, although their calculations revealed a full and correct understanding. The results of the Understanding Group are therefore presented again in the following corrected table.

shows that the correct results were not always arrived at by the same method. During all the tasks there were only two subjects who repeated in all its details the scheme presented during the learning period. One subject introduced abbreviations in attempting to solve the first task. In the course of the experiment the number of subjects making use of abbreviations and omissions increased considerably. The changes in the scheme to which the subjects resorted consisted not only of omissions. In the second task two subjects began to write the letters below one another (not beside one another as they had been instructed to do in the training period) and followed that method during the whole experiment. Only in attempting Task 3 did all the subjects make calculations in several rows as was done in the training period. In the second easy task two subjects were already able to arrive at the result by compressing their calculations into one single row. In working on Task 4 several subjects introduced entirely new methods. One subject was able to find the correct result by crossing his fingers; he did not need any calculations on paper.

The main result of the experiments with the Understanding Group can be summarized in stating that about the same number of subjects solved Task 1 as solved the other tasks. Although solving Task 1 was the only matter actually practiced, in the tests Task 1 had no advantage over the other tasks.

It was different with the Memorizing Group, for whom the

ITEMIZED RESULTS OF THE UNDERSTANDING GROUP
Number of Subjects

Task	Correct Solutions	Mistakes Due to Carelessness	Complete Failures
1	6	0	3
2	6	2	1
3	5	3	1
4	6	3	0
5	6	1	2
6	9	0	0

In studying the solutions of the first task we find that three subjects did not have full understanding of the principle. But two subjects were able to correct their misunderstanding when working on Task 2, an easy application, which they completed without a mistake. In this task the mistakes due to carelessness were made by two subjects who correctly solved Task 1. Thus, there was only one subject in the Understanding Group who failed entirely in each of the first three tasks.

solution of the tasks whose results were learned was much easier than was the solution of new tasks. Trick A was solved by eight and Trick B by seven members of the group which consisted of nine students. But only one and two subjects, respectively, succeeded in solving variations of Trick A (Tasks 2 and 3 in the table on page 39). These subjects adopted during the tests a problem-solving attitude instead of merely using what they had learned in the training period. Thus we may state that for members of the Memorizing Group who were "pure memorizers" the variations caused insurmountable difficulties.[7] The transfer of knowledge from one material to another was observed only in Task 4, whose solution, however, can be considered not different from the well-practiced result of Task 1. Many essential elements vere identical in both tasks. But it must be noted that even Task 4 was solved by only five out of the nine subjects of the group.

In the experiments in which the principle of the card trick was explained to individual subjects, abbreviations and changes of the scheme similar to those in the group experiment were observed. Only in a few exceptional cases did it happen that the subjects repeated exactly the procedure followed by the experimenter. Yet while working on the solution of a new task the subjects often stopped and seemed to think. When asked whether they were trying to remember how the experimenter proceeded at that special point, they indignantly denied such an assumption and asserted that they were trying to figure out the next step. Subjects who were asked eight days or more later than the learning period whether they still recalled the details of the "instruction" generally gave a negative answer. They were not able to tell how the experimenter had started, what he had said next, and so forth. By introspection, at best, such answers were obtained as "I remember the general scheme," "I know the principle," and so forth. But the tests permitted the experimenter to observe what the subjects actually did remember.

---

[7] The behavior of the few members of the Memorizing Group who were not satisfied with memorizing is described in Appendix 1.

Three subjects to whom the principle of performing the trick with thirteen spades was explained were not tested at all immediately after the learning period. Four weeks later they were asked to perform the trick with ten spades. Two of the subjects declared that they were unable to do it, having forgotten the explanation. They did not seem to recognize even that the task now given differed from that originally learned. When the experimenter asked the subjects to try to perform the trick even though they had forgotten "everything," the result proved that their statement was not accurate. After a few minutes both subjects obtained the correct results, in much shorter time than was ever experienced in unassisted problem solving, that is, without any previous learning. Observation of the procedure followed by the subjects showed that it was similar to the procedure of problem solving, but nevertheless the effects of the preceding practice were very noticeable. The subjects did not at first use question marks as was done in the training period, and did not repeat the details of the practice procedure, but when they had made a mistake they noticed it very quickly. (In solving the problem without previous practice, a mistake was usually followed through much longer before it was noticed.) The subjets were aware of their goal in a much clearer way than were those who had no previous understanding. Each step was better related to the whole procedure, its correctness or its falseness was quickly seen, the periods of hesitancy were shorter, and regression to the beginning was less frequent. By enumerating these differences between the discovery of a solution and the recollection of our subjects, the similarity of both processes becomes obvious. There are only differences of degree and of time. Only in one respect do greater differences appear: once in a while in the course of the work a subject recalled the exact details of the learning period. Thus, one of the subjects said when half-way through the task "last time you showed the trick with thirteen cards"; another subject suddenly fell back to the previously unused method of an additional row containing question marks, and so forth. But correct solutions are possible when none of the details of the learning process is apparent. One of the subjects, taught by the usual method, ten days later solved the trick with four red and four black cards in the following way: he wrote first R Bl R Bl R Bl R Bl. Then he slowly made the four lines shown below. The subject did not number the lines; the numbers are added by the author to show in what order the lines were drawn.

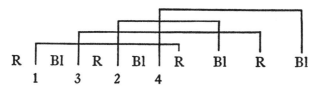

After having finished the fourth line the subject declared that he was ready, and he read to the experimenter the correct result— R R Bl R R Bl Bl Bl.

In spite of the fact that this proceeding differs from that previously learned, it would be incorrect to state that the subject solved the trick unassisted by former training. The formal principle, the proper arrangement or classification of the last four cards in the order of the first four cards, was discovered in a much shorter time and with the aid of a smaller number of incorrect trials than is usual in pure problem solving.

These observations help us to characterize the process of reproduction on the part of the "meaningful learners." The subjects proceeded to discover or to construct the solution, and the preceding training helped them in doing so. Reproduction was not at all similar to a door bursting open, because a button has been pressed —it did not consist of the presentation of an ever-ready response to the appropriate stimulus. It was more like the processes of discovery, of problem solving, and of construction. Remembering can here be best characterized as a rediscovery—a *reconstruction*.[8] The effect of learning was ability to reconstruct.[9]

[8] Cf. the reference to Bartlett's views on pp. 291 f.

[9] In a few cases reproduction in the usual sense of the word was also encountered in delayed tests of a trick learned by understanding. As mentioned above, the experiment in which the subjects were tested four weeks after they had learned the trick with thirteen spades, was made with three subjects. The results with two subjects have been described, but not those of the third subject, who seemed to remember the

Preliminary Survey of Results

Duration of learning.—In memorizing the time required for learning depends on the number of repetitions. Learning takes longer for much material than for a small amount. On the other hand, learning by understanding is independent of the amount of material, since the understanding of a trick with a few cards is sufficient to ensure knowledge of the trick with a very large number of cards. Therefore memorizing is a quicker method of learning only when a small amount of material is concerned. For a large amount and for more complex material meaningful learning is much easier and much more acceptable to the subjects than memorizing. In addition, it must be kept in mind, as proved by many old experiments, that in memorizing a considerable amount of over-learning (repetitions beyond the point of first mastery) is required to ensure retention after a long interval. Thus, even with comparatively simple materials memorizing is often not a quicker method of learning than understanding, if retention over a long period of time is desired.

Reproduction time.—When in the tests the subjects were asked to perform a task which they had learned in the training period, the members of the memorizing group completed their work quicker than the members of the understanding group. Memorizing may therefore have some advantages over understanding if for any reason it is necessary that reproduction time be very short.

Retention.—After an interval of one week or more retention re-

---

trick best. She immediately started to write letters, numbers, and question marks, as she had experienced it in the learning period. But in writing the second row she made mistakes, and she arrived at last at an incorrect result. She was unable to correct it in spite of the fact that she remembered correctly a large number of details taught in the learning period. The recall of these details seemed almost to prevent the subject from finding the solution of the problem.

The recollection of specific details rather than the principle was a more frequent occurrence in a few experiments, in which the subjects were unable to perform the trick immediately after the end of the learning period. Naturally the presentation of material in a meaningful way does not assure meaningful learning. It is possible to memorize a text which the experimenter wants to be understood and to memorize some of the steps leading to the solution instead of endeavoring to understand the principle. However, precise recollection of a detail may also occur in the case of real understanding.

sulting from meaningful learning was better, and after memorizing forgetting occurred sooner. These results were obtained even with short and simple material.

Applications.—Memorizing permitted transfer of training from one material to the other to a very limited extent only. When the tests consisted of tasks different from those which were practiced, the memorizers often were at a complete loss, while most subjects who learned by understanding succeeded easily. Often it is no more difficult for meaningful learners to deal with variations of the material and to apply a principle than to deal with the practiced material.

Transitions.—When the experimenter asked his subjects to memorize the order required for a card trick with twenty or more cards, the subjects frequently objected and expressed their intention to discover the principle of the trick instead of to learn by heart the order of the cards. The subjects who were not compelled to proceed with pure memorizing often resorted to other methods of learning. On the other hand, it sometimes happened that a meaningful method did not result in understanding, but that the material was partly recalled because certain details had been memorized.

A Quantitative Experiment

The qualitative experiments just described yielded two results which can be measured easily. By using different learning methods we arrived at different results with regard to the applicability of the knowledge and the rate of forgetting. The following experiment with about one hundred subjects was made to check and to verify these results.

The main difference between the new experiment and the experiments formerly reported is that now only a two-minute test period was given to solve each task. As a result of shortening the working time a much greater number of mistakes was made by the subjects than were made in the previous experiments. We here call "mistake" any result except the correct solution, even though the correct solution was missed only because of lack of time. The test papers were simply divided into two groups—those showing and those not showing a perfect solution.

The experiment [10] was divided into "fore-test," "practice," and "test," which followed each other without pause. Fore-test and test were identical for the three classes used. In the fore-test the trick was shown with thirteen spades. Then the question was asked whether any subject knew or had seen the trick or similar tricks. The few subjects who answered the question in the affirmative were not used in the experiment. The practice period differed for the three classes. Group Mem. (memorizing) learned by heart for four minutes the correct orders required to perform the trick with four red and four black cards (Task No. 3) and the trick with eight spades (No. 4). Group Und. (understanding) listened to the explanation of the method of arranging four red and four black cards (No. 3). This instruction also lasted four minutes. Group Con. (the control group) had no practice period at all. Three tests were given immediately after training. First No. 1—an easy application (three black and three red cards, omit one card); then No. 2—a difficult application (four red and four black cards, omit two cards); and finally No. 3—the test of the task which both learning groups have practiced (four red and four black cards, omit one card).

After the test the subjects were asked not to discuss the experiment with fellow students and not to show the trick to anyone. Four weeks later the groups were surprised by a second test. It began with the "fore-test"—the demonstration of the trick with thirteen spades. Then the students were asked whether they had thought of the card trick since the former test or had tried it out or showed it to anybody. The test papers of those who answered in the affirmative were not scored.

The "retest" consisted of three tasks to be performed in two minutes each. At first No. 3 was presented, the same task which had been practiced by both groups and which had been tested once four weeks ago. Then followed No. 4—eight spades—the task

[10] Carried out in undergraduate classes of Brooklyn College.

which had been learned by Group Mem. but not by Group Und. for which it was an easy application. No. 5 was the last test—three black and three red cards were to be arranged by omitting two cards each time. That test was an application of medium difficulty which had not been used at all. The retest was performed by three groups, Und. and Mem. consisting of the same subjects who participated in the experiment four weeks earlier, while the control group was different from the Group Con. which was used in the first tests. The same subjects cannot be used several times as an "unpracticed" control group. The following table contains the results.

TABLE 2. GROUP EXPERIMENT WITH CARD TRICKS

	PERCENTAGE OF PERFECT SOLUTIONS		
Test	*No. 1*	*No. 2*	*No. 3*
Group Mem. (26 subjects)	23	8	42*
Group Und. (25 subjects)	44	40	44*
Group Con. (32 subjects)	9	3	9
Retest	*No. 3*	*No. 4*	*No. 5*
Group Mem. (22 subjects)	32*	36*	18
Group Und. (21 subjects)	48*	62	52
Group Con. (22 subjects)	9	14	9

The asterisks indicate that the test refers to a task which has been shown in the practice period. All other numbers refer to new tasks. If we first compare the achievement of Group Mem. with that of Group Und. in performing practiced tasks (represented by the numbers followed by asterisks in the table above), we do not find much difference. But new tasks were solved by 23, 8, and 18 percent of the members of Group Mem. as against 44, 40, and 52 percent of the members of Group Und. In solving new tasks Group Und. is distinctly superior to Group Mem.

The differences between the achievements of the control groups and the groups Mem. and Und. indicate the effects of learning. Should a certain test be passed by half the members of a practice group and by only 10 percent of the members of a similar control group, then the superiority of the first group must be due to the effects of the practice.[11]

We analyze the results of the experiment first from the viewpoint of the applicability of knowledge. The results of Group Mem. conform to the usual assumptions. The group has learned how to solve Task 3, consequently 42 percent of its members were able to find the solution a few minutes after the learning period. Other unpracticed tasks were solved by a much smaller number of subjects. The score for the difficult new task No. 2 was only insignificantly higher than that of the control group. Similarly, in the retest many more subjects were able to solve the two tasks which were practiced than could solve the new task, No. 5.—Group Und. showed entirely different results. The three tasks of the tests were solved by about the same number of subjects. A similar result was obtained with the three retests given four weeks later. (That Task 4 was easy may explain the high score obtained in performing it.) Thus here it is not possible to differentiate between learning effects on practiced and on new tasks. Apparently Group Und. had learned something which permitted the solution of all the tasks, old or new.

In the test the grade of learning achieved by Group Und. for all tasks was as high as the direct memorization effect shown by Group Mem. As a consequence of learning how to solve Task 3 about the same result was obtained with regard to Tasks 1, 2, and 3, as was obtained in a different group by the memorization of Task 3 for that one task.[12]

---

[11] That is the only legitimate use of the results obtained with our control groups. The scores of the control groups are too small to prove the grade of difference existing between the various tests. Thus, both Task 1 and Task 3 were solved by only three of the thirty-two subjects (9 percent), which because of chance solutions possibly arrived at by some of the subjects, does not prove that the tasks are of equal difficulty.

[12] It may appear surprising that a short time after the memorizing only eleven of the twenty-six subjects (42 percent) were able to reproduce what they had learned. It appears that ten subjects did reproduce correctly what they had memorized, one solved the problem, four made mistakes in the reproduction, and eleven did not recognize that they had been asked to solve the task for which they had learned the solution.—In studying the test papers of Group Und. we find that the number of perfect solutions would have been increased considerably if a longer working time had been granted to the subjects. But, as stated above, it was within the plan of the experi-

These results hold true only of tests made immediately after training. Four weeks later the scores of Group Mem. in performing the two practiced tasks were lower than were any scores of Group Und. If we study the achievements of the individual subjects (instead of the group averages), we find that of the members of Group Und. nine subjects solved all the tasks in the test, and ten subjects all the tasks in the retest. In Group Mem. only one subject had a perfect score in the test and three such subjects in the retest. (The last result cannot be considered significant, because Group Mem. was tested by only one new task at the occasion of the retest.) Among the members of the control groups there was one subject with a perfect score in both test and retest.

With regard to the rate of retention the results of Group Mem. conform to expectations. The solution of Task 3 was accomplished by 42 percent of the group in the test and by 32 percent in the retest, indicating that forgetting occurred with the passage of time. On the other hand, the performance of Group Und. indicates that there had been no progressive deterioration, although the problem was not practiced during the four weeks between test and retest. The same Task 3 was solved by 44 percent of the subjects in the test and by 48 percent in the retest. In new tasks, too, we find indications for an improvement in the performance of the members of Group Und. Four subjects scored higher on the later than on the earlier occasion, but of course the tests are not strictly comparable.[13]

The problems referred to above—the apparent lack of forgetting after learning by understanding, the relation of direct practice to applications, the question of transfer—will be topics of special investigation in the next chapters. It has been found that in

---

menter to arrive at low scores. The range of the difference between the two groups would have been obscured if we had obtained a 100 percent score in any of the tasks.

[13] The scores of Group Und. in the retest would have been still higher if it had not been necessary to exclude those subjects who had practiced the card trick in the period between test and retest. Of the twenty-five members of the group, one was not present at the time of the retest, while the results of three were not included in the table because of intervening practice. All three had high scores at the test. Of the two subjects of Group Mem. who were excluded at the retest for the same reason, one had a high and one a low score four weeks earlier.

using senseless methods and meaningful methods of learning there is much quantitative difference concerning the retention of the material and its applicability. It has been proved that the results of learning by understanding are not the same as the results of learning by memorizing.

Qualitative Analysis

We shall use the card-trick experiment for one more purpose. It shall help us to achieve a more complete description of the process of meaningful learning. The similarity of remembering to unassisted construction has been previously established, and therefore we have used the term "reconstruction." But is the similarity between unassisted problem solving and learning by understanding restricted to the after-effects (the remembering), or is the process of learning itself similar to that of solving a task without any assistance? The analysis of the process of problem solving shall help us to answer that question.

In addition to learning experiments individual experiments were made in which the subjects were shown the trick and asked to find out how it was performed. According to these experiments (1) it is possible for some subjects to discover the principle of the card tricks without any instruction (especially if the trick is presented in or reduced to a simple form); [14] (2) if the principle has been discovered without assistance, retention seems to endure even longer than after learning by understanding. Tests made two months after the learning (or solving) periods with a few subjects showed that the best results were obtained by those who had solved the problem alone.

The processes by which the subjects arrived at a solution of the problem did not reveal any new or surprising features. It is not necessary to describe in detail the steps taken by the subjects or to analyze the differences in the behavior of various subjects. Our

---

[14] It happened once in a while that a subject found by chance, that is, after a number of uncoördinated trials, the correct arrangement required for the performance of a trick. This is not what we mean when we speak of "discovery of the principle." This term should denote a rational process leading to a more-or-less articulated knowledge of the principle.

intention is to compare the process of problem solving with that of understanding, and for that purpose it is sufficient to give a schematic description of the discovery of the principle. By the following simple example of a card trick with three alternating red and three black cards it will be possible to differentiate between unassisted solving and assisted learning.[15]

SYMBOLS USED IN OUR DESCRIPTION

M_b Material at the beginning in arbitrary order; for example, a a a b b b

M_c The correct order of the material which is required to perform the task; a b b b a a

M_e Material at the end of the experiment, as placed on the table when the task is correctly performed; a b a b a b

P The performance of the trick which results in M_e: to lay the first card on the table, the second card under the deck, the third on the table, and so forth

Op Various operations performed in the course of the learning or solving process

I. The process of discovery.—P is shown, M_b is given to the subject. First step: M_b P. The question is how to

. . . . ? . . . .

change M_b in order to arrive at P.

Second step: M_b P → Op_1. The performance requires that the first, third, and fifth cards alternate, while nothing is as yet known about the second, fourth, and sixth cards. Op_1 is a ? b ? a ?.

Third step: The three gaps must be filled in according to the requirements of the task. It happens that the third step consists in deriving a new Op_2 from Op_1. Op_2 is the alternation of the three missing cards as follows: ? b ? a ? b. Op_2 is proved to be false by actual trial or by reasoning. It becomes apparent that the missing members of the series (the question marks in Op_1) must be filled in the same way as was done with the first three cards, that is, by again constantly omitting one card. The order of the three miss-

---

[15] The author is indebted to Professor M. Wertheimer for the principles of the following description. For earlier literature on problem solving see Wertheimer (103), Duncker (15), and Maier (66).

ing cards is therefore b $?$ a. We call this operation of constant
                    b
omissions Op_o, which when understood comprises Op_1. It is difficult to express Op_o in words: it includes the knowledge that all gaps must be filled in by cards of alternate colors and that between each two cards we must leave a gap by placing a card at the bottom of the deck.

Fourth step: $P \rightarrow Op_o \rightarrow M_c$. Op_o leads to the order M_c, and the problem is solved.

Between P and Op_o there exists an intrinsic relationship. If this relationship is understood, it is independent of the specific features of M_b and M_c. It is valid for all cases, not only for the example in which it has been discovered. Only the structural interrelation of the items is important, while the items themselves are variable.[16]

II. Learning by memorizing.—The given elements are M_c and P. M_c is repeated several times and learned by heart. The subject is told that M_c makes P possible. But the learning process, the repetition of M_c, does not create and does not reveal any structural relationship between the elements. There remains an "and sum" of items. In this learning process Op_o is never referred to.

The term "memorizing" is used here and will be used in the course of the entire investigation in the sense of pure memorizing (p. 41), or mechanical memorizing; that is, learning by heart without understanding why and how the various parts of the material are connected with one another. It would not serve to clarify the fundamental differences in the learning processes to use a concept such as "substance memorization," which involves the processes of both understanding and memorizing.[17]

III. Learning by understanding.—The given elements are Op_o and P. The material of learning is Op_o; the subjects listen to the description of Op_o in the terms of an example. If that were the

[16] It should not be inferred that the process of "discovery" assumes in every case the more-or-less straight and rational form described above. But such cases exist, and the phases described are essential phases in each process of discovery, even if they are interrupted by several more or less unnecessary "detours."

[17] The final clarification of the relationship between understanding and memorizing will be attempted in Chapter X; there we will discuss also the joint use of both processes of learning.

complete description of meaningful learning, the results of the experiments would not be understandable. Even exact recall of every detail told to the subjects in the instruction period cannot insure their ability to apply their learning to different materials. They must have done more in the practice period than merely to listen to the instructor. The subjects must have realized how the sequence M_e is determined by the sequence M_c. They understood how the arbitrary and irrelevant M_b was transformed into the required M_c; which means that they established an interrelation between the material, the operation, and the performance. A new and hitherto unknown oganization of the material was achieved and understood. The organization consisted of the insight into the relationship between the performance and Op_o, from which M_c follows by necessity.

$$P \to Op_o \to M_c$$

The process of understanding by means of reorganizing the material yields something which is not identical with learning the words which were taught. The subjects understood the intrinsic relationship between Op_o and P, a relationship independent of the material with which it has been demonstrated.[18]

In establishing the schemes for problem solving, memorizing, and learning by understanding, we had to use the same letters in order to describe the first and the third process correctly, but different letters were to be employed for the second process. Thus we arrive at the following summary of our investigation:

1. Learning by memorizing is a different process from learning by understanding.

2. Learning by understanding involves substantially the same process as does problem solving—the discovery of a principle.

3. Both problem solving and meaningful learning consist pri-

---

[18] It can be shown that it is not an arbitrary relation between Op_o and M_c which is grasped by the successful learner who is able to apply his knowledge. Suppose the instruction was made with four cards. Then M_b may be a b b a; M_e is a b a b; and M_c is a a b b.

Transfer to other materials would be possible by learning a senseless relation. Such a transfer, say to six cards, could result in the order a a a b b b, which is incorrect. But this senseless transfer only occurs after memorizing and does not occur if the principle is grasped, that is, if Op_o is understood in its intrinsic relation to P.

marily in changing, or organizing, the material. The role of organization is to establish or to discover or to understand an intrinsic relationship. Hereby the findings of the previous chapter are confirmed—that learning by understanding consists of grouping (organizing) a material so as to make an inner relationship apparent (p. 19). If the essence of learning by understanding is organization of the material, it is understandable that remembering is reconstruction, that is, the "revival" of the process of organization.

Chapter III

INTRODUCTION TO THE PROBLEM OF
TRANSFER OF TRAINING

IN DRAWING CONCLUSIONS from the experiments with card tricks, we have perhaps proceeded too rapidly. The quantitative differences between the results of memorizing and the results of understanding and the qualitative differences between these processes must be investigated in greater detail.

The Problem

Following are the main questions involved which will be studied in experiments now to be described: Which methods of teaching and learning result in the greatest measure of applicability? By what methods can the transfer effect be increased? How can methods of teaching and learning be improved? The main goal of this research, the establishment of different results obtained from different learning methods, will constitute the means by which we shall attempt to answer the aforementioned questions. A decision concerning the differences in the learning effects of different methods of teaching and learning is important not only for educational practice but also for the discussion of the basic assumptions of the theory of learning. By experiments we shall endeavor to clarify certain controversial problems of theoretical importance and shall therefore begin our discussion by presenting counterarguments derived from other viewpoints. This is the appropriate procedure, since in describing the experiments with card tricks and in drawing conclusions resulting therefrom we did not consider possible objections to our statements.

It may be objected that the learning materials used in the card experiments were not "identical." The different groups learned to perform the same card trick, but they were not taught the same procedure. In analyzing the differences between the parts or elements of the learning materials it may be argued that considerably more material or a larger number of elements was presented to the meaningful learners than to the memorizers. The latter group obtained specific instruction which held good for only one situation, while the learning material of the first group contained many elements which recurred in the various card tricks. The presentation of common elements may have led to the solution of variations of the original task.

An objection to our explanation of the card-trick experiments may be derived also from an entirely different psychological theory. The fact that certain learning methods make it possible to solve variations of the problem is then explained by former experiments which revealed that the development of concepts and the formulation of principles constitute conditions of transfer in contrast to the memorization of raw facts and to routine training. Judd (36) showed in 1908 that by acquiring knowledge of a theory (of the principle of refraction) we can learn to overcome an illusion and to adapt our behavior to new conditions. Ruger (82) proved in 1910 that a general formula for puzzles spreads from one puzzle to another. It was therefore assumed that general ideas can be transferred and that conscious formulation of the guiding principles is required for transfer (Orata, 78). Generalization, the aim of all good teaching (Judd, 37), is the method of arriving at such principles or ideas and is therefore the basic condition of transfer.

This is not a complete answer to our problem, however. The term "generalization" may have different meanings. It may be that one must first apprehend or learn the various specific contents, in order to infer the principle or the guiding idea by generalization. Or it may be that a formulated general idea must be present as a common component of the various specific contents in order that one may resort to generalization and application. There are other possibilities, too, which will be discussed.

For the present let us concede that the results of the card-trick experiment alone do not prove the correctness of the given interpretation. They should be confirmed by further experiments with different materials before we attempt to decide between the possible explanations. We shall try to answer the following questions by further experimentation. Of what significance is the number of the elements presented in the practice period? Must the elements be identical in the practiced tasks and in the test tasks, or must the principle be identical? Must the principle be formulated and understood in order that the practice should result in transfer? To answer these and similar questions the comparison of the effects of two methods of learning is not sufficient. In the new experiments we shall teach the solution of a task in several different ways and shall try to determine which of the learning methods is the best.

The criterion for the best learning method will be, for the purposes of our investigation, its effect on retention (after eight days or more) and on the ability to apply it. In this and the next chapter the various learning methods will be compared by applying the second criterion: which method enables the largest number of subjects to solve the greater number of tasks which have not been practiced?

In order to identify the best, the second best, and the worst learning methods the new experimental set-up must fulfill another condition. It must be possible to measure the extent of the ability to solve new tasks after various kinds of practice. To measure the extent of the transfer effect, a task is needed which can be presented in many different forms—some very similar to each other and some not so similar. We will differentiate between similarity of the elements and similarity of the principle, which distinction adds considerably to the number of possible variations.

The number of elements presented in the practice period will not be found decisive for the quality of the learning method. We will show that improvement in learning results is brought about, not by merely increasing the number of elements presented, but by grouping or organizing them in a certain way. Furthermore, the best learning method will still not be attained by stating the principle of the task in the practice period, that is, by furnishing the subjects with the formulation of the guiding principle recurring in every task. Other methods which we shall call "learning by examples" and "learning by help" will prove to be the superior forms of learning, provided that they lead to the discovery or the development of essential whole-qualities by means of the "right" grouping of the steps of learning or the "right" organization of the learning process. Organization suitable to the structure or to the inherent relations of the material will be found essential and will lead to questions about the meaning and role of a principle, the nature of the whole-qualities, and their relation to the elements.

Search for Methods of Teaching, I

As the subject matter of the experiments a problem-solving situation has again been selected. The experiment will be divided into fore-test, practice, and test, and thereby we shall ascertain the occurrence of a process of learning: in the fore-test there is something unknown to the subjects (namely, how to solve the task), while in the test they may know it as the result of what occurred during the practice period.

The problem presented to the subjects concerns an unusual task with geometrical figures. It can be performed with matches or with pencil and paper. The individual experiments were done with matches, the group experiments with pencil and paper; but we shall call the problems briefly "match tasks."

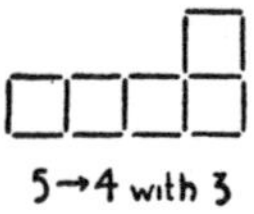

5→4 with 3

Fig. 1

The subjects are given the following task: Here are five equal squares (fig. 1); make four squares out of the five squares by changing the position of three sides.

The subjects are told that the squares are equal. The new figure should also consist of equal squares of the same size as those in the original figure. The subjects are told also of the following conditions which restrict their freedom of action. 1) All the side lines must be used in composing the new figure. (In speaking of matches one may formulate this requirement by saying: it is not permissible to take any matches away from the table.) Thus fig. 2a, which is shown to the subjects, does not represent a solution of the task. 2) The new figure should consist, as does the original, of squares only, not of squares and unused lines, which are not the sides of any squares. Fig. 2b is shown as another example of a procedure which is forbidden. 3) Duplications are not permitted—each square must have only four sides. Thus fig. 2c exemplifies another proceeding that should not be adopted by the subjects.

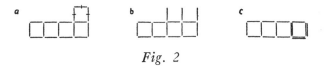

Fig. 2

In the fore-test the subjects are given a short time (one or two minutes) in which to solve the task. They are also asked whether they know the task or similar tasks. When someone solves the problem in the fore-test or reports that he knows the task, he is not used as a subject in the following learning experiments. Less than ten of about four hundred subjects had to be excluded for this reason from the experiments described in Chapter IV. In view of this negative result the main purpose of the fore-test is to provide an opportunity for the subjects to familiarize themselves with the task.

In the first few experiments made with the geometrical tasks the two tasks shown in fig. 3 were used. The instruction was the same for both tasks: to make four squares out of the five squares by changing the position of three lines. Fig. 3 also shows a correct solution [1] of each of the tasks.

---

[1] Task 1 has three other and Task 9 two other correct solutions. Some of these solutions involve the separation of the original figure into two noncontiguous parts.

Task 1

Task 9

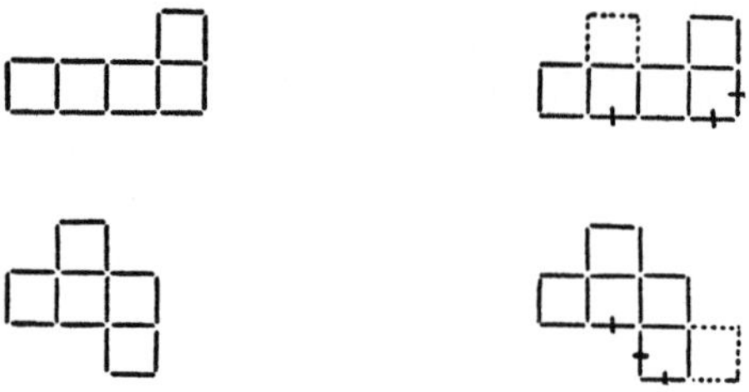

Fig. 3

How can we teach the subjects to solve these tasks? Recalling the memorization procedure used in the card-trick experiments, the presentation of a figure showing the correct solution of one task appeared to be a possible method of teaching. We want the subjects to learn how to solve Task 1; therefore we teach them precisely what we want them to learn by showing repeatedly the design of Task 1 (five squares) and the design of the "solution," which consists of four squares only. This method was tried out in the following way.

Learning Method I: result is taught.—First step: Task 1 is given to the subjects; it is not solved within two minutes. Second step: Task 9 is given; it is not solved within two minutes. Third step: The solution of Task 1 is shown to the subjects. Test: Task 9 is given again for three minutes.

The third step, comprising the practice or training, may have different forms: the task and its result (the final figure consisting of the required number of squares) may be shown, then removed, then shown again, and so forth. Six repetitions of the process were used to memorize the figures and to strengthen the connection between them. In a few other cases the result was shown and its elements were memorized: "The lower match of the second box from the left is to be taken away and placed . . ." It is easy to lengthen in this way the period of learning and to ensure a quick and exact reproduction (solution of Task 1) within the next twenty-four

---

Since (except in one experiment to be reported later) the subjects were not instructed to construct only one figure consisting of four squares, the solutions involving separations were also accepted as correct.—The numbers of the tasks refer to fig. 15 at the end of this chapter.

hours. However, none of the first few subjects who underwent practice of this kind was able to solve the similar Task 9. The fourth step of the experiment brought an entirely negative result: the knowledge of the solution of Task 1 was not sufficient to make solving of Task 9 possible. Moreover, with the learning method just described forgetting set in quickly: a week later four subjects were retested, and only one was still able to solve Task 1 within two minutes.

What method of instruction ought to be substituted for the memorization of the result, which appeared to be so unsatisfactory? Recalling the lasting effects of the discovery of the solution, the author made various tests in which he gave no instruction at all. Task 1 was presented to the subjects in a problem-solving situation in the assumption that they would solve this task without assistance and would be able to transfer to Task 9 the knowledge acquired during the process of solving Task 1.

The first subject with whom these assumptions were tested fulfilled the expectations, although it took him ten minutes to solve Task 1. Afterward he was able to solve Task 9 in three minutes, and a week later two minutes each were sufficient to solve both tasks.

After this initial success one disappointment followed another. Most of the subjects tested were unable to solve Task 1 even within ten minutes. Moreover, some subjects produced correct solutions of Task 1 and were nevertheless unable to solve Task 9 and even forgot the solution of Task 1 after eight days had passed. Thus it became necessary to distinguish between genuine and chance solutions. Even if the subjects succeeded in furnishing the correct solution of Task 1, there was no assurance that they had gained understanding of the match tasks.

But also for subjects whose unassisted solutions fulfill all requirements it is important to find out how the period of instruction can be shortened, controlled, and directed. Can a method of *teaching* be found which will convey understanding of the match tasks? In the first few experiments we contrasted Learning Method I, in which the result was taught, with a second learning method in which the principle of the match tasks was taught. In analogy to the procedure with card tricks it appeared that the explanation of the mathematical principle which forms the basis of the match tasks should be used as a method of teaching.

Learning Method II: principle is taught.—The first and the second steps are the same as in Method I. The third step is different. Task 1 remains before the subjects while the following explanation is given:

Here are five squares composed of sixteen equal lines. We want to change these five squares into four similar squares. Since we have sixteen lines and want four squares, each square must have its four independent side lines, which should not be side lines of any other square at the same time. Therefore all lines with a *double function,* that is, limiting two squares at the same time, must be changed into lines with a *single function* (limiting one square only).

For a few subjects the above explanation, given once, proved to be a good form of instruction. They listened to the explanation and then quickly solved both tasks. After an interval of eight days most of the subjects who immediately after the explanation were able to solve the tasks were again successful. But for only a minority of the subjects was the explanation of the arithmetical principle sufficient instruction, as will be shown in Chapter IV. Many subjects, although understanding the meaning of double and single functions, were unable to apply the information in solving either Task 1 or Task 9. With these subjects Method II was less effective than Method I.

This result was unexpected, inasmuch as some of the arguments brought forward to provide alternative explanations for the card-trick experiment appear to apply to the comparison of Method I and Method II. One may maintain that by listening to the principle the subjects learned "more" than by experiencing the solution of one task. The elements presented in Method II are those which recur in both tasks, while those given in Method I (for example, "take the second match from the top . . .") are unique. In Method II an explicit formulation of the principle is given, and recalling the general terms "double function" and "single function" may assure success; while Method I provides no hint for generalization.

In the card-trick experiments observation of the subjects' behavior and data obtained from introspection weakened the validity of such an interpretation. Most subjects solved the card tasks without being able to formulate the principle which guided them, and they used methods which differed from the practiced methods. But when a new task was given to the subjects a month later many who were taught the match-task principle promptly replied that "the double functions must be eliminated," and they then began to count the lines, following exactly the scheme of Method II.

By analyzing Method II in greater detail we find some causes for the relatively unsatisfactory performance of the subjects with this method. The principle stated in Method II, the elimination of sides having double functions, may be considered a principle concerning the whole figure, that is, the qualities of several squares and their mutual relation. But the explanation of the principle started from the elements of the material (by counting the lines or matches) and proceeded step by step toward larger units (the squares and their requirements). Is this the correct and natural description of the process involved in solving and understanding the problem? Various observations point to the fact that the unassisted solution of the problem and its full understanding involve "whole-principles" that are different from principles which deal with the elements. Below are recorded a few indications that successful solving of the problem is determined by procedures which are not expressed by the arithmetical principle.

1. In the problem-solving experiments, in which Task 1 was given for fifteen minutes to the subjects, eight of fifteen subjects were able to solve the task. The matches were then taken away, and the eight successful subjects were asked how many matches the figure contained. Only two promptly answered "sixteen." The others were silent for some time; they tried to visualize or to reconstruct the squares. Finally some arrived at the correct result, while others, unable to finish their counting, answered: "I do not know." These answers prove at least that it is possible to solve the problem in another way aside from the arithmetical principle given above.

2. The subjects of the problem-solving experiments proceeded by trial, touching first one and then another match. The trials were not evenly distributed to the various parts of the figure. Matches belonging to the upper square and to the first square on the left were seldom moved. When they were, it was only at first, and they were quickly replaced. The trials were, therefore, not arbitrary, but were guided by some principle which restricted the choice to the middle of the figure.

3. Children can learn how to solve the tasks and find the solution without assistance, although they are usually unable to understand the deduction given in Method II. In various experiments this result was obtained with children between nine and thirteen years of age. The instruction given to children will be described later.

4. The knowledge of the principle as presented in Method II is not sufficient to solve the problem. According to this principle all lines with double function should be changed into lines with a single function, but in reality none of the sides with double function is moved! Some matches with a single limiting function are moved in such a way that all double function is eliminated. The principle, however, does not indicate which sides should be moved. In successful cases of learning by Method II the subjects nevertheless are able to select the sides which they must move, probably because they understood something which is not expressed by the abstract principle.

Because of these observations we must assume that the explanation of the arithmetical principle as presented in Method II is not the only method by which the understanding of the match tasks can be taught.

How is it possible to teach or to facilitate the understanding of a difficult problem? In order to answer this question a comprehensive analysis of the problem itself is necessary. Our investigation of different forms of grouping in Chapter I illustrated the thesis that organization according to the requirements of the material is the key to any meaningful method of learning. In searching for such a meaningful method we must, therefore, first inquire into the nature of the requirements, the principles, and the laws of the material to be learned. This investigation will necessarily lead into problems of perceptual organization and thus to some the search will perhaps appear irrelevant to problems of learning. The distinction, however, between perceptual organization and higher mental processes is artificial. Methods devised for finding the requirements of the material have a proper place in the psychology of learning.

Digression: Sensory Organization

One of the first applications of gestalt principles led to the discovery of the "problem of *unum* and *duo*." Perception is articulated according to the laws of sensory organization. Under certain circumstances the articulation may determine that an individual sees only one object (or figure or drawing), while in other cases, which are only slightly different, the articulation of the perception may be altered so that two clearly differentiated objects are seen at the same time. Perception of depth (of perspective) furnishes a good example of the different forms of articulation.

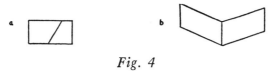

Fig. 4

Fig. 4a may be seen as one rectangle with a line passing through it, whereas fig. 4b can only be seen as two planes meeting at an angle. Even if fig. 4a is seen as two quadrilaterals, it remains flat, and the articulation in two objects is not completed. Another example follows.

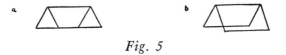

Fig. 5

Fig. 5a is usually seen as one figure consisting of three subdivisions, while in 5b may be seen a roof, by which word we express the perception of two separate planes.

The main factor in the distinction of a *unum* or a *duo* perception is the role played by the boundaries. A contour may have a single limiting function, for example, when it encloses one square, which in this case is seen as a figure on a neutral ground. But in other cases the contour may appear to be limiting two figures at the same time, that is, to be performing a double function.[2]

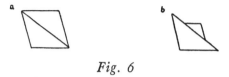

Fig. 6

Fig. 6*a* is usually seen as one object divided by a line, while fig. 6*b* is seen as two triangles, and one part of one side line performs a double function.[3]

The changes required in the function of points, lines, or planes because of which the number of objects perceived increases or decreases can be studied by beginning with elementary cases. In fig. 7*a* are two lines which are not connected and thus have four end points.

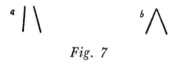

Fig. 7

If we identify the upper end point of the right line with that of the left line, we obtain two lines and three points (7*b*). The middle point limits both lines; it has a double function. Thus it is possible to change two lines with four points into two lines with three points and vice versa. The operation consists in uniting (joining) two points or in dividing one double point into two points. The same principle applies to geometrical figures (triangles, squares, and so forth) if we treat the sides as the points were treated above. From two triangles and six lines can be made two triangles and five lines (fig. 8*a* and 8*b*).

[2] The problem of *unum* and *duo* was first formulated by Wertheimer (105), who studied the laws of articulation responsible for the number of objects seen. Kopfermann (51) continued the experimental research. Koffka (50, p. 153) gives a detailed account.

[3] But in perception the common side line appears to limit either the left or the right triangle of fig. 6*b*, as found by Rubin (81) and by Koffka, who speaks of the "one-sided function of contour" (50, p. 181).

Fig. 8

Or from three triangles and nine lines can be made four triangles and nine lines (fig. 9a and 9b). This example can be described by stating that the three lines a, b, and c, each with a single limiting function, were transformed into three lines with a

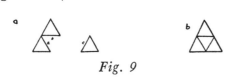

Fig. 9

double limiting function. Or in the reverse operation, the double limiting function of all lines was eliminated, and by this process the number of triangles was reduced.

The description just given is the result of an analysis performed by someone who after completion of the process was able to compare all its phases. However, it is at least questionable whether the description is commensurate with the psychological process which accompanied the changing of the figure consisting of three triangles into one of four triangles. We should ask first: Was the example with the two lines described in the right manner by stating that two points were united? Would it not be better to say that in transforming fig. 7a into 7b an angle was formed? In looking at fig. 6b an unbiased observer perceives two triangles; this description differs from the other, which asserts that the subject sees the short line in the center as having a double limiting function. Similarly, in fig. 9b the unbiased perception consists of a big triangle containing a smaller triangle. If somebody calls the figure "four triangles," the perception changes; if the task of making three triangles out of the four is presented, the solution may be arrived at by a further change of the perceived forms. By breaking up the figure we can complete the task without dealing with the single or double limiting function of the separate lines.

Similarly, in transforming fig. 9a into 9b we have not invested certain lines with a double function, but have made a triangle out of a "hole." The left side of fig. 9*a* contains two triangles; that is one possible description. Another way to describe the figure is to say that it contains two triangles and a hole; there is a third "triangle" on the left side, but one side is still missing. The third "triangle" is not yet "closed." To see the left side as just described rather than as two triangles is to take a decisive step in solving the problem: a fourth triangle is created if the hole is closed, and to close the hole all that is necessary is to push the triangle on the right against the figure on the left.[4]

In the two "match tasks" which were described above and in the various other tasks which will be described shortly the problem is always to increase or to reduce the number of geometrical figures without changing the number of the sides. The same problem is involved in the transformation of fig. 9*a* into 9*b* and 9*b* into 9*a*. If one is asked to change the four triangles of 9*b* into three triangles, the task is analogous to Tasks 1 and 9. Should we present the "solutions" of Tasks 1 and 9, containing four squares, and demand that they be transformed into figures containing five squares, we should have an analogy to the problem of fig. 9*a*.[5]

By using our description of the actual psychological process we are able to qualify the achievement required in the solution of the match tasks. The tasks are solved by discovering holes which can be closed if the task is to increase the number of triangles, squares, and so forth, or by breaking up the figure through the creation of holes where there were none if the task is to reduce the number of triangles, squares, and so forth. Task 4*b* (fig. 15) is a good example of the first procedure. Seven squares are to be made out of five. The task is solved by seeing the holes between the squares as prospective squares. Three holes can be closed by destroying only one square, thus the number of squares is in-

---

[4] To see an object in a new way which is structurally more adequate, is the essence of "recentering," a process which was described by Wertheimer (103) as one of the most important steps in productive thinking.

[5] Therefore the problem of figs. 9*a* and 9*b* appears as Task 3 in fig. 15. Page 79 contains the designs of all the tasks referred to in the following pages and in the experiments discussed in the next chapter.

creased by two. Task 4 (to make five squares out of seven) and Task 5 are examples for the opposite procedure, the creation of holes. Task 5 contains four squares which can be transformed into three squares by a process of disintegration, of "breaking up."

The description just given (closing of holes, creation of holes) differs from that with which we started (elimination or creation of the double function of lines). The correctness of this assertion can be tested by experiment. If there is a difference between the whole-principle of condensing or disintegrating geometrical figures on the one hand and the procedure of changing the function of certain lines on the other hand, then there must be tasks which are "arithmetically" of equal and nevertheless "structurally" of unequal difficulty. (The procedure which follows the principle described in Method II, that is, counting the functions of the side lines, is called "arithmetical," and the other directed by the apprehension of certain qualities of the whole figure is called "structural.") Moreover, there must be tasks which are structurally easy, but arithmetically difficult, and others which are arithmetically easy, but structurally difficult.

What is a structurally difficult task? Articulation of a sensory field depends on principles which in recent years have been demonstrated in great detail.[6] The laws of field organization, such as the laws of proximity, equality, good continuation, closure, and pregnance, determine what we perceive, that is, how we organize the distribution of the stimuli in perceiving. Conversely, if a perceived content corresponds to the requirements of the laws of articulation, for example, if it is a closed figure in which the lines near to each other belong to each other, and if one line or its good continuation is the contour of the same figure and does not belong to two different figures, then the perception gains in stability and it is difficult to see the figure in any other way. It is especially difficult to see in such cases the same stimulus pattern in an articulation which conforms less to the principles of perception. In order to solve Task 4 one must destroy a good closed

6 Wertheimer (105), Köhler (45), Koffka (50), especially pp. 98–210; Metzger (69) gives a good summary of the experiments of Wertheimer and his pupils.

figure and divide and break straight lines into parts. It is difficult to imagine and to perform these actions. Therefore Task 4 is structurally a difficult task. The following small experiments were undertaken for the purpose of investigating the difference between the arithmetical procedure and the structural procedure:

First Experiment: Problem Solving in Five Minutes

a) Five subjects (never before used in any match experiment) are asked to solve Task 4*b*: to make seven squares out of five by changing the position of three sides.

b) Five other subjects are asked to solve Task 4: to make five squares out of seven by changing the position of three sides.

Prediction: From an arithmetical point of view Tasks 4 and 4*b* cannot be considered different. But structurally Task 4*b* is easy, while Task 4 is difficult. In Task 4*b* the apprehension of holes is made easy by the general form of the figure presented to the subjects; the solution requires only the closing of well-defined holes. In Task 4, however, a complete and satisfactory figure must be broken up into parts which in the whole figure do not play an independent role.

Since most subjects proceed structurally, not arithmetically (compare the first observation on p. 63), it may be predicted that more subjects will succeed in Experiment *a* than in Experiment *b*.

Result of Experiment *a*: Correct solution achieved by all five subjects.

Result of Experiment *b*: Correct solution not achieved by any subject.

The same result was obtained also with Tasks 2 and 2*b*, for which the characterizations given above fully apply.

Second Experiment: Problem Solving in Five Minutes

c) Six subjects (never tested before) are asked to solve Task 6: to make five squares out of six by displacing three sides.

d) Six other subjects are asked to solve Task 7*b*: to make four triangles out of three by displacing three sides.

Prediction: Task 6 is arithmetically difficult and structurally easy, while Task 7*b* is arithmetically easy and structurally difficult. To say the least, from the arithmetical point of view Task 7*b* is not more difficult than Task 6, while structurally it is more difficult. Therefore a smaller number of subjects should solve 7*b* than should solve 6. While in Experiment 1 it was easier to increase the number of squares than to decrease them, in Experiment 2 the reverse is true.

Arithmetically Task 6 consists of seventeen lines, while five separate squares would require twenty lines. Therefore the solution must contain three lines with double function, whereas the original figure contains seven such lines. Task 7*b* requires the transformation of nine lines, none of which has a double function, into nine lines three of which have double function.

Apart from the destruction of a good symmetrical figure, the structural difficulties of Task 7*b* consist in the elimination of the common base line of the triangles. It is hardly possible to see a hole in Task 7*b*. The transformation of Task 6 into 6*b* again destroys a good gestalt, but the destruction may occur in a way corresponding to the structure (the axis) of the figure, which makes the procedure comparatively easy.

Result of Experiment *c:* Correct solution achieved by four subjects.
Result of Experiment *d:* Correct solution achieved by one subject.

The two experiments should be sufficient to show the differences between solving a task by the arithmetical procedure and by the application of a structural "whole-principle." The latter brings about the elimination of the double function, whereas the former must not bring about an understanding of the essential points of the problem. If in discussing the requirements of the problem we do not deal in terms of "lines," but in terms of "squares" and "holes," we find that the following qualities of the figures are of importance for the operations involved.

1. "Corner squares" (fig. 10*a*) and "center squares" (fig. 10*b*) can be destroyed by removing two lines, "inner center squares"

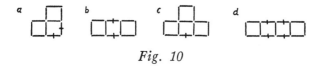

Fig. 10

(fig. 10*c*) by removing one line. By this operation a square is transformed into a hole. To destroy any of the other squares we must remove at least three lines, which is inadvisable in view of the requirement that the task should be solved by changing a limited number of lines.[7]

2. Conversely, in order to form a new square the addition of one line is sufficient when the hole is surrounded by three squares,

---

[7] In destroying center squares we must be careful, because the destruction of two center squares, which are neighbors, usually does not serve our purpose. In this case an unused line would remain between the destroyed squares, as shown in fig. 10*d*.

and the addition of two lines is sufficient when the hole is surrounded by two squares. These cases are illustrated in the drawings given above. It is inadvisable to form a new square at a place which is not surrounded by other squares (that is, where there was no hole), because in such a case we would have to add three or four lines.

The operations just described indicate the "detour" principle involved in solving the tasks. Instead of changing the position of lines, as we were told to do, we first destroyed certain squares and formed later new squares. Such detours do not concern the elements, but can be derived only from the whole problem and its requirements.

The expressions "corner square" and "center square" refer to whole-qualities. The same applies to the concept of the "hole." The arrangement of the entire figure and the position of the parts within the whole determines these qualities. To be "in the center" must not imply the identical position in the case of several individual figures, but it is nonetheless a concrete and precise determination. Thus we observe that principles and whole-qualities in the sense just described are not vague or hazy general ideas, but that they refer to concrete operations determined by the structure of the entire figure. Such operations are fundamentally different from specific operations, such as: taking the second vertical line from the left and placing it . . . and so forth.

It must now be remembered that we undertook the investigation of the principles of the match task in order to find the right methods of teaching and of learning these tasks. The results of this investigation may be summed up as follows:

1. When presented with the task, the subjects are confronted, not with a sum of lines, but with a consistent figure divided into sub-wholes according to the laws of gestalt. 2. The process of transforming Situation 1 (the task) into Situation 2 (the solution) is not necessarily determined by operations with one or the other side line, but is usually derived from the whole situation, which is recentered by apprehending "holes," or "possible holes," where there were none before. 3. The latter operation is not arbitrary, but

is governed by an intrinsic relationship between Situation 1 and Situation 2.[8] Therefore, knowledge of the operation may be acquired in a meaningful way. In problem-solving experiments there is the possibility of rational, rather than chance, solutions; and in learning experiments understanding in addition to memorizing may play a role.

Search for Methods of Teaching, II

The analysis of the principle and of the procedure involved in the solution of the match tasks should help us in devising new methods of teaching the mastery of the tasks. But before we do this we want to characterize the methods which we have applied in the preliminary experimentation. Method I appears to be a senseless method. The subjects were not taught any relation between the task and its solution (between Situation 1 and Situation 2), but a specific experience of one solution was created by memorization without understanding. Method II cannot be regarded as the only meaningful method. To some subjects it may not convey understanding, but may merely furnish them a formula (counting the lines, dividing them by the number of squares, and so forth) which may or may not help them. For other subjects, however, Method II may be meaningful. These are the subjects who when given the formula grasp the main point of the problem that the double function of the lines disappears if the figure is disintegrated.

These remarks confirm the old truth that methods of teaching may have different effects corresponding to the grade of understanding on the part of the pupils. But in searching for the best learning method we must restrict as far as possible variations in understanding the instruction. Teaching should if possible insure the right or the intended kind of understanding in the greatest possible number of subjects.

It may be possible to arrive at that goal by following Method II, inasmuch as the instruction is again based upon words which should convey understanding of the problem involved. But in-

[8] The term "intrinsic relationship" is used here in the sense applied by Wertheimer.

stead of using words significant for the arithmetic procedure, words which express the structural solution have been selected. These words are exemplified in a structurally easy task. This procedure shall be called Method II*b*.

Using as an example Task 4*b*, a structurally easy task, it is explained to the subject that in order to increase the number of squares he must *close the holes* and *condense* the figure. Then the reverse task (Task 4) is presented, and it is explained that in order to reduce the number of squares he must *create holes* and *loosen* the figure.

Method II has been transformed by introducing a structurally easy task. Similarly the method which was used in unassisted problem-solving experiments at the beginning of this chapter may be changed. To solve a structurally difficult task (for example, Task 1) without assistance proved to be too difficult for many subjects, or it required too much time to make it a practicable method of learning. One or more structurally easy tasks may therefore be presented to the subjects, who solve them without assistance. The question is whether or not difficult tasks can be solved as the result of such training. This procedure will be tried out with Tasks 4*b*, 3, and 3*a*. Each of these tasks was solved by most subjects in less than five minutes.

What further methods can be applied in addition to memorizing the solution, unassisted problem solving, and instruction by means of general formulas? We search for a meaningful method, that is, a method by which the transformation of Situation 1 into Situation 2 will be understood. The question arises: will the presentation of the solution of several structurally easy tasks serve that purpose? It seems justifiable to call the structurally easy tasks instructive, because the working of the principle is easily discernible in them. Should the solution of instructive tasks facilitate the understanding of the principle, it would be quite easy to devise a new method of instruction. It would only be necessary to show the subjects several instructive tasks and their solutions. Because the tasks are instructive, understanding them will lead to the knowledge of the principle. Instead of teaching the principle abstractly in words, the new method enables the subjects to develop it from a series of instructive concrete examples and their solutions. In addition, to further facilitate the understanding, the order in which the examples are presented can be chosen in such a way that the subjects are led from easier to more difficult problems.

This method of learning could also be called "learning by discovering," because during a successful learning period the subjects gain knowledge of the principle without its being explained by words. We prefer, however, to speak of "developing" the principle by means of simple examples and to reserve the word "discovery" for unassisted problem solving.

Another method will be tried so that its results may be contrasted with those obtained by the presentation of instructive examples. Suppose we follow the same system, but substitute structurally less instructive tasks and their solutions for the instructive ones and present them at random instead of proceeding from easy to difficult tasks. Will it be more difficult to develop the principle in the course of such a method of instruction?

"Learning by examples" is not the only method which should enable the learner to understand the transition from Situation 1 to Situation 2 without a formulation of the principle. Another method of instruction developed from our analysis of the tasks may be called "learning by help." The subjects arrive at the solution with the aid of certain hints given by the experimenter. Of what should the help consist? Our investigation of grouping may furnish the answer. There are several steps which lead from Situation 1 to Situation 2. These may be grouped either in a senseless way, that is, in a way which does not bring about an understanding of the reason for each step, or in a structurally adequate way, in which the role and the function of each step are determined by the task.

Beginning with the whole figure, we may contrast two different

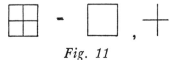

Fig. 11

situations. Suppose the figure shown in fig. 11 (Situation 1 of a structurally difficult task) is seen as a big square which is subdivided by a cross. As long as a subject sees the figure in this way, he will not be able to transform the four squares into three squares (Task 5). Should the subject, however, see the figure as indicated in fig. 12, he would have made an important step toward the solution of the task.

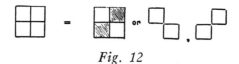

Fig. 12

The original figure of four squares is now seen as two pairs of squares which touch each other diagonally. Most subjects to whom this help is given, by shading two squares, quickly find the solution of the task. They preserve one set of squares and demolish the other. Thus, four lines are removed from which a new square can be formed.

These considerations led to the following method of teaching. The two series of steps (or movements or actions) shown in fig. 13 are contrasted. The first series, indicated by the steps *a*, *b*, *c*, and

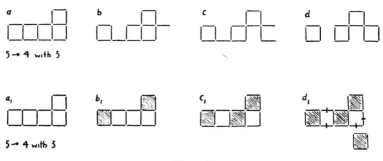

Fig. 13

d, represents a grouping of the steps bringing about the solution without regard to the structure of the material. The second series, indicated in fig. 13 by the steps a_1, b_1, c_1, and d_1, is an example for an adequate organization. In the method which we call "learning by help" the subjects are asked to solve a task. Their efforts are assisted, however, by presenting to them every half minute one of the consecutive steps a_1, b_1, c_1, and d_1.

A fifth step is required after step d_1 in order to solve the task by moving three instead of four lines. But in learning by help it is usually not necessary to present the fifth step. Often the third step leads to understanding, and if not, the fourth step does. After grasping what has been done in the third and fourth steps, most subjects discover that in order to solve the task with three lines they must simply leave any one of the four lines (removed in the fourth step) at its old place.[9]

In devising the cues shown in the lower part of fig. 13 we wanted to convey the idea that the closed unified figure must be broken up and expanded in order to solve the task. A second form in which learning by help was undertaken emphasizes the possible transformation of a square into a hole. A new cue is introduced in this method. In order to open the eyes for certain structurally important qualities of the task, we show the task once by paper squares and once by outline drawing. Fig. 14 in-

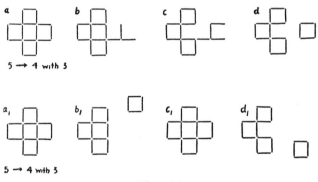

Fig. 14

dicates in the upper part how one can arrive at the solution of a task by grouping the necessary steps in an inappropriate way. The lower part of the figure also shows four steps. Fig. $14a_1$ is presented in the form of five paper squares. Fig. $14b_1$ shows that

---

[9] The task can therefore be solved in four ways.

five squares remain on the table if one paper square is separated from the rest. Fig. $14c_1$ is presented with matches or drawn on the blackboard in outline. If one square is separated from the rest—fig. $14d_1$—there remain four squares, and thus the number of squares is reduced by one.[10]

One procedure of memorizing, which was called Method I at the beginning of this chapter, consisted of the frequent repetition of the task and its final solution. The upper series in figs. 13 and 14 represent another procedure used in memorizing. In this procedure the steps leading to the solution are memorized. It is improbable that there will be understanding if the steps are inadequately grouped, as steps a, b, c, d are. Understanding would probably be excluded if the designs of the task were not presented at all—each step being described by words only (such as "Take first the top line of the second square from the left; put it . . . ; take the line . . ." and so on).

The lower series in figs. 13 and 14, however, indicate that it is possible to organize the transition from Situation 1 to Situation 2 in a different way. With a series of numbers we have discussed the difference between grouping according to and grouping against the structure of the material. The distinction made between the grouping 581 215 . . . and 5 8 12 15 . . . can be repeated with the match tasks. Steps a_1, b_1, c_1, d_1 exemplify grouping the steps in agreement with the principle of the task. The steps are chosen, not arbitrarily, but according to the inherent qualities of the problem. No repetition is used in this method, the helps (the individual steps) are presented only once.

The instructions shown in figs. 13 and 14 will be given in the experiments without using such words as "double function" or "hole." The guiding general idea is not formulated. Will learning by help nevertheless yield significantly better results than memorizing? By providing the answer to this question the methods of learning just developed will permit a comparison of the effects of senseless organization and meaningful organization.

---

[10] Here again a fifth step is required in order to solve the task by changing the position of only three lines instead of four lines.

Task

1

Task

1b

Task

9

Task

9b

2

2b

10

10b

3

3b

11

11b

3a

3c

4

4b

12

12b

5

5b

13

13b

6

6b

14

14b

7

7b

15

15b

8

8b

16

16b

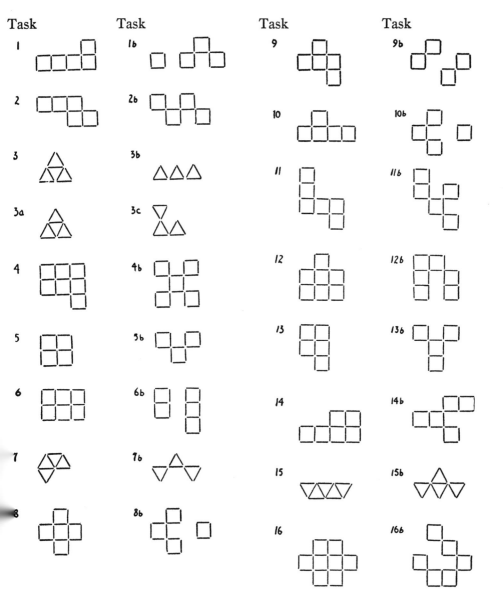

Fig. 15

The Match Tasks

Fig. 15 on the preceding page contains the designs of the match tasks which were used in this investigation. Task 1*b* represents the solution of Task 1, and vice versa. The same applies to the other tasks. All tasks must be solved by changing the position of three lines, except Tasks 2, 2*b*, 3*a*, 3*c*, 12, 12*b*, 15, and 15*b*, in which the position of two lines only must be changed. Some of the tasks have several solutions. The solution shown is the one given during the instruction period. In the tests and in the problem-solving experiments any correct solution was accepted.

Chapter IV

EXPERIMENTS CONCERNING TRANSFER
OF TRAINING

THE MATCH TASKS were used as the subject matter of several quantitative experiments, most of which were administered to comparable undergraduate classes in colleges of New York City and vicinity. The various experiments whose results are reported in this chapter differed mainly with respect to the method of teaching. The tasks used in the tests differed as well.[1]

[1] The identical features of the experiments will be briefly summarized here. The first experimental session consisted of introduction, fore-test, practice period, and test; the later session of introduction and test (called delayed test, or retest).

Introduction: "I shall show you a few tasks dealing with geometrical figures. Try to solve the tasks to the best of your ability. But you should know that the experiment is not a test of your ability or intelligence. What I want to test are various methods of presenting and explaining the tasks, because with the help of this experiment I hope to gain some knowledge of the psychology of learning. I shall tell you more about our problems after the experiment is finished."

After these words the design of Task 1 was drawn on the blackboard. "Here are five equal squares. The task is to make four similar squares out of the five by changing the position of three sides." Then the three types of wrong solution were explained by drawing on the blackboard, as shown in fig. 2. (In Experiment C, Task 2 was used instead of Task 1. The numbers of the tasks refer to fig. 15.)

Fore-test: "Should some of you know the problem or know similar problems, please write down what you know about it. If you already know the solution, draw it on the paper. If not, try to find it." After one or two minutes the work was interrupted and the papers were collected. The subjects who asserted that they knew the problem or who solved the task were not used in the experiment which followed.

Practice period: Description in the text.

Test: Test papers were distributed, each task on a separate mimeographed sheet. Each sheet contained in addition to the instruction (e. g., "make four squares out of five squares by changing the position of two sides") two copies of the task's design. The subjects were told to change one drawing, but to preserve the second in the original form for purposes of comparison. They were encouraged to make any number of other drawings. The solution (i. e., the design of the figure consisting of the required number of squares), as well as the lines whose position were to be changed, was to be indicated clearly. The working time allotted for the tasks varied.

At the end of the test the subjects were asked not to show the tasks to anybody, not to try to solve them, and not to think of them. At the beginning of the second test they were asked whether they had obeyed this instruction. The test papers of

Experiment A

The aim of the first quantitative experiment with match tasks was to compare the results of a senseless and of a meaningful method of teaching the task. As the senseless method, the memorizing of a solution was selected. The method used differed from that described as Method I in the preceding chapter in that the the number of details and variations presented had been greatly increased. Learning by examples was selected as the method for meaningful learning. It was intended that the subjects should develop understanding of the problem by watching the solution of several instructive tasks presented in a carefully chosen order. It is difficult to count the number of elements contained in an instruction period, but they were about equal in both methods, and the instruction took the same amount of time in both cases. The tests were devised so that the effects of the two methods on transfer and the curve of retention might be compared.

Three undergraduate classes of Brooklyn College were subjects for this experiment. The first class—we shall call it Group Mem. (memorizing)—practiced for eight minutes. The subjects were told to watch the experimenter carefully in order to learn how to solve the tasks, because they might be asked to solve them on a later occasion. Just one task (Task 1) and one of its solutions were shown. But the task was presented in the four different forms shown in fig. 16.

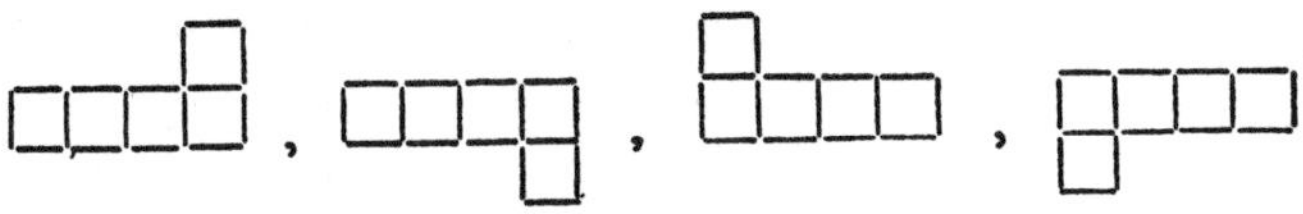

Fig. 16

First the experimenter drew the design of the first form on the blackboard, and then he drew its solution beside it.[2] The black-

---

subjects who admitted that they had tried to solve the task in the meantime, and so forth, were not scored.

[2] The term "solution of a task" as used here denotes only the final drawing consisting of the required number of squares, and implies no presentation of the intermediate steps by which this final form is achieved.

board was then wiped clean, and the procedure was repeated with the second design; and so forth. Because the same kind of solution occurred in each of the four forms the subjects obtained the impression that they were learning by repetition. After the fourth repetition, the reverse of the task was shown in the form of a "story." [3]

The second class, Group Ex. (examples), was told in the practice period (eight minutes): "In order to teach you how to solve such problems, I will show you some similar ones. Try to solve them. If you do not succeed in a short time, I will show you the solutions. Please watch carefully and try to understand what I have done." At first the design of Task 8 was drawn on the blackboard, and a half minute later its solution was drawn, that is, one whole square was removed far away from the other squares, thus making a "hole" of the center square. "We have solved the problem by moving four lines." After another half minute a solution was shown which required the moving of only three lines. Task 4b was next shown and solved. The reverse operation, Task 4 and its solution, was then demonstrated. Task 5 and its reverse form ended the instruction. The subjects thus experienced six transitions from one situation to another.

The third class was used as a control group (Group Con.). The practice period was omitted with this group, and the experiment consisted of introduction, fore-test, and test.

The test, in which four tasks (Tasks 3, 2, 4, and 1) were given, allowing two minutes for each, followed immediately after the practice period.[4] For Group Con., of course, all four tasks were

---

[3] The procedure was as follows: "Here we have the diagram of the house of a poor man in Japan. The man must have a new room in his house. He has one of those Japanese houses with movable paper walls and can't afford to buy any more walls. So what shall he do to make a five-room house out of a four-room house? Which walls shall he move in order to do it with as little work as possible? By moving only three walls he can make his house big enough for his larger family. By pushing these three walls he made a five-room house out of a four-room house."

[4] In this experiment rather short time limits were set throughout in order that many mistakes might be made, thus avoiding the frequent attainment of a 100 percent score, which would have been incomparable with other scores, since the solution time of the individual subjects was not measured. The fore-test was restricted to one minute. The subjects were asked to solve Tasks 3 and 2 by changing the position of three lines, and if they had time, also of two lines.

new. Group Ex. had seen Task 4 in the practice period, and Group Mem. Task 1. Thus both groups had to solve one old and three new tasks. Tasks 1 and 4 were, according to the results of problem-solving experiments, of about equal difficulty; therefore the three new tasks presented to Groups Ex. and Mem. were comparable.

Four weeks after the first experiment a second test was made. We shall call it simply retest, although most of the tasks presented were new. It consisted of four tasks, and two minutes were allowed for each.[5] For Group Con., a new control group, all four tasks were new. The old groups Ex. and Mem. were asked to solve three new tasks, and in addition one task which had been solved for them in the practice period four weeks earlier.

Table 3 (p. 85) shows what percentage of the subjects in each group solved the various tasks. We omit the records of the two "easy tasks" included in the experiment.

Practiced tasks.—Group Mem. worked on Task 1, the solution of which was learned in the practice period, for the entire eight minutes of that period, while Group Ex. devoted only one-third of that period to Task 4 and its reverse form. Nevertheless, as the table shows, the respective scores are about equal in the test. In the retest the practiced task is solved by more subjects of Group Ex. than of Group Mem. If we compare the test and the retest scores of the latter group, it is apparent that forgetting had occurred, while the table does not permit the same conclusion for Group Ex.

New tasks.—The scores of Group Mem. are, with one exception, higher than those of Group Con., but the scores of Group

---

[5] The scheme of the experiment was the following:

	Tasks Assigned to Group Ex.	*Tasks Assigned to Group Mem.*
Practice period	8, 4, 5	1 (in several forms)
Test	3, 2, *4*, 1	3, 2, *1*, 4
Retest	14*b*, *5*, 9, 10	14b, *1*, 5, 9

Task 3 and Task 14*b* were, according to the results of problem-solving experiments, distinctly easier than any of the other tasks. They are structurally easy tasks, while the other tasks are structurally difficult.

TABLE 3. PERCENTAGE OF PERFECT SOLUTIONS IN EXPERIMENT A[a]

	Group Con. 33 Subjects	Group Mem. 24 Subjects	Group Ex. 26 Subjects
Test			
Task 2	6	21	34
Task 4	9	8	46*
Task 1	6	42*	31

	Group Con. 20 Subjects	Group Mem. 19 Subjects	Group Ex. 21 Subjects
Retest			
Task 5	10	15	43*
Task 1	10	33*	. .
Task 9	15	21	52
Task 10	10	. .	35

[a] The numbers marked by asterisks indicate a practiced task. The number of subjects was smaller in the retest than in the test because of the absence of a few subjects and the exclusion of others who had familiarized themselves with the tasks in the interval.

Ex. are still higher. A comparison of the scores of Group Con. and Group Mem. shows that Group Mem. was most successful with Task 2. Here we should note that the design of Task 2 is very similar to that of Task 1, the practiced task of Group Mem. Moreover, Task 2 has a solution of exactly the same form as one of the solutions of Task 1. Nevertheless, even for Task 2 Group Ex. had the highest score.

Relation of practiced tasks to new tasks.—With Group Mem. the practiced task shows a substantial advantage both in test and retest. With Group Ex. the practiced task has a slight advantage in the test, while in the retest it appears to have neither an advantage nor a disadvantage.

These results must be considered as tentative and in need of confirmation by further experiments. The low scores of the control group do not permit an exact comparison of the achievements with regard to the individual tasks.[6] If we now attempt to compare the total accomplishment of the three groups, we are in a

[6] It cannot be assumed that one task is easier than another because it was solved— in two minutes—by three instead of two members of the control group.

somewhat better position. By introducing a scoring system we obtain a measure for the three respective performances.[7]

TABLE 4. SCORES OBTAINED FOR THREE NEW TASKS IN EXPERIMENT A

	Group Con.	*Group Mem.*	*Group Ex.*
Test			
Average score per subject	1.06	1.79	3.92
Standard error of average	0.27	0.26	0.46
Retest			
Average score per subject	2.20	2.84	6.24
Standard error of average	0.44	0.48	0.69

In solving new tasks Group Ex. is far superior to Group Mem., which is only slightly superior to Group Con. Thus the method of learning by examples (without the formulation of general principles) proves to be a good preparation for a test with new tasks. Memorizing the solution of one task (in its various forms) appears, on the other hand, to be only an insignificant aid in solving new tasks.

The statistical discussion of the results in Appendix 2 will afford further confirmation of these statements. The overlapping of the individual scores of Groups Con. and Mem. was very extensive. Among the members of Group Ex. there were also nine in the test and five in the retest who apparently did not profit from the instruction. But the other seventeen and sixteen subjects, in test and retest, respectively, show substantial learning effects; their performance was much better than that of the control group, which had no training. In the retest there were seven members of Group Ex. who obtained perfect scores with the three new tasks.

That the scores of all three groups were higher in the retest than in the test is due first to the fact that the tasks presented on the later occasion were the easier ones (cf. the difference in the

---

[7] The scoring system is explained in Appendix 2, which also contains the statistical discussion of the results. Whereas for the compilation of Table 3 only the perfect solutions were taken into account, for the purposes of Table 4 small scores were awarded also to "probable solutions." We explain that term on p. 270 in Appendix 2. The maximum score attainable by one subject was 10 for the three new tasks of both test and retest.

scores of the two control groups). But even if we deduct the scores of the control group from those of Group Ex., there are indications that the achievement of the latter group in solving new tasks had improved after the passage of four weeks. We shall discuss this point in Chapter VI.

Individual Experiments

In Experiment A two methods of learning, which brought about greatly different results, were employed. But in our introductory discussion many more types of learning method were discussed. Thus the question arises as to the place in the system of learning methods of the ways in which Group Ex. and Group Mem. were taught.

Experiment A was not the first experiment to be performed with match tasks by the author. In order to clarify the methods and their mutual relations and to observe the subjects' behavior while working on the tasks a great number of experiments were made with individual subjects instead of with groups. We shall report only a few of the results of these experiments, in which the subjects were intelligent adults, mostly students and professional people of different ages. The learning method assigned to each subject was decided by chance. Although the author believes that the various groups were comparable, he has no assurance that they were. Therefore we cannot make use of all the details in the results of the experiments.

In these experiments the fore-test lasted two minutes and the practice period eight minutes. In the test, following immediately after the practice period and uniform for each method, three minutes were given for each task. Four tasks were presented, none of which was shown in any of the practice periods. In the scoring system used, eight was the maximum score (perfect solution of all tasks), and zero the minimum score. It can be stated fairly accurately that all subjects who obtained a score of six or more understood the problem of the match tasks; they have acquired knowledge of the main points. On the other hand, scores of two or less indicate that the preceding instruction period had had no effect;

scores of one or two were due to chance and were often attained by subjects who had had no instruction at all.

TABLE 5. AVERAGE SCORES OF EIGHT LEARNING GROUPS AND PERCENTAGE OF SUBJECTS WHO OBTAINED HIGH AND LOW SCORES

METHODS OF LEARNING	NUMBER OF SUBJECTS	AVERAGE SCORE	PERCENTAGE OF SUBJECTS HAVING	
			Scores 6, 7, 8	*Scores 0, 1, 2*
Method I*a*	6	1.66	0	74
Method I*b*	6	1.83	0	74
Method II*a*	12	3.83	42	42
Method II*b*	12	4.00	42	33
Method X*a*	6	4.17	33	50
Method X*b*	6	4.67	50	33
Method III*a*	12	4.83	42	16
Method III*b*	14	5.43	57	14

METHODS OF TEACHING USED

Method I*a*.—Result was taught. Task 1 and its solution were repeated six times, using always the same task design and the same solution design. (Method described on p. 60.)

Method I*b*.—Result was taught. The solution of Task 1 was memorized in five different forms. Method is identical with that of Group Mem. in Experiment A.

Method II*a*.—Principle was taught in arithmetical form involving double function, as described on p. 62. Example: Task 1.

Method II*b*.—Principle was taught in structural form involving holes, as described on p. 74. Example: Task 4*b*.

Method X*a*.—This method consists of unassisted problem solving. Task 1 was presented, and the subjects were instructed to "try to solve the problem." After eight minutes the work was interrupted regardless of success.

Method X*b*.—This method also consists of unassisted problem solving. Three structurally easy tasks were presented in succession. At least two tasks were solved by all subjects. Method is described on p. 74.

Method III*a*.—The subjects learned by examples; noninstructive examples were presented at random. Examples: Tasks 9, 7*b*, and 13.

Method III*b*.—The subjects learned by examples. Instructive examples were given in planned succession. This is the same method which was used for Group Ex. in Experiment A, only this time Tasks 8, 4*b*, and 6 were chosen as the examples. The difference between III*a* and III*b* can best be expressed in the following way: in III*b* the experimenter intended to use those examples which he thought best for the purpose of teaching, while for IIIa he selected examples which he believed less suitable.

A comparison of the scores shows that Methods Ia and Ib were the worst methods of teaching and learning. Memorizing the connection between one task and its solution resulted only in a very restricted ability to solve new tasks. On the other hand, Methods IIIa and IIIb (learning by examples) were the best methods of teaching. Teaching by the formulated principle and unassisted problem solving have brought intermediary results, which are, however, more nearly comparable to the results of learning by examples than of memorizing. In view of the fact that the results of Method IIIa and Method IIIb are better than those of Method IIa and Method IIb we must conclude that formulating the general principle in words is not indispensable for achieving applications.[8]

As stated above, these experiments may be called crude when compared to the best methods of experimental technique, but the results are in full agreement with those of Experiment A—a group experiment. Methods Ib and IIIb even showed somewhat greater differences than the methods used with Groups Mem. and Ex., respectively. Thus experiments conducted with individuals, in which the subjects worked with matches in the presence of the experimenter only, brought about the same result as did group experiments conducted in the classroom, in which the subjects had to solve the tasks with paper and pencil. A few further results of the experiments with individuals should be mentioned.

Methods Ia and Ib.—The scores obtained by Methods Ia and Ib were about the same. By using different forms of a task and by presenting many details we secured results which were only slightly better than those obtained by strict repetition of one unchanged task and its solution. After the conclusion of the four

---

[8] We are, however, not permitted to draw another conclusion, namely, that learning by words is always less efficient than learning by examples. As discussed in the previous chapter, Method II was not exhaustive, insofar as the formulated principle did not tell the subjects exactly how to proceed. The inferiority of Method II may be due to some extent to this factor.

standard tests the same subjects were tested with Task 1. Most of them were able to solve that task, showing that the training had had a direct effect. Task 1 was presented in its different forms (p. 82), which were taught only in Method I*b*, not in I*a*. Nevertheless, the great majority of both groups succeeded with all forms of the task. There was no difference in this respect between the results of Groups I*a* and I*b*.

Methods II and X.—The Methods X*a* and X*b* appear to be somewhat better than the Methods II*a* and II*b*. The best of the four methods is unassisted problem solving, with the aid of structurally easy tasks. But the average scores tell only a part of the story. They are not much lower than the scores of Method III, and with respect to the percentage of the subjects who attained a high score, the difference between the six methods is still smaller. But we find in the case of Methods II and X a great number of subjects with a score of 0, 1, or 2. Thus, for certain subjects Method II, the learning of the formulated principle, and to a still higher degree Method X, unassisted problem solving, proved to be ideal methods of instruction. These subjects achieved scores of 7 and 8 points in tests which included only tasks they had never before seen. But the number of such successful subjects does not exceed 50 percent and is in some cases surpassed by the number of those who did not profit at all from the instruction. For a comparatively large number of subjects the application of the principle taught caused insurmountable difficulties. Similarly, for a comparatively large number of subjects unassisted problem solving had no instruction value at all.

Methods IIIa and IIIb.—These methods proved to be the best methods of learning, as measured by the high average score per subject and by the low percentage of subjects who in spite of instruction failed to learn anything. With Method III*b* a higher score was attained than with III*a*, but the difference is not very significant. That Group III*a*, instructed by "bad" examples, obtained a higher score than Groups II and X was an unexpected result. It indicates that our method of teaching by several examples is a rather good method even if the examples are not selected with great care. One single example may be noninstructive and may be presented in a way which is not helpful, as proven by the results of Method I, but several uninstructive examples watched attentively in succession may bring about a different result than can be obtained from each one alone. Due to the succession of several tasks exemplifying the same principle, understanding of that principle may arise. Method III*b* was tried out also with several children. Children between nine and thirteen years of age often made very high scores. In general these experiments indicate that our method of teaching by examples is suitable for teaching children.

Further experiments were made with the subjects who failed in the tests after having been taught by Method III. A repetition of the practice period resulted in all cases in a sharp increase in the scores. It appears probable that the main reason for their failure was that the instruction time was too short for them.[9]

Experiment B

Experiment A shows that two groups, Group Ex. and Group Mem., taught by different methods, behaved differently with regard to practiced and to new tasks. Group Mem. solved the practiced task much more easily than it could solve any new task, while the performance of Group Ex. was as good with new tasks as with practiced tasks. May we trace this result to the distinction between meaningful and senseless methods of learning?

[9] Following the plan of the individual experiments, group experiments were carried out with three of the methods in undergraduate classes at Newark University. The instruction of Method II*a* was presented on paper to each member of the group. The results, given in the following table in the form chosen for the individual experiments, brought a confirmation of what was previously established.

Methods of Learning	Number of Subjects	Average Score	Percentage of Subjects Having Scores 6, 7, 8	Percentage of Subjects Having Scores 0, 1, 2
Method II*a*	6	3.65	33	50
Method III*a*	15	4.44	31	12
Method III*b*	16	4.87	40	13

Somewhat lower scores were obtained than were obtained in the individual experiments, but the relation of the results remains similar. Learning by examples again proved to be a good method of instruction, even in case of poorly selected examples; whereas one-half the subjects who listened to the arithmetical principle of the task failed in the test with new tasks.

The following counterargument may be raised against our explanation of the results in Experiment A: Both Groups Mem. and Ex. learned for the same length of time, and both were presented in the practice period with the same number of figures and solutions. Yet Group Ex. was taught more than Group Mem. The latter group experienced only the solution of one task (although this task was presented in several forms), while Group Ex. observed the solution of three tasks. It seems probable that a new task is more similar to or more related to any one of three practiced tasks or to a common component of the three tasks than to the one practiced task. Therefore the superiority of Group Ex. with regard to new tasks may be due to practice with common or related elements.

In order to test such an argument a new experiment must be made, in which the same number of tasks and the same group of tasks are taught by different methods. In this case neither the greater number of the practiced tasks nor a greater similarity between practiced tasks and new tasks may account for the result. Should such a new experiment yield the same or similar results as did Experiment A, then we would be entitled to explain both experiments with the aid of the same principle—the quality of the learning methods—instead of emphasizing the importance of the number of the tasks in the first experiment and the qualities of the learning methods in the second experiment.

In the new experiment further possible flaws of Experiment A will be eliminated. In Experiment A there was a difference in the tasks used for testing the two experimental groups. In the new experiment we use the same tasks not only in the practice period but also in the tests and the retests. Moreover, in Experiment A some of the practiced tasks were also used in the test. Thus, in the retest they were doubly familiar as compared to new tasks, being both practiced and tested. In Experiment B the tasks chosen for the instruction period will not be tested in the first experimental session at all. As we have already explained in the first chapter, the value of the different learning methods cannot be decided merely on the basis of the results of immediate recall. Therefore the following experimental set-up was devised.

Practice period: Tasks 1 and 8

Test (following immediately after the practice): four new tasks—Tasks 10, 6, 9, 16

Retest (four weeks after the practice): *a*) the two practiced tasks— Tasks 1 and 8; *b*) two new tasks—Tasks 5 and 4; *c*) two tested tasks —Tasks 6 and 9. The latter six tasks were given in the order 6, 5, 8, 1, 4, and 9.

The practice period of ten minutes was used differently for the four groups:

Group Mem.—The senseless method of learning made use of the "inadequate grouping" of the steps, shown in figs. 13 and 14, above. The design of Task 1 was drawn on the blackboard. "To solve that problem, we proceed in the following way." Then steps *b, c,* and *d* (fig. 13) were drawn. The blackboard was wiped clean. "We shall repeat the solution in order that you should know it well." There were six repetitions of Task 1 and six repetitions of Task 8 (fig. 14*a*).

Group Help.—Task 1 was given. "Look at the blackboard and try to find the solution of this task." Thirty seconds later the experimenter said: "Try to understand what I am doing." With these words the experimenter shaded the corner squares on a new drawing placed beside the first. After another thirty seconds the second help was given—as illustrated in the lower part of fig. 13. The only words used by the experimenter were "Now we have solved the task by changing the position of four lines" (and later, "of three lines as required"). There was no repetition, each step being shown only once. The blackboard was never wiped clean, so that at the end of the instruction with Task 1 all the drawings representing all the steps could be examined simultaneously. The procedure with Task 8 was similar.

Group Arith.—The text of the arithmetical principle (elimination of lines with a double function, p. 62) was slowly read to the subjects. Then Task 1 was shown. "Let us see how the principle works." The solution was shown. "Now we have eliminated all the lines with a double limiting function." The principle was then read again and exemplified on Task 8.

Group Con.—This control group was given no instruction.

In all three learning methods the same two tasks were solved by the experimenter before the eyes of the subjects. Nevertheless, the methods of teaching differed: the steps leading to the solution of the tasks were grouped or organized each time in another way. Group Mem. was repeatedly presented with a ready-made pattern —which led to the correct result, but in which there was no understandable relation between the consecutive steps. Group Arith. was taught a principle and was also shown how to apply it; but here again the links between the well-formulated abstract principle and the structural whole-qualities of the task did not form a part of the instruction. On the other hand, the organization of the successive steps presented to Group Help was structurally consistent: the function of each step and its role in solving the task may have been understood by attentive listeners.

Of course, no strict correspondence can be assumed between methods of teaching and methods of learning. Some of the subjects to whom senseless repetitions were presented may have speculated during that time about the reasons for the various steps taken; conversely, instead of understanding the successive steps, some members of Group Help may have merely memorized the one or the other help without its function in the whole process. Therefore it was not to be expected that all the subjects of each group would achieve results corresponding to the methods of teaching. The question raised by the experiment was whether the averages would show significant differences.

There was some reason to expect smaller differences in the averages than those arrived at in the experiments previously reported. The method of teaching Group Arith. was better than Method IIa in that two examples were given for the elimination of the double function. The results with Group Mem. in Experiment B were also expected to be better than those with Group Mem. in Experiment A, because this time the solution of a structurally clear task (Task 8) was taught, in addition to that of a structurally difficult task (Task 1). On the other hand, the best method of teaching· was expected to be less efficient in Experiment B than in Experiment A, because only two, instead of three, examples were included in the practice period.

The experiment was carried out in sections of the same undergraduate course in the College of the City of New York, taught by the same instructor.[10] The records of those students who were not present at the retest and those who reported in the retest that they had thought of the tasks or shown them to someone during the time between test and retest were eliminated. The following table contains the results of the four groups with the four new tasks in the test, in which three minutes were allowed for each task. The total scores of each group are computed on the basis of a scoring system in which the minimum score (no task solved) was zero and the maximum score (all tasks solved perfectly) was thirteen.

TABLE 6. RESULTS OF THE TEST IN EXPERIMENT B

PERCENTAGE OF PERFECT SOLUTIONS

	Group Con. 29 *Subjects*	*Group Mem.* 27 *Subjects*	*Group Arith.* 24 *Subjects*	*Group Help* 25 *Subjects*
Task 10	14	30	35	40
Task 6	43	61	50	72
Task 9	14	19	54	48
Task 16	11	16	16	28

AVERAGE SCORES PER SUBJECT

	Group Con. 29 *Subjects*	*Group Mem.* 27 *Subjects*	*Group Arith.* 24 *Subjects*	*Group Help* 25 *Subjects*
Score	2.92	3.82	5.00	6.00
Standard error	0.61	0.63	0.83	0.83

The order of the four groups is: Help, Arith., Mem., Con. The differences in the average scores of two neighboring groups (Help and Arith., Arith. and Mem., Mem. and Con.) are not significant; but Group Help, taught by a meaningful method, is again significantly superior to Group Mem., which was taught by a senseless method. The differences between the groups are, as expected, somewhat smaller than in Experiment A. But even between the neighboring groups there are differences worth mentioning: in Group Help there were eight subjects who had a perfect or an almost perfect score; in Group Arith., however, there were only

---

[10] Cf. Appendix 2 on the question of the comparability of the groups, on the reliability of the differences, and for the explanation of the scoring system used.

five such subjects, in Group Mem. three, and in Group Con. two. Two subjects of Group Help failed completely (zero score); but in Group Arith. there were six, in Group Mem. seven, and in Group Con. fourteen such subjects.

Scrutiny of the performances with respect to the four individual tasks indicates that one of the four tasks, No. 6, was much easier than the others. It was solved by 43 percent of the members of the control group. It seemed advisable to include one easy task in the test in order to avoid as far as possible the depressing effect which is usual if a subject fails to solve a single task. Task 16 was the most difficult task, while Tasks 9 and 10, being structurally of about the same difficulty, differed in one important respect: Task 10 and the practiced Task 1 both consisted of four squares in one row and one square above one of the squares in the row, and Task 10 had one solution similar in form to that of the learned Task 1. On the other hand, there was no such similarity between Task 9 and Task 1.[11] Nevertheless, for Groups Arith. and Help Task 10 was not easier than Task 9. Members of these groups who solved Task 10 used several forms of correct solutions without any preference. Of the eight subjects of Group Mem. who solved Task 10, however, seven produced that solution which had the form of the learned solution of the practiced task (see fig. 19 on p. 120). Group Mem. had the most significant advantage over the control group in Task 10. There is reason to believe that it was due to the similarity just described. The inclusion of Task 10 in the test thus served to increase the total score of Group Mem.

Group Arith. fared best with Tasks 9 and 10 and much worse with Tasks 6 and 16 (always comparing its scores with those of the control group). Here again a simple explanation presents itself: in Tasks 6 and 16 only some of and in Tasks 9 and 10 all the

---

[11] The similarity between Tasks 1 and 10, which we have just described, we shall call "piecemeal," because it is reducible to the identity of parts and solution designs. Structurally both Task 9 and Task 10 are similar to Task 1, because the same kind of operation, such as the destruction of noncontiguous center and corner squares (p. 71), is used in all these tasks. Task 16 is, from a structural point of view, somewhat different from Task 1, because the operations required to solve Task 1 must be changed to some extent in order to solve Task 16.

lines with a double limiting function were to be eliminated. Therefore the first two tasks were arithmetically more difficult than the latter. With the exception of Task 9, the results of Group Help were the best in all the tests.

In the retest, made four weeks after the first experiment, six tasks were used. The time limit for the solution of each task was reduced from three minutes in the test to two and one-fourth minutes in order that we might obtain comparable scores which should as far as possible not attain the maximum range of the score. The following table shows the total accomplishment of each group in the retest. The range of the possible scores was zero to fifteen; the score fifteen representing perfect solution of all tasks.

TABLE 7. AVERAGE SCORES OF THE RETEST IN EXPERIMENT B

	Group Con. 29 *Subjects*	*Group Mem.* 27 *Subjects*	*Group Arith.* 24 *Subjects*	*Group Help* 25 *Subjects*
Score	2.38	4.41	5.67	8.08
Standard error	0.61	0.55	0.73	0.65

The same order of groups was obtained as in the test. Group Help had the highest score, Group Arith. the second highest, while the score of Group Mem. was again nearest to that of the control group. In the test, however, there was only a comparatively small difference between Group Help and Group Arith., while in the retest that difference increased greatly. The results of Group Arith. were now much nearer to those of Group Mem. than to those of Group Help. All the differences are significant with the sole exception of that between Group Arith. and Group Mem.[12]

[12] The shift in the performance of Group Arith. can also be demonstrated in another way. We may ask: have the subjects who had high scores in the test fared well again in the retest, and have those with low scores in the test failed in the retest? Rank correlations determined between the performance in test and retest answer that question. The correlations were fairly high in the case of Groups Help and Mem. (.43 and .48, respectively), but rather low in the case of Group Arith. (.24). Even in the first two groups there were many exceptions to the rule of uniform performance in test and retest. But with Group Arith. sharp improvements and unexpected deteriorations in the accomplishment of individual subjects were the rule rather than the exception. Learning by the abstract principle is thus characterized in our case by a certain degree of instability.

The above table does not answer the main question investigated in the retest: have the various groups, that is, the subjects taught by different methods, fared equally well with practiced, tested, and new tasks? Table 8 gives the detailed results of the retest and thus permits us to answer the question. Since there were two practiced, two tested, and two new tasks,[13] we have three possibilities in each subdivision: a subject either solved both tasks or solved one of the two tasks or solved none of them. The table shows the number of subjects in each of these classes. This distribution of frequencies permits the calculation of a measure for the accomplishment of each group, which is given in the last two columns of the table. The number of correct solutions in each subdivision of each group was divided by the number of possible solutions.[14]

TABLE 8. SOLUTION OF NEW TASKS, PRACTICED TASKS, AND TESTED TASKS IN EXPERIMENT B

	NUMBER OF SUBJECTS WHO SOLVED			PERCENT	NET
	No Task	*One Task*	*Two Tasks*	OF SOLUTIONS	SCORE
NEW TASKS					
Group Mem.	20	7	0	13.0	−0.8
Group Arith.	10	11	3	35.4	21.6
Group Help	7	12	6	48.0	34.2
Group Con.	21	8	0	13.8	. . .
PRACTICED TASKS					
Group Mem.	11	10	6	40.8	25.3
Group Arith.	9	13	2	35.4	19.9
Group Help	4	15	6	54.0	38.5
Group Con.	21	7	1	15.5	. . .

[13] For the sake of statistical comparability of results it would have been better if each of the subdivisions had consisted of three or four tasks. But exploratory experiments proved that a test could not be prolonged beyond the time and the effort required for the solution of six tasks. Even with eight tasks (all rather similar) new uncontrolled factors entered into the picture: fatigue, loss of interest, and effects of practice due to the work on the previous tasks of the same test.

[14] To give an example: the twenty-five subjects of Group Help who were tested with new tasks produced six test papers with two solutions each (twelve solutions) and twelve papers with one solution each (twelve solutions). Twenty-four correct solutions instead of the fifty possible solutions represent an accomplishment of 48 percent. Thus, 100 percent in the table would mean that every subject of the group solved both tasks; 0 percent, that no subject solved any task.

TABLE 8 (*Continued*)

TESTED TASKS

Group Mem.	3	13	11	64.8	38.9
Group Arith.	5	12	7	54.2	28.3
Group Help	1	7	17	82.0	56.1
Group Con.	18	7	4	25.9	...

The last column of Table 8 contains a measure of the learning effect. We obtain the "net scores" by deducting the score of the control group from the score of each learning group.[15] The net scores of Group Help in new and practiced tasks are about equal, but Group Mem. has a much higher net score in the practiced tasks than in the new tasks.

This comparison of the performances of Group Help (meaningful method of learning) and Group Mem. (senseless method of learning) with respect to new and to practiced tasks constitutes the main result of the experiment. Group Help solved new tasks as well as practiced tasks; for members of this group it made no difference whether a task had been practiced four weeks earlier or had never been seen before. Group Mem., however, scored much higher with practiced tasks than with new tasks. In the first case the score indicates a substantial learning effect; while in the second case the performance of Group Mem. is not better than that of the control group.

The performance of Group Arith. was also equal in new and in practiced tasks, but in both cases it was inferior to that of Group Help. With practiced tasks and to a still higher extent with tested tasks Group Arith. fared worse than even Group Mem.

The data of Table 8 will permit us to measure the transfer ef-

---

[15] It is possible to calculate "net scores" in another way, namely, by computing the ratio of the scores of the learning and the control groups. In this way we obtain the following measures of the learning effect:

RATIO OF IMPROVEMENT

	New Tasks	Practiced Tasks	Tested Tasks
Group Mem.	0.94	2.64	2.50
Group Arith.	2.56	2.28	2.09
Group Help	3.48	3.48	3.17

The net scores in Table 8 and these ratios point to the same regularities in the case of the new and the practiced tasks. With regard to tested tasks certain differences appear which are due to the much higher control score in this subdivision.

fect (see Appendix 2), which is very substantial in the case of Group Help and Group Arith. Group Mem., on the other hand, was unable to transfer to new tasks what it had learned. The scores of the control group show that the difficulty of the new and the practiced tasks was about the same. Similar operations were required for the solution of these four tasks provided that the operations are understood in the sense of whole-principles.

With regard to tested tasks, the comparison is more complicated than with regard to the other two subdivisions. The control score is here much higher, because an easy task (No. 6) was included among the tested tasks. Whether under these circumstances the "net scores" are strictly comparable with those of the practiced and new tasks we do not dare to decide. Nevertheless, the result, as available in the data of Table 8, may be stated as follows. The three learning groups had higher net scores with the tested tasks than with the practiced tasks. The second type of calculation, as computed in the footnote, brings about a somewhat different result; but even there, in the scores of Group Mem., the tested tasks had a substantial learning effect. This fact will be confirmed by later experiments; earlier tests improve the scores of later tests, and testing means practicing.

After the completion of the retest the subjects were asked to go quickly through their test papers to find out whether or not they recognized any of the tasks from the previous experimental session. The subjects were asked to write "o" (old), "n" (new), or a question mark on each page—"o" being used for assured recognition, "n" for a task which was certainly not seen before, and a question mark for inability to decide.

TABLE 9. RESULTS OF THE RECOGNITION TEST

Groups	Percentage Giving Correct Answers [16]	Percentage Giving False Answers [16]	Percentage Giving Question Marks
Mem.	46	24	30
Arith.	44	30	26
Help	47	21	32

[16] Correct answer means "old" for old tasks and "new" for new tasks; false answer, "old" for new tasks and "new" for old tasks.

The correct recognitions amounted to less than one-half of the judgments given. More than one-quarter of the judgments were false. There was no significant difference in the performances of the three groups in the recognition test, except that Group Arith. gave the largest number of false answers.

The last question asked by the experimenter at the end of the retest was:

> Try to formulate in a few words the main point or the principle of the tasks on which you have just worked. What is the essential thing you have to know in order to be able to solve such tasks? I do not need exact definitions; a hint at certain ideas you have in mind will suffice. You will have three minutes in which to write.

The answers collected from the seventy-six subjects of the three learning groups were rather unsatisfactory. A few blank papers were returned, a few contained generalities such as "you must be able to think clearly," and "inquisitive ability is essential," while the great majority of the descriptions given were inaccurate or dealt with minor points or were so vague that it was hardly possible to decide whether the writer had the right idea. A lenient judge might have considered only about ten answers satisfactory. Many subjects declared after the experiment that they found it impossible to express in words what they had in mind, and most answers showed clearly the difficulty under which the subjects labored. The subjects no doubt succeeded in conveying only a part of what they knew. There was no correlation between the few satisfactory answers and the performance of the same subjects as revealed by their scores. Many subjects who solved all or most of the tasks were, nevertheless, unable to give an account of the problem's main points.

This result reveals that it is very difficult to express in words what is required to solve such tasks. The ability to solve the tasks can be acquired without verbal formulation of what has been learned and successfully performed. Conversely, formulation alone is no guarantee of good performance.

Experiment C

From the two group experiments just described we may conclude that the ability of the subjects to solve new tasks differs greatly according to the method of instruction. When the "good" method of teaching was administered in the form of three different examples and when the "bad" method was restricted to the repetition of the solution of one task (Experiment A), the differences were very significant. There were also great differences when the various methods of teaching were applied to the same tasks and the same solutions (Experiment B). A further experiment should serve to verify the latter result and to clarify the relationship between the methods of learning and the ability to solve practiced and new tasks.

In the new experiment we repeated the procedure of Experiment B in that the same tasks were included in the different training periods. But the senseless learning method was changed to some extent in order to insure that one of the groups should learn in a stereotyped and routine way. The other group was taught with the intention that it should understand the role of the various steps of the instruction within the whole process. The tasks selected for the practice period, as well as for the tests, differed from those in Experiment B. Furthermore, in the new experiment the groups were not tested by match tasks immediately after the practice period, in order to eliminate the possible practice effect of the test. Finally, Experiment C was made with time intervals between practice and delayed test which were not investigated in the previous experiments.

The scheme of the experiment was: fore-test, Task 2; practice, Tasks 2 and 10; delayed test, Tasks 2, 10, 11, and 16. The practice period lasted eight minutes; in the test, in which two practiced tasks and two new tasks were given, the subjects had three minutes for each task. The test was made in the order 10, 16, 11, and 2 for half of each group and 16, 10, 2, and 11 for the other half of each group. The delayed test was administered to half the groups one week after the practice period and to the other half three weeks after the practice period. We shall speak of Experiment C1 and Experiment C3 in order to indicate that different subjects were used in the two tests.

For Group Help the methods described in Experiment B were adapted. Task 2 was first shown with the cue of shading certain squares; then followed Task 10, which was solved by using five squares made out of paper. Thus the difference between Group Help in Experiment C and in Experiment B consisted mainly in a change of tasks, which, however, were taught in a similar way. Group Mem. was taught in Experiment C by using solutions which were identical for the two tasks.

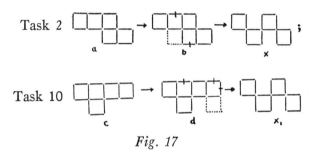

Fig. 17

Fig. 17 illustrates the procedure used with the group. First the connection a–b–x was formed and strengthened by six repetitions; then the connection c–d–x_1 was formed and strengthened by six repetitions. Due to the fact that fig. 17x is identical with fig. $17x_1$, the members of Group Mem. obtained the impression of a stereotyped learning process having the character of drill.

After the training it was necessary to provide some kind of conclusion to the experiment in order to satisfy the subjects that the purpose for which they learned the solution of the tasks was attained. Therefore a test was made which consisted of difficult problems of an entirely different kind.[17] The subjects believed that the purpose of the experiment was to find out whether instruction in solving the match tasks helped or retarded the ability to solve "reasoning" tasks.

[17] For example, the nine point task of Maier (66, p. 142) was used. The test was the same for all training groups.

The results of one control group, which received no instruction whatever, may serve as a control for both subdivisions of the delayed tests with the learning groups. The control group consisted of thirty students. If these students had solved all the tasks, the test papers would have contained sixty solutions for the so-called practiced tasks and sixty solutions for the so-called new tasks. Actually only seven correct solutions were found for the one kind and seven for the other kind of tasks.[18] Thus, Group Con. achieved a 12 percent score both with those tasks which served as practiced tasks and with those which served as new tasks in the learning experiments. The results of the learning groups will be reported in the same brief manner by giving the proportion of the solutions to the possible maximum number of solutions.

TABLE 10. PERCENTAGE OF SOLUTIONS IN EXPERIMENT C

	Group Mem. 26 Subjects	Group Mem. 28 Subjects	Group Help 22 Subjects	Group Help 27 Subjects	Group Con. 30 Subjects
Test after one week					
Practiced tasks	67	..	58	..	12
New tasks	25	..	55	..	12
Test after three weeks					
Practiced tasks	..	53	..	52	12
New tasks	..	14	..	55	12

The two memorizing groups scored high when tested with practiced tasks (67 and 53 percent, respectively), but very low when tested with new tasks (25 and 14 percent, respectively). In the scores of the two understanding groups we find no appreciable difference; both one week and three weeks after training about the same scores were obtained with the new and the practiced tasks. Forgetting is indicated by the fact that the scores of Groups Mem.

[18] The low control score in spite of the three-minute time limit for each task is due to the fact that we used only structurally difficult tasks in this experiment. In order to avoid the annoying effect of zero scores, a fifth easy task was added to the test of the control group, which task, however, was not taken into account in the scoring.

become lower with the passage of time, while the performance of Groups Help does not justify such a conclusion.

The frequency distribution of the individual scores of Experiment C is included in Appendix 2, p. 272. We find there, and also in the frequency polygons, that of all the scores of the learning groups only two, designated by figures 25 and 14, are significantly different from the other scores. The differences between the percentages 52, 53, 55, 55, 58, and 67 cannot be considered significant. Similarly, there is no significant difference between the control-group score of 12 and Group Mem.'s "new" score of 14, and only a slightly reliable difference between the control-group score of 12 and Group Mem.'s other "new" score of 25.

We learn from the experiment that memorizing brought about a small transfer effect if the test was made one week after the practice period and practically no transfer effect if the test was made three weeks after the practice period. On the other hand, Group Help showed on both occasions the familiar result of previous experiments; that is, the ability to solve old and new tasks was about the same. Learning by understanding proved to be a much better method than learning by stereotyped repetitions, provided the ability to solve new tasks was used as the measure of the learning effect. But even with regard to the solution of practiced tasks, memorizing had no advantages over understanding, provided the tests were made a few weeks after training.[19]

Experiment D

In a last experiment the problem of transfer of training from practiced to new tasks was subjected to inquiry. The following considerations influenced the devising of this experiment.

In previous experiments we tested the counterargument according to which the "good" methods of learning consisted of learning more than the "bad" methods (or the good methods meant learning recurring elements). We therefore performed the experiment by using the same number of tasks and the identical

[19] In Chapter VI we shall discuss these results with regard to the curve of forgetting.

tasks in the practice period of both learning groups. But in these experiments we gave certain "helps" in the one method of teaching which were not given in the other method. It may have been that these cues comprised components which recurred in an identical way in the new tasks. In that case the same argument which we raised against the validity of the card-trick experiment may be repeated against the achievement of Group Help in solving new match tasks: certain "concrete particulars," acquired in the practice period, were carried over to the solution of the new tasks. We shall attempt to determine the weight of this proposition by a new experiment.

Let us analyze the method of help from the drawings of fig. 13 on p. 76 (shaded squares). We could assume that the three cues given in that series meant for the subjects the following three specific statements: step b_1—those squares of the figure which are most remote from each other (the "end-squares") must remain intact; step c_1—the center square is to be preserved; and step d_1—two squares, not contiguous and surrounded by intact squares, are to be demolished.

Suppose the subjects to whom the method of help was presented would have learned these three specific statements. In that case we would have to conclude (1) that they would be able to apply their knowledge to those tasks in which the solution requires the preservation of squares most remote from each other and the demolition of two noncontiguous squares, and (2) that they would fail in those tasks in which that particular procedure is of no avail. We have tasks of both types and have used them in previous tests. Thus a thorough analysis of the results of the previous experiments may answer the question now raised. The result of that analysis is that no significant difference in the ability to solve the two types of tasks is found. We arrive at the same result by a new experiment made expressly for the purpose of determining the function of the cues. The experiment had the following form.

Introduction: This differs from the usual introduction in that a further condition is added—the problem is solved only if the parts of the new figure remain contiguous.

Practice: Task 1, method of help. Because of the new condition the task now has only two, not four, solutions.

Test (one hour later, allowing three minutes for each task): Tasks 4, 9, 5, 16.

Tasks 4 and 5 belong to the first type of task: the description of the method of help, given in the form of three specific statements, may be applied to these tasks, in which the end-squares must be preserved.[20] On the other hand, the cues, when they are dealt with piecemeal, cannot be applied successfully to Tasks 9 and 16, in which the center square must be demolished, contiguous squares must be demolished, and, in Task 9, one of the end-squares must be demolished in order to solve the problem.[21]

The experiment was made with nineteen subjects. The number of correct solutions was seventeen for Tasks 4 and 5, and sixteen for Tasks 9 and 16 (45 and 42 percent, respectively). A control group, without any instruction, also obtained about the same score in both groups of tasks.

The experiment indicates that the difference in solving Tasks 4 and 5 on the one hand and Tasks 9 and 16 on the other, is very small and unreliable. There were two subjects whose test papers may confirm the assumption that the "helps" were effective in that they caused the remembering of several specific statements. But for the other seventeen subjects it holds true that solutions which involved different operations were arrived at as frequently as solutions corresponding to the specific statements. Therefore it cannot be assumed that the subjects who learned by the procedure described as method of help acquired and carried over information of the preservation of end-squares, of destroying two noncontiguous squares, and so on. We must search for a different explanation.

[20] There are no tasks in our collection for which the specific description of the help given would apply more fully than for Tasks 4 and 5. A scrutiny of the designs of the tasks reproduced in fig. 15 may help to clarify this assertion.

[21] The design of the solution of Task 16 is to be found in fig. 15, while for the only correct solution of Task 9 under the conditions given the reader should turn to fig. 3. Task 9 has no other solution unless the figure is separated into two noncontiguous parts.

Chapter V

THEORY OF TRANSFER OF TRAINING

Direct Practice

FOR ONE TYPE of learning we may adopt the current designation "direct practice." This method has been characterized as the shortest road to a specific goal, as learning precisely what we want to know. I hear in a foreign language a word which I do not understand. I look it up in the dictionary and repeat it several times, together with its English equivalent. I need the area of the trapezoid. My teacher tells me that it is $\frac{1}{2}h \ (b + b_1)$, and I repeat this formula several times. Or I want to learn how to solve Task 1. The experimenter shows me the solution of Task 1, and I repeat it several times. These examples illustrate what we mean when we say that we learn specific data without a detour.

A theoretical explanation of this kind of learning can be summed up in a few quotations. "The mind is on its dynamic side a machine for making particular reactions to particular situations. It works in great detail, adapting itself to the special data of which it has had experience" (Thorndike and Woodworth, 88, p. 249). The consequence of strictly coördinating particular situations and particular reactions has been strongly brought out by Thorndike: "Any disturbance whatsoever in the concrete particulars reasoned about will interfere somewhat with the reasoning, making it less correct, or slower, or both" (91, p. 33, also 92, p. 458). If only specific abilities are acquired, and if every change disturbs somewhat the learning effect, practice cannot spread, or it can spread only insofar as the task has not changed at all: "Spread of practice occurs only where identical elements are concerned in the influencing and influenced function" (Thorndike and Woodworth, 88, p. 250). "One mental function or activity improves others in so far as and because they are in part identical with it, because it contains elements common to them. Addition improves multiplication because multiplication is largely addition" (Thorndike, 89, pp. 243 f.).

We dealt with specific effects of learning when we studied the process of memorizing. The solution of one particular match task or card trick was shown and learned by mechanical repetitions; the memorizers had no understanding of the relation between the task and the solution. This learning had sometimes the advantage of speed both in the learning process and in the reproduction of what had been learned, but it had the disadvantage that it did not spread (or that it spread only to a small extent). To solve new tasks proved to be very difficult for subjects who were given this kind of training.

What we call direct practice was not uniform in all our experiments. In Experiment A several variations of one task were practiced (even a "meaningful" form of the Japanese house was introduced), and in Experiment B the solution of two different tasks was memorized; while Method Ia in the individual experiments represented the least complex way to arrive at a specific goal—the memorization of one task design and one solution design. In some experiments the final solutions were memorized, and in others an arbitrary order of arriving at the solutions. The results of these methods of training differed only slightly. Therefore direct practice cannot be characterized by the scarcity of details presented in the training period. We may vary the learning material in many ways and still have direct practice of specific subject matter, as long as the subject memorizes the material without understanding the relation between the items or the steps which are repeated one after the other.

It must be understood that the term "repeating" in the last sentence permits the inclusion of the extensively varied Method Mem. of Experiment A in the concept of direct practice. Direct practice does not require identical repetition of identical material.

The material may be presented for each repetition in a different way, and nevertheless it is possible to practice the same material.

There is a further reason why the concept of direct practice must be understood in a rather broad sense. No narrow parallelism between the object of practice and the knowledge acquired can be assumed. Even taking it for granted that any change in the particulars makes the application of the knowledge more difficult, certain applications remain possible in spite of the changed conditions. In the match-task experiments certain changes in the conditions caused no observable difference in the results. Apparently it was immaterial whether Task 1, learned by frequent repetitions by Group Mem., was presented in the tests in any of its possible forms (shown in the drawings on p. 82). Furthermore, knowledge acquired by memorizing figures drawn on paper could be transferred without apparent deterioration to the actual use of matches on a table. But other more important bits of experimental evidence seem to confirm Thorndike's statement that a change in particulars (of the memorized material) interferes with the results. In most cases memorizing brought about a very small transfer effect. But in Experiment B, Group Mem., which had memorized the solution of Task 1, had a fairly good performance with the similar Task 10. Yet they had still greater ability to solve the practiced task than to solve the similar task. The same was true of Tasks 1 and 2 in Experiment A. Similarly, when in the card-trick experiments the red-black alternation was changed into the even-uneven distinction Group Mem. had a rather high score, yet not as high as before.

Let us recall the form of the transfer from "red-black" to "even-uneven" (pp. 38, 266):

TRICKS

First Trick	*Second Trick*	*Third Trick*
Four red and four black cards, "omit one"	Four cards with even numbers and four cards with uneven numbers, "omit one"	Four red and four black cards, "omit two"

SOLUTIONS

Cards	*Cards*	*Cards*
2 red	2 even	1 red
1 black	1 uneven	3 black
2 red	2 even	1 red
3 black	3 uneven	1 black
		2 red

Many (but not all) subjects who had memorized the solution of the first trick solved the second trick; but they were unable to solve the third trick. Those who had learned by understanding solved all three tasks, because "structurally" all three tricks are similar; that is, the same principle applies to all of them. But in learning without understanding transfer seems to occur only if piece by piece there is a similarity between the unpracticed task and the practiced task. In the match experiments the new Task 10 and the practiced Task 1 both had four squares in one row and one square above another square. In these cases we can substitute the new for the old situation (the second for the first trick), because the memorized components which differ in the two tasks are not essential features of the whole figure or operation, while many other features are the same. Thus in the few cases in which direct practice brought about a transfer effect, transfer may be understood as the carrying over of certain specific similar components from the practiced tasks to the new tasks.

Summarizing the qualities of direct practice, as revealed in our experiments, we do not find that there was only one specific response connected with one specific situation. But a more-or-less diversified practice, which was not understood, had a specific effect—which means that certain specific data are retained and that transfer occurs by carrying these data over from one situation to another. Similarity of specific components appears to facilitate the substitution of one situation for another.

The Doctrine of Identical Elements

Transfer, as we found it in our experiments on direct practice, has thus been explained in a way which may appear to be related to the theory of identical elements. We must now ask whether that theory may be applied generally to all types of learning and to all forms of transfer effect.[1] What does the theory of identical elements state?

The general background of this theory is given in the quotations cited above. This is the thesis of the specific nature of the learning effect.[2] If practicing A results in knowing A, it is important to find out whether this practice also contributes to knowing X. Knowledge of A not only must be the specific effect of the practice but also must be superior to the knowledge of X. This implication of the theory has been clearly stated by one of its critics, Orata. He believed that there was experimental evidence for it: "Thorndike has shown conclusively, I believe, that the amount of improvement effected by practice directly is greater than the amount of indirect or transfer effect" (78, p. 23). We learn from these considerations that the usual transfer theory involves the assumption that the transfer effect is in all cases and by necessity not greater than the direct effect.[3]

Up to this point there seems to be general agreement as to the implications of the theory of identical elements. But now we must distinguish between two ramifications. One interpretation is that the theory really implies the negation of transfer. Bode quotes the main statements of Thorndike and adds: "That is an elaborate way of saying that there is no such thing as transfer" (10, p. 169). Orata explains in greater detail that according to the theory "the only kind of transfer that is possible is that of doing over again what has been done before in another situation" (78, p. V). But "doing over again what we have done before in another situation is not transfer" (p. 158). We are not interested in the question

[1] The importance of that question was pointed out by G. W. Allport in the following way: "The most prevalent doctrine of mental organization in American psychological theory is the doctrine of identical elements or, as it is often called, of partial identity" (5, p. 259).

[2] Cf. the following formulation of the thesis: "The first point to be noted is that training in any subject is specific, not general . . . Thinking, like training, is always specific, i. e. connected with some particular situation and dependent upon the specific nature of the situation as a whole" (Mann, 68, p. 183).

[3] Therefore Woodworth states that "We cannot expect a greater gain in any other task than we find in the one directly practiced" (112, p. 180). The greatest possible transfer effect is the "complete transfer effect of 100 percent."

whether the term "transfer" is used here rightly or wrongly. There is, however, a real problem involved in the statement that spread of practice occurs only when the same thing is done over again. This statement means that if there is transfer from a learned task A to an unlearned task B, it is due to the fact that certain phases of task B are the same as certain phases of task A and can therefore be repeated. It follows that the extent of identity determines the transfer effect. Should we have a transfer effect of 20 percent, then we should assume that (about) 20 percent of the elements of the two tasks are identical, because "one mental function improves others *in so far* as . . . they are . . . identical with it" (as quoted from Thorndike at the beginning of this chapter). A constant correlation between the similarity of the two functions and the magnitude of the transfer effect is demanded by the theory. Allport uses the word "proportionality"—the amount of transfer must be proportional, according to the theory, to the number of identical elements present in two situations (5, p. 273).

We do not propose to review the entire body of transfer research in order to determine whether or not a correlation between the degree of similarity and the magnitude of the transfer effect has been established. It should suffice that it was found in some cases, while it was lacking in others (cf. Orata's review). The establishment or the negation of such a correlation is, however, not a simple mathematical procedure. The measurement of the number of identities or the degree of similarity very often involves an interpretation of the results. How shall we decide whether in the example discussed a few minutes ago the third or the second trick is more similar to the first trick which was practiced? By qualitative analysis of the processes we may arrive at a decision, but hardly by counting the identical and the different elements in each of the tricks. There are instances in which the change of a very small number of elements alters the structure of the task and thus makes the transfer of memorized data very difficult; while in other instances the change of a great number of elements does not alter the problem, which therefore is solved as well (or almost as well) in its new form as the practiced problem was solved.

But there is also a second interpretation of the theory of identical elements. We are told that we need not restrict the identities to individual elements. Woodworth, in his most recent exposition, proposes that we should use the term "component" in place of the term "element." Then he proceeds in this way: "What the theory of identical elements demands is that transfer should be of concrete performance" (112, p. 177). Should we therefore assume that the theory is proved if it holds true that in all cases of transfer there is some kind of concrete identity or similarity between the original and the new situation? In this form the theory appears to be too general. Ruger remarked as early as 1910 that "the conception of identical elements does not seem to have much value as a criterion for the existence of transfer since it covers so wide a range of phenomena as: general principles of method, special information processes, and eye movements" (82, p. 85). Some kind of identity must indeed be present. The practice of the match tasks does not "transfer" to knowledge of, let us say, historical facts. But a theory of transfer should give us a more specific clue to the nature of the identical factors.

Woodworth shows in greater detail how the criterion of concrete performance should be applied. After analyzing the experiments of Ruger, who found a general formula most helpful for the transfer from one puzzle to another, he concludes:

The more definitely the principle is isolated, even to the extent of formulating it in words, the more chance of transfer . . . We think of principles as 'abstract' . . . But if they are embodied in words, they are concrete bits of behavior and their transfer from one situation to another creates no difficulty for the theory of identical elements [112, pp. 206 f.].

We are now confronted with a definite formulation of the theory. In order to obtain transfer it is not necessary that some elements of a new task should be the same as some elements of the practiced task, but concrete *words* used in the practice period may bring about transfer. The identity of two situations consists then in the words by which a principle is formulated. Instances ostensibly validating this theory were found in our experiments: the words "double function" and "hole," learned in the practice period, were sometimes recalled in new situations, in which a transfer was noticeable.[4]

The difference between the two theories, or interpretations, just described is not fundamental. Both seem to assume the existence of direct effects which are carried over to new situations by means of a specific vehicle—concrete individual elements in the one case, words in the other. Both theories may serve to explain some of our experimental results: the reference to the individual elements may explain the rare transfer effects in the case of direct practice, and the identity of words may explain certain results obtained by Method II*a* and Group Arith., in which expressions used in the training period were recalled. But our main experimental evidence points to extensive transfer made by the "understanding groups," even though the members of these groups had been taught no words, formulas, or principles and had forgotten the particular content of the instruction period, the method of solving the tasks was changed, and the tasks were not recognized as the original tasks. Variations of a task were solved, as a consequence of learning by understanding, with the same ease, regardless of whether the elements of the new situation were more or less similar to the old situation. We shall not discuss now how the theory of identical elements would have to be interpreted in order to be applied to these results, but shall proceed to the analysis of learning by understanding and its results.

Learning by Understanding

Our first objective is investigation of the process of learning that took place when our subjects acquired knowledge of the

---

[4] The theory which posits words as the carriers of transfer can be viewed from the angle of behavioristic identification of verbal responses with that which introspectionists call consciousness or memory. J. B. Watson wrote "memory is really the functioning of the verbal part of a total habit" and "thinking is largely subvocal talking" (100, chap. xi). From this theory one may deduce that these all-important verbal responses make transfer possible. Thus we read in a more recent behavioristic educational psychology: "Language is the means or medium of the recall of past experience which is then concretely used in the solution of the problem" (Leary, 57, p. 200).

match tasks by being given examples in one of our meaningful methods of teaching. How did the numerous successful learners in Group Ex. proceed?

The practice period was devoted to gaining an understanding of the solution of three tasks and their reverse forms. The result was that the subjects proved able to solve these tasks and many other tasks. Can we assert that the subjects learned A, B, C, D, E, F (each letter representing one of the six "solutions" shown to the subjects), and as a result of that learning came to know A, B, C, D, E, F, and also G, H, I, and so forth? This view of the learning process would be difficult to defend. We should have to assume that the subjects first learned a concrete solution A. That would be direct practice of the solution of one specific task, similar to the procedure in Method Mem., except that the practice was inadequate because it was confined to only one repetition. According to the experience with Method Mem. we must assume that direct practice of A resulted in practically no transfer and in quick forgetting. The same would be true of the practice of each of the tasks B, C, D, E, and F. According to such a view of the learning process, there would have been six separate learning objects, of which each is impressed in an insufficient way that does not yield appreciable transfer effects. The results of the experiment contradict such a characterization of the learning process.

From introspective reports we may describe what actually happened during the practice period to the learners whose training by examples resulted in understanding and application.[5] From the first solution shown (Task 8) the subjects got a clue that a square can be transformed into a hole and vice versa. They then acquired the notion that the precise number of matches displaced was not very important; the same effect could be achieved by moving four or three matches. The experience gained from the solution of Task 4b was, first of all, that the closing of holes resulted in an increase of the number of squares. Task 4 gave them some notion about the results of breaking up a compact figure. Finally, Task 5

[5] The description was obtained for the most part after applying Method IIIb in the individual experiments (cf. p. 88), which method was essentially the same as that of Group Ex.

showed them how a good unified figure can be torn apart in order to solve the problem.

These data were obtained by questioning the subjects both after practice and after test. But the questions and the ensuing attempt to remember undoubtedly falsified the reports to a certain extent. The clear-cut, well-defined concepts used in the above description were in part constructed later. The words "hole," "breaking up," and so forth, rarely came to the mind of the subjects—they were used only in a few introspective reports, of which we have given a summary. Instead the subjects often felt them vaguely or noticed something which was "difficult to express in words." But of all cases it holds true that certain formal principles (structural principles) were developed from the successive steps of learning. Instead of having learned first one, then a second, then a third of a series of consecutive data, the subjects developed an integrated knowledge to which all parts of the practice period contributed.

To correctly describe the learning process we must consider that the training period consisted of a unit; that as the result of this training the subjects learned "X," the intrinsic relationship between Situation 1 and Situation 2. Here Situation 1 represents a figure with a larger and Situation 2 a figure with a smaller number of squares, triangles, and so forth, formed by the same number of side lines. Learning resulted, not in the knowledge of the specific solutions of several tasks which had been shown in the practice period, but in something different. The effect of practice was not specific,[6] it was not limited to the specific learning materials. The principles developed were rooted in the role and form of the various operations, but not in the specific material from which they were derived.

By studying the method of help and its results we arrive at the same conclusion. In a negative way we investigated that method in Experiment D. There it was found that the consecutive steps had not brought about the knowledge of the specific data which the individual steps supplied. The subjects did not learn

---

[6] For the determination of the meaning of the expression "nonspecific learning effects" see the examples given on p. 122 and compare especially the discussion on p. 126.

from the first step of Task 1 that the two squares being most remote from each other must be preserved intact, but they saw the steps in relation to the goal of a figure consisting of a smaller number of squares, and they grasped the various steps in their mutual relationship. It was a unitary process of disintegrating the original figure, of seeing it in a new and different way, which took place as the result of the entire method of help. Learning was a development. What was developed was rarely expressed in words; it was a formal principle of a unitary operation, which is applicable to all kinds of figures in which the number of squares is to be decreased or increased and therefore to some extent independent of the individual figures used to exemplify the process. What happened in the tests was, then, a process of reconstruction (cf. p. 43); the subjects attempted to construct a new figure, behaving as in a problem-solving situation. They were, however, much more successful, because their construction was aided by a more-or-less distinct structural principle. In our experiments we found manifold further indications which support the assumptions just made.

a) *Observation of the subjects during the tests.*—When asked to solve new tasks the subjects who learned by the method of help did not grasp their pencils immediately to draw the figure representing the correct solution, and they did not begin by erasing a line and drawing one elsewhere. Instead they first scrutinized the figure without using their pencils. Then some of them covered with their fingers or hands some part of the figure. Thus, the parts of the figure which remained visible differed from the original figure. Some, after a pause, erased several lines (often four or five) without transferring them at all. Thus, again the original figure was changed into a new form. Later a new square was drawn, and some of the lines previously erased were restored. All this was done by frequently comparing the "new" figure with the original figure.

We may call this procedure trial and error. But the trials were not random trials. They were directed by a definite goal or plan, even though the plan was not consciously formulated. The number of possible errors, that is, erasures of lines that should have remained in their original places, was very extensive. But only a certain kind of error was made. Even the subjects who ultimately failed to find the correct solution committed errors which could for the most part be understood, not errors which were "out of place." [7]

b) Scrutiny of the correct solutions.—In studying the test papers gathered in the various experiments, which contain several hundred correct solutions, we find confirmation of the distinction between the memorizing of specific solutions on the one hand and the gaining of understanding of the essential features of the match tasks on the other hand. In the tables computed in Chapter IV all correct solutions of a task were scored in the same way. But most of the tasks had several correct solutions. If we now ask which of the possible correct solutions (all being of the same value) did the subjects produce, we find certain regularities. Below we give a few typical examples for these regularities; many more could be given from the extensive material gathered in the experiments.

In Experiment B, Task 1 was one of the practiced tasks. This task has four correct solutions, which are shown in fig. 19. The memorizing group repeated the task and the first of its correct solutions (fig. 19*a*) several times, while with the help of certain carefully chosen cues the understanding group found the way to solve the task. Task 1 was again presented in the retest four weeks after the practice period. It was then solved by 37 percent of the members of Group Mem. and 48 percent of those of Group Help.

[7] For example: the test papers of the subjects of Group Help who did not solve Task 1 were most frequently left in the first form but never in the second form (cf. fig. 18*a* and 18*b*).

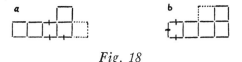

Fig. 18

The statements in the text should not be taken as implying that no subject possibly solved a task by pure chance, that is, by hitting on the solution after planless trials and errors. But chance should have been as "helpful" to members of Group Con. or Mem. as to those of Group Help.

Task 1

Correct Solutions

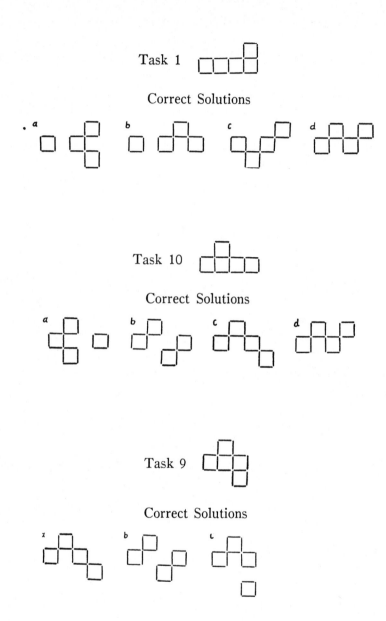

Task 10

Correct Solutions

Task 9

Correct Solutions

Fig. 19

The following table shows how these correct solutions were distributed among the four possible solutions indicated in fig. 19.

TABLE 11. CORRECT SOLUTIONS OF THE PRACTICED TASK 1

	FREQUENCY OF				TOTAL NUMBER OF SOLUTIONS	PERCENTAGE OF SOLUTIONS
	Solution a	*Solution b*	*Solution c*	*Solution d*		
Group Mem.	7	3	0	0	10	37
Group Help	3	4	3	2	12	48

These solutions of a practiced task shall be compared with those of new tasks. We select two examples from the same experiment. In the test the two groups mentioned above were asked to solve, among other tasks, Task 10, a task which we called similar to the practiced task by dealing piecemeal with the figures, because both Task 1 and Task 10 have four squares in one row and one square above another. The subjects were also asked to solve Task 9, which is somewhat less similar to the practiced task. The final results of these tests were given in Table 6 of the preceding chapter; the frequencies of the various correct solutions are shown in Table 12.

TABLE 12. CORRECT SOLUTIONS OF NEW TASKS

	FREQUENCY OF				TOTAL NUMBER OF SOLUTIONS	PERCENTAGE OF SOLUTIONS
	Solution a	*Solution b*	*Solution c*	*Solution d*		
Task 10						
Group Mem.	7	0	0	1	8	30
Group Help	3	2	3	2	10	40
Task 9						
Group Mem.	1	2	2	. .	5	19
Group Help	5	4	3	. .	12	48

The test papers of Group Mem. show what is meant by "learning a specific solution." The solution of the practiced Task 1 had the form of reproducing the learned solution or (in a few cases) a very similar solution, but never that of finding somewhat different solutions. In Task 10 the learned solution was again reproduced almost exclusively by the subjects who were able to solve the problem. The performance of the group was here not much inferior to that in Task 1. But Task 9 was solved by a small number of subjects, because those who solved this task could not just reproduce a learned solution. They had to find a new solution, which was apparently a difficult problem for the subjects who learned by memorizing.

If we now scrutinize the various forms of correct solution presented by members of Group Help, we obtain a different picture. We may first state again the performance of Group Help which was emphasized in Chapter IV: there is no significant difference in the total number of correct solutions obtained for the three tasks. For the moment we are more interested in the frequency of the various correct solutions. The result can thus be formulated: there is a learning method which does not bring about the acquisition of just one specific solution (or just one specific response). Subjects who learned by understanding and who thereafter were able to solve certain tasks used all kinds of correct solution without any preference. The instruction given to Group Help appears to have had no specific effect favoring one kind of procedure. In individual experiments made with several tests it happened often that the same subjects solved the same task once in one way and a few weeks later in a different way, without noticing the difference. The diversity of correct solutions was greatest for Task 11, which was a new task in the tests of Experiment C. This task has seven different correct solutions. It was solved by twelve of the twenty-two subjects of Group Help. The twelve solutions were distributed among the seven possibilities thus: 3, 1, 2, 3, 1, 1, 1. All the subjects had received identical instruction, but they solved the same new task differently. On the other hand, in a small experiment not previously mentioned five subjects learned one solution of Task 11 by mechanically repeating it. The subjects had seen no other match task and no other solution of Task 11. Three weeks later three subjects again solved the task, using exactly the same solution as the one learned. The other two subjects failed to solve the task. Thus, no subject found any of the six "different" solutions.

c) *Recognition test.*—The number of mistakes made in the recognition test was very large in both groups (p. 100), and many subjects failed to recognize those tasks which they had practiced four weeks previously. We may explain the entire behavior of Group Mem. in a simple way. Some members of this group forgot what they had learned; therefore they failed to recognize the practiced tasks and were unable to solve them. Some members of Group Help, however, solved correctly various old as well as new tasks, at the same time mistaking old ones for new and new ones for old. They did not remember the actual shape of the figures seen four weeks earlier, but they remembered something else that helped them in solving the problem. The principle involved must consequently have been more-or-less independent of the specific learning material.[8]

d) *Invention test.*—After the conclusion of some of the experiments the subjects were asked to invent a new match task. They were told to use the same principle (which was not explained to them), but to draw a design different from those the experimenter had shown them. Altogether the subjects had been shown six tasks —four tasks four weeks earlier and two old and two new tasks on the day of the "invention test." Numerous subjects who had learned by the method of examples and help were able to act on this instruction. Some few new designs drawn were slight alterations of tasks previously seen; some were even exact copies of tasks seen, but the subjects asserted that they had not seen them before. Others were good new tasks—some of which were unknown to the experimenter and were used in later experiments. Subjects who invented such tasks were then asked to reproduce one of the tasks exhibited to them in the practice period several weeks earlier. For many subjects the invention of a new task was

---

[8] Of course there were also instances of correct solutions of correctly recognized tasks and of inability to solve unrecognized tasks.

an easier job than the reproduction of the design of a task seen several weeks before. The exact design of the individual tasks, which were seen for only a short time in the practice period, did not stick in the memory. Learning was directed toward a principle, not toward the reproduction of the design of any one task.

e) Formulation of the principle.—The test reported at the end of the description of Experiment B must be mentioned again. The number of subjects able to formulate the principle of the match tasks in a satisfactory way was quite small and was greatly exceeded by those who learned how to deal with such tasks but were not able to give an account of the principle. There are subjects who resort to words and for whom verbal formulas constitute a help. But it seems that it is not so much the mental type of the subject (for example, whether he is the visual or the auditory type) that determines whether or not he uses words in learning, but rather the nature of the problem. With many learning materials the use of words is the natural and most appropriate procedure. Apparently the match tasks do not belong in that category. Nevertheless mastery of them could be acquired easily. One could gain knowledge of the structural principle, and it could guide one's actions without being formulated.[9]

The differentiation between specific and nonspecific learning effects, it appears, should be confused neither with verbal—nonverbal nor with concrete—abstract forms of learning. Both verbal and nonverbal learning can be specific. But concrete words may also serve to express nonspecific learning effects, just as may unformulated structural principles.[10] For our purposes it is immaterial whether what has been learned is called "concrete" or "ab-

[9] The knowledge of a principle may be helpful without being formulated, and, on the other hand, even a formulated conscious knowledge must not be of help, as Maier has found: "Mere conscious presence of the necessary experiences or data is not sufficient to solve certain problems" (66, p. 133).

[10] It must not be assumed that all the members of Group Arith. who recalled the words "double function" had acquired knowledge of specific data only; the extensive individual differences found in this method and the inconsistency between the results of the test and the retest indicate that the subjects taught by a formulated principle may have learned in many different ways (cf. p. 97, above).

stract"; the question is whether or not particular reactions have
been acquired.

We conclude that in the case of meaningful methods of learning
it was not the specific learning material that was learned and retained by the subjects. The function of the concrete learning material may be described by introducing the term "example": the
individual tasks, or the various helps, served as examples. That
means that the subjects were concerned mainly with what the
tasks exemplified and less with their particular features.

When they were learning by understanding, the subjects saw
certain tasks in the practice period; but the specific solutions of
these tasks were not what they learned and remembered later. The
tasks which we called briefly "practiced tasks" served as examples through which the principle or the essential point of any
such tasks was to be (and was) understood by the meaningful
learners. We do not learn the examples; we learn *by* examples.
The material of learning is not necessarily the object of learning:
it may serve as a clue to a general principle or an integrated
knowledge.

This description of the learning process implies that it is possible to learn by examples or by illustrations—not only by the direct
method of a lexicon or a dictionary. In meaningful learning, instead of defining or translating we may choose detours or cir-
cuitous ways to acquire knowledge—and they often prove to be
the simpler, the more natural, and the more efficient ways. The
term "efficient" refers again to retention after a long interval and
to the ability to apply what has been learned.[11]

What do we learn with the aid of the examples? Relations or
qualities of the process; the form or the main point of the operation; the essence or the principle of the problem. All these ex-

[11] In our experiments learning by examples seemed to be such an efficient method
of acquiring knowledge that it was difficult to hit on bad examples which would not
help one to acquire knowledge (cf. p. 90). Many of our subjects performed better
in the retest than in the test—as we will show in the next chapter—because the tasks
given in the test served as examples by means of which additional training was
obtained.

pressions describe whole-qualities (qualities of the gestalt), not those of pieces and elements. Learning in these instances is a development or a crystallization of whole-qualities. We often do not express such whole-qualities in words, but in determining our actions they are precise and definite, even though nonverbal and abstract.

The last analysis implies that the differentiation between the acquisition and the retention of specific data on the one hand and nonspecific data on the other hand—with which we started our analysis of the effects of learning by understanding—is essential, but that it is not sufficient for distinguishing senseless from meaningful learning. First, direct practice, too, is often not the formation of a bond between just one specific stimulus and one specific response, and the retention of specific data may also involve a certain degree of (piecemeal) variability (p. 111).[12] Secondly, the expression "general, nonspecific effect" of learning by understanding must be understood to denote an integrated learning effect which is adequate to the structure of the process.[13] In this case the nonspecific effect of learning embraces essential qualities or principles of the whole process.

What about those instances of learning for which our description of meaningful learning does not hold true and in which we do actually learn the examples, that is, acquire specific data? We shall return to this question in later chapters, but on the basis of our analysis of direct practice we may already say that these instances of learning are characterized by a special kind of organization. To obtain direct practice we had to isolate the material of learning, interfere with the possibility of its spreading, and exclude the understanding of inherent relations. By mechanically repeating one solution or by learning in different ways the very same solution (as was done by Group Mem. in Experiment C) we

---

[12] In the research on conditioned responses it was established that no differences are caused by certain changes in the stimuli (e. g., when an animal is conditioned to a tone of a certain wave length, certain tones of different wave lengths also acquire the capacity to evoke the response). This type of fact is often designated as "irradiation," but frequently also as "generalization."

[13] We shall return to the discussion of the different meanings of the term "generalization" on p. 135.

achieved such a restricted result. In direct practice we do not learn less (a smaller number of elements) than in other kinds of learning, but we learn in a special way.

"Carrying Over" or "Applying"

Do we find "transfer of training" in consequence of learning by understanding? We know that the subjects who learned by meaningful methods solved new tasks as readily as they solved practiced tasks. With this evidence the question is not yet answered. An affirmative answer would mean that no transfer or only slight transfer resulted from memorizing; understanding, however, has brought about very extensive transfer. But there is also another possibility. It may be that we must differentiate between two forms of solving new tasks. If this is true, we should not use the same concept in describing the two different performances.

If transfer is defined, as it often is, as the "carrying over" of an act, a performance, a bit of knowledge, from the original situation to a new situation, we can hardly avoid restricting that term to the few and inconsiderable transfer effects of direct practice. For no specific acts or data have been carried over to new tasks by the subjects who understood the geometrical problem. In meaningful learning the practiced tasks served as examples, not as the objects of learning; an integrated knowledge (a whole-principle) was acquired and was later applied to all tasks involving the same principle—to the so-called "practiced tasks" as well as to new tasks.

The question of terminology is not of great importance.[14] Let us therefore omit here altogether the use of the word "transfer" and summarize the arguments in favor of a differentiation between "carrying over" and "applying." In the following pages we discuss the considerations that prompt us to assume that the difference is fundamental and does not consist merely in the extent of the transfer effect.

a) With increasing similarity between new and practiced tasks

---

[14] But let us note that by investigating latent learning Koffka also arrives at the conclusion that the term "transfer" is inadequate (50, p. 546). On the other hand, Allport points out that the term transfer suggests "change of vehicle" and not "identical vehicles" (5, p. 268).

the solution of new tasks becomes easier—in case of carrying over a performance (cf. the question of proportionality, p. 113). But apparently similarity of the parts plays a small role if the effects of meaningful learning are studied.

Experimental evidence for the first statement has been given in our investigation of direct practice. Here we point only to the fact that when the subjects who memorized the solution of Task 1 attempted new tasks, they scored highest with the "partially identical" Task 2 (in Experiment A) and the "partially identical" Task 10 (in Experiment B). The form of the solutions chosen for Task 10 (cf. fig. 19, above) illustrates what is meant by carrying over specific data. The second statement can be proved by the entire performance of Group Help. We now emphasize only that Task 10 did not prove to be easy for the subjects who learned to understand the problem of the match tasks on the basis of Task 1. Of course, there were new tasks in our experiments which gave the meaningful learners greater difficulty than certain other tasks. But merely by studying the number of identities and similarities between the parts, or components, of the various task designs we can reach no conclusion about the degree of difficulty. What mattered was whether a new task was "structurally easy" or "structurally difficult"—that is, whether or not the principle could be applied easily.

b) If the "carrying over" of an act depends on the similarity between two situations, it must be greatest when there is perfect similarity, that is, identity, of the two situations. In that case, then, we cannot expect an indirect effect greater than a direct effect. But if we apply a general method to practiced tasks as well as to new tasks, there will be instances in which the new tasks will cause greater difficulty and others in which they will cause less difficulty than do the practiced tasks, dependent upon the structural difficulties of the respective tasks (which may be unequal to individual learners in spite of equation by control groups).

In summarizing the calculations presented in Appendix 2 we

find the following transfer coefficients.[15] Each number represents the average transfer effect obtained in one experiment.

	Transfer Coefficients in Percentages				
Direct practice	— 0.3	7	16	21	24
Learning by understanding	63.0	89	90	92	107

In the case of direct practice we find a confirmation of the statement that "the transfer effect is usually much nearer to zero than to 100 percent" (P. Sandiford, 84, p. 293), or that "in general there will be little transfer effect if the learning takes place in a memoriter, mechanical fashion" (A. M. Jordan, 35, p. 231). After learning by understanding, however, the average transfer effects were near 100 percent. There is no significant difference between solving new tasks and practiced tasks.[16]

The main confirmation of our conclusions, which assume a fundamental difference between the effects of carrying over and applying, is to be found in the analysis of the individual transfer ratios computed in Appendix 2. In Table 13 on page 130 we present a summary of the data of Tables 26 and 30 by determining the number of subjects whose scores in new tasks were higher than, equal to, or lower than their scores in practiced tasks.[17]

We have recorded the scores of 85 subjects who in four experiments underwent a memorization training. In tests made one, three, and four weeks after memorizing, for the great majority of the subjects the practiced tasks proved to be much easier than the new tasks. Only three subjects scored higher in new tasks, and only twelve subjects made equal scores in new and practiced tasks. These subjects can be treated as exceptions. As stated before, it

[15] The transfer coefficient is computed by dividing the average score obtained in new tasks (minus the control score) by the average score obtained in practiced tasks (minus the control score). The formula and the calculations are explained on pp. 274 ff.

[16] An explanation for the low transfer coefficient of 63 percent will be attempted on p. 132.

[17] Table 30 refers to Experiment E, which will be discussed in the next chapter, since its main purpose was not connected with the question of transfer. But in that experiment the question about the extent of the transfer effect in the case of different methods of learning was again answered.

TABLE 13. TRANSFER EFFECT IN DELAYED TESTS

SCORES IN SOLVING "NEW" TASKS IN RELATION TO
SCORES IN SOLVING "PRACTICED" TASKS

	Number of Subjects		
	Higher	*Equal*	*Lower*
Understanding Groups			
Experiment B	6	9	8
Experiment C1	7	4	8
Experiment C3	8	8	8
Experiment EI	7	4	8
Experiment EII	8	8	6
Total	36	33	38
Memorizing Groups			
Experiment B	1	1	15
Experiment C1	0	7	18
Experiment C3	2	3	17
Experiment EIII	0	1	20
Total	3	12	70

happened in the memorizing methods used in our experiments, which we attempted to make comparable to the understanding methods, that a subject learned something different from that which he was taught. A few individual subjects arrived at an understanding of the tasks in spite of the memorization method.

Of the 107 subjects who were taught by the methods of help and examples only one-third found the practiced tasks easier than the new tasks. The number of subjects for whom new tasks were easier about equaled the number for whom new tasks were more difficult than the practiced tasks. Here 100 percent transfer is the rule, not the exception; it is almost the mid-point of the distribution.

The achievement of the 36 subjects who scored higher in the new than in the practiced tasks must be taken into consideration. Even if we omit the discussion of the occurrence of "infinite transfer effects," [18] we must refer to the considerable number of subjects belonging to the understanding groups who scored twice as high in the new tasks as in the practiced tasks. Shall we here

[18] Positive score in new tasks, zero score in practiced tasks, cf. p. 278.

speak of "200 percent transfer effect"? Two-hundred-percent transfer is, according to customary theoretical assumptions, a contradiction. The fact that new tasks were solved better than practiced tasks indicates that there was no carrying over of knowledge from the latter to the former. The practiced tasks had no advantage; their solution could not be the direct effect of the training. The results can be explained only if we abandon the thesis that practicing A always leads to the knowledge of A, and assume that in meaningful learning both the so-called "direct" effect and the so-called "indirect" effect constitute instances of application of a principle.[19]

c) The transfer coefficients obtained by the memorizing groups were about the same in the immediate tests and in the tests made after several weeks. When we carry over a memorized response from one situation to another, the performance deteriorates with the passage of time, yet forgetting affects the reproduction of the practiced solutions in a similar way. On the other hand, certain considerations suggest that the transfer effects due to learning by understanding will be different in test and delayed test of our experimental set-up. Only in a delayed test made several weeks after training can we expect to find pure cases of application. There the absence of specific effects and the perfect distribution of the transfer ratios as just set forth are to be expected. Extraneous factors, however, may affect the result of testing the subjects' knowledge immediately after the conclusion of training, at least in some individuals. Suppose a member of Group Help is asked to solve a new task in the immediate test; he tries to apply his integrated knowledge. Then he gets a practiced task. He had seen it only ten minutes before; in spite of the insufficient specific training (no repetition) the subject might have recognized the task and remembered its solution. Therefore, in the test some sub-

---

[19] Under this assumption the occurrence of a "200 percent transfer effect" is not surprising. We must recall that all subjects who had perfect training, that is, who solved in later tests all tasks without exception, had a "100 percent transfer effect": their new-task score was equal to their practiced-task score. When the subjects missed the solution of a task, it happened that the mistake was committed almost as frequently in practiced tasks as in new tasks.

jects will make a better score with a practiced task than with a new task. We must expect that the transfer coefficient, the average ratio of a group, will be higher in the retest than in the test. This expectation was fulfilled in the one experiment in which it was submitted to scrutiny: in Experiment A the transfer coefficient rose from 63 percent in the test to 90 percent in the retest.

We attempted to show that the assumption, that the indirect effect is inferior to the direct effect and that "any disturbance whatsoever in the concrete particulars" of the specific learning material interferes with the performance, cannot be applied to learning by understanding. It was possible to change the practiced tasks in many respects without interfering with the performance of the subjects. Yet in spite of the various changes there was an "identity" in the practiced and in the unpracticed tasks. The subjects acquired knowledge of whole-qualities representing the principle of the task. They learned to perform certain operations with "center squares" and "corner squares" which were the same for all the tasks. Can we reformulate this statement and assert that there were identical "abstract elements" in all the tasks which the subjects learned when practicing with examples? Such a formulation would hardly be to the advantage of the doctrine of identical elements or similar theories. Our main contention would be accepted: that by practicing a number of specific tasks the subjects did not learn the solution of these tasks, but that they did acquire knowledge of something different from the specific learning material. The difference would be only that while we argued that the subjects learned a capital X, the critics would plead that they learned a small x (or small x, y, z). But is the x an element—whether represented by a capital letter or a small letter? For an answer we must refer to our analysis of the learning process. "Destroying center squares" and making "holes out of squares" are, not elements, but qualities within the whole process. And these qualities are not necessarily abstract—they may be concrete as well.

An analogy to our discussion of the use of examples in widely applicable meaningful learning may be found in passages by J. L. Mursell, who states that "transfer can be increased by having the pupils learn and apply the ability in question in a variety of contexts" (76, p. 101, and p. 184).[20]

In order further to clarify our position, we must examine a theory of transfer that is of great importance for educational psychology. This theory assumes that the content of learning is mainly specific, whereas certain procedure values are general.[21] It is then assumed that by memorizing the multiplication table or by practicing (in psychological experiments) crossing out every "s" and "t" on a printed page the students learn precisely what they are trained for. But in addition they acquire an attitude which is valuable in innumerable tasks of learning. The attitude of attentiveness, concentration, accuracy, neatness, fairmindedness, logical approach, can be acquired by practicing A, and can also be applied to B, C, D, and so forth.

The merits of this approach for educational psychology cannot be praised sufficiently; but a theory that restricts generalization to attitudes and admits the specific nature of every kind of learning content does not go far enough. The same holds true of the generalization theory of C. H. Judd. A valuable confirmation of our analysis of direct practice is that Judd describes the effect of a stereotyped and clumsy way of teaching, which does not result in transfer, in the following way: "[the pupil] reproduces that which comes into his experience in the form in which he receives it" (37, p. 107). Judd argues that there is no automatic transfer of training, that no subject of instruction guarantees mental training, and that if anyone asserts that mathematics or Latin

[20] The use of a variety of contexts is only one of the methods recommended by Mursell, with the view of increasing the transfer effect. The other methods are conscious generalization and leading the pupil strongly to desire transfer.—In referring briefly to a variety of contexts Mursell does not distinguish between a senseless and a meaningful use of the examples.

[21] Thorndike accepts transfer of training both when the elements are identical in content and when they are identical in method of procedure (89, p. 244). Allport argues that this statement involves "a complete surrender" of the original theory (5, p. 274). But the emphasis on methods is also to be found in theories of transfer which are based on different assumptions.

will train the general powers of discrimination or reasoning, that person is wrong. But "if anyone asserts that all training is particular . . . that person is just as wrong" (p. 432). Judd's transfer theory may be summed up in the following quotations:

Any subject taught with a view to training pupils in methods of generalization is highly useful as a source of mental training [37, p. 432].

[We must distinguish between] content of experience and the mode of intellectual treatment of this content. Content of experience is of necessity specific [p. 438].

Trained intelligence is *particular in its contents but general in its methods* [p. 417; italics not in original].

Mental development consists . . . in equipping the individual with the power to think abstractly and to form general ideas. When the ends thus described are attained, transfer of training . . . has taken place because it is the very nature of generalization and abstraction that they extend beyond the particular experiences in which they originate [p. 441].

In our experiments it was not only an attitude or a "mode of intellectual treatment" that was acquired, independent of the actual learning material. The meaningful, as well as the senseless, learners may have gained in the practice period a new mode of behavior with regard to match tasks. But the former also acquired the knowledge of certain formal or structural moments of the contents, which they applied later to various tasks. The condensing or disintegrating of a geometrical figure—and the principle of alternately omitting a card in the card-trick experiments— are not merely attitudes, they have to do with insight into structural features of the contents. Therefore the thesis that in certain cases the effect of practice is general must be applied to contents as well as to methods.[22]

---

[22] Judd's thesis that the contents of learning are particular seems to be derived from the assumption that "memory is the one mental function which is altogether particular" (37, p. 424). That statement is illustrated by the example of learning and remembering a telephone number. By restricting the validity of the statement to one form of memory function (as will be done in later chapters of this book) and by substituting the expression "material of learning" for Judd's "content of experience," a somewhat greater similarity between Judd's views and our views could be construed than is apparent from the text.

Is "generalization" the solution of our problem? Wertheimer distinguishes between two meanings of this concept, the first of which cannot be applied to the effects that are here attributed to learning by understanding. Generalization may mean to form senseless sums which are "blind" to the inherent structure of the greater whole, and generalization may be appropriate to the structure, in which case it brings about an adequate, meaningful organization.[23] As an example for a generalization which is inadequate because it is "senseless" or "blind" to the essence of the problem, we may mention the behavior of a subject who after memorizing the solution of Task 1 always destroyed the second square from the left because he generalized one feature of the learned procedure without regard to the whole operation. A better example was given in the footnote on page 53: after memorizing "a a b b" as the solution of a card trick with four cards, some subjects wrote "a a a b b b" as the solution of the trick with six cards. The subjects themselves noticed later that this generalization is senseless, that is, it is contrary to the requirements of the new problem; they crossed out the arrangement, but were unable to find the correct one, which would have conformed to the requirements. Thus, in spite of having made a generalization the memorizers were unable to solve new problems. Not generalization in itself, but only a structurally adequate generalization can serve to explain those different instances in which meaningful learners solved the new tasks by applying in a reasonable way what they had learned.

It has often been said that the establishment of mechanical habits is the opposite of transfer.[24] This statement may be called correct if we attribute to the term "transfer" the meaning for which we have used the word "application." But when the term is employed with its other, more customary meaning, we must emphasize that acquisition of mechanical habits (memorization) and transfer (carrying over) are intimately connected, because,

[23] Wertheimer's differentiation between these two meanings of "generalization" will be expounded in his forthcoming book on productive thinking.

[24] Cf. Orata (78, chap. vi). Mursell writes: "The way to *avoid* transfer in our teaching is to direct learning as if it were a matter of forming fixed habits" (76, p. 103).

as we have seen, they both imply the establishment of specific learning effects. With meaningful learning most highly developed, we find that there is a plasticity or flexibility of learning which permits reasonable applications on a wide scale. These applications are due, not to the transfer of specific data from an A to a B, but to the fact that meaningful learning results in the acquisition of integrated knowledge, which is usable under different circumstances.

Transfer in the sense of wide applicability is a concept related to transposition. When learning consists of acquiring whole-qualities, reproduction often takes the form of transposition—the elements are changed, but the whole-qualities, the essence, the principle are preserved in recollection. This rule holds good of "transfer," too. When whole-qualities are better preserved than the elements, we may apply them under changed circumstances.

Chapter VI

FORGETTING AND THE EFFECT OF REPETITION

WE HAVE DISCUSSED at length one important difference between the effects of memorizing and understanding. There was found to be a limited amount of transfer in the one case, whereas in the other case the knowledge acquired could be applied on a broad scale. A second possible distinction between the two processes of learning was treated only briefly. Is the rate of retention and are the qualities of the curve of forgetting alike in the two cases?

The Curve of Forgetting

Experimental investigations concerning forgetting are very numerous. The beginning was made in 1885, when Ebbinghaus published his book on memory, in which he established laws of forgetting. They can be summarized as follows: (1) Reproduction deteriorates with time. (2) The rate of forgetting is very rapid in the early stages. (3) The curve of forgetting can be expressed by a mathematical formula; it is a negatively accelerated logarithmic curve. (4) Forgetting becomes less rapid if the number of repetitions used in learning is increased.

Ebbinghaus arrived at these results by memorizing lists of nonsense syllables. His laws were generally confirmed by later investigators, who used many subjects, different materials of learning, and various methods for testing retention.[1] In 1929

---

[1] Ebbinghaus (17) measured the time saved by relearning rote series of nonsense syllables. Twenty minutes after memorization the saving amounted to only 58 percent—more than 40 percent of the learning effects were lost. One day later the saving amounted to only 34 percent (six days later, to 25 percent). Radossawljewitsch (79) repeated the experiments with both nonsense syllables and poetry, with a large number of subjects. He confirmed the main point of Ebbinghaus's findings—the quality of the curve of forgetting—although he found somewhat better

Hunter summarized the results of a large number of experimental investigations by stating that there are many curves of forgetting; they vary with such factors as the character of the material learned, the degree of mastery of initial learning, the speed of initial learning, the amount and character of the following interpolated work, and the method by which retention is tested (34, p. 605). But all these curves are similar to each other; entirely different curves were found only in "reminiscence" experiments with children (34, p. 608). In the same way McGeoch states that "the classical Ebbinghaus curve was, until recently, thought to represent a universal principle"; at present an exception is known—reminiscence (62, p. 397).

The recent extensive investigations on the improvement in recall after an interval of time, for which the term "reminiscence" is used, will not be reviewed here. It suffices to state that at first ascending curves of forgetting could be considered as exceptional instances due to very special circumstances. They were found only in children and in connection with the learning of poetry or other interesting material which was not completely mastered. In the light of more recent investigations a larger scope must be attributed to reminiscence, since adults who learned different kinds of material showed improvement in recall.[2] Some methods developed especially to find reminiscence are of interest for us. When instead of group averages individual results were studied, and when instead of the total amount of recall the individual items

---

rates of retention (68 percent saving after twenty-four hours, 49 percent after six days). The difference may be due to the fact that Ebbinghaus learned many series one after the other. Among the many investigations on forgetting we cite next that of Luh (60), who used different methods of measuring retention and used different degrees of learning. The method of recognition resulted in the slowest rate of forgetting; next followed the method of reconstruction (of individual items); then that of written reproduction, whereas the method of anticipation brought about the quickest rate. In all four cases, however, the curve of forgetting proved to be logarithmic and similar to that of Ebbinghaus.

[2] But it has not been proved that there is any reminiscence for rote learning of nonsense material, except after very short intervals (less than two minutes after the end of the learning period, cf. 98). According to most recent investigations by E. B. Newman (American Journal of Psychology, October, 1939), however, interference due to crowding of items appears to cause "reminiscence" in nonsense syllables.

recalled were compared on various occasions, more frequent instances of improvement in recall were established. Woodworth (112, p. 68) summarizes our present knowledge of reminiscence by emphasizing the possibility of reviewing between earlier and later tests and by pointing to experiments which make it seem probable that recall "acts upon the learning material as a whole, and not only upon the units that are reproduced" (80, p. 837).

Do the phenomena of reminiscence constitute the only restriction to the universal validity of the Ebbinghaus curve? Many old investigations show an extremely slow deterioration of habits. Watson (99), in emphasizing the difference between verbal and nonverbal habits, states that there is scarcely any forgetting in typewriting or in ball tossing after one year, whereas with regard to language habits deterioration sets in very quickly. Book (11) found that after six and twelve months students of typewriting showed almost no forgetting and the ability to relearn very rapidly. These findings indicate that forgetting of skills sets in later than demanded by the Ebbinghaus curve, but their bearing on the form of the curve of forgetting is not quite clear. Yet, the old statement that we learn skating in summer and swimming in winter seems to imply the occurrence of an entirely different type of curve. On the other hand, investigations of McGeoch and Melton (65) revealed that Watson's distinction between verbal and nonverbal habits cannot be generally valid. Forgetting was as rapid after the learning of mazes as after the learning of nonsense syllables provided learning was equally thorough. There are indications that the lasting retention of such skilled acts as typewriting is due at least to some extent to overlearning: in contrast to verbal material, skills learned by drill are usually repeated over and over again even after they are known, with the result that they are practiced to a much greater extent than is the language material with which they are usually compared.

To decide whether the Ebbinghaus curve must be altered for certain types of material, we refer next to the investigations concerning retention of meaningful material. Here, again, most authors recognize a difference only in the speed of forgetting and not in the quality of the curve.[3] We mentioned that the Ebbinghaus curve was found valid in experiments with poetry (except for occasional reminiscence). Forgetting of meaningful texts proceeded in the same way as that of "overlearned" nonsense material, provided that verbatim learning was applied. Thus meaningfulness of the material alone does not appear to change the curve of forgetting. McGeoch states in agreement with the older thesis that "meaningful material is better retained than non-meaningful material" (62, p. 407), referring to experiments made by McGeoch and Whitely (64). In studying these experiments it may appear possible that it is not the meaningfulness of the material which changes the curve of retention, but certain methods applied in learning and testing.[4] The importance of methods of testing is shown in recent investigations of English. He found that tests of verbatim learning are not adequate for determining the rate of retention of substance:

The same subjects, learning the same material at the same time and under the same conditions, on the one hand forget rapidly, or on the other retain what is learned depending upon whether our criterion of learning is a fixed routine response or a grasp of the meaning or substance [19, p. 258].

---

[3] Cf. Woodworth, "The curve of forgetting shows the same general character with various types of material" (112, p. 69), Bean, "The rate of forgetting is slower for meaningful than for nonsense material" (7, p. 43), and Jordan, "Meaning makes the curve of retention drop slower" (35, p. 101).

[4] In the experiments of McGeoch and Whitely a cardboard with several different objects—photos, stamps, money, buttons, and so on—was observed for thirty seconds, and the recall was tested immediately after the observation and 30, 60, 90, and 120 days later. When the tests were made in the form of what is called "interrogatory recall" (the subjects had to answer fifty questions about the card), a very slow rate of forgetting was found (after 120 days the accuracy of recall was 93 percent of the immediate recall), and the curve was highly irregular; some of its phases were level and even ascending.

We cannot apply our concept of meaningful learning to the experiments of McGeoch and Whitely. It seems that in their experiments there was no understandable relation between any of the objects recalled. But the method of learning and testing differed from that used in most experiments establishing the curve of forgetting. Instead of memorizing by repetition, the subjects observed the cards only once and for thirty seconds. The large number of questions following immediately after the short observation may have had an effect on the retention by organizing the material. Thus a certain amount of constructiveness may have characterized the learning as well as the reproduction process.

A definite correlation does exist between forgetting and whatever is specifically and differentially measured by the V-items [V stands for verbatim], and between reminiscence and that which is differentially measured by the S [summary] -items [20, p. 262].

In these experiments the subjects read aloud a difficult, meaningful text. Later either verbatim recognition or recollection of substance was tested. The first kind of test yielded a curve of forgetting similar to the Ebbinghaus curve, whereas in the second case frequent instances of reminiscence were found.

The assumption that methods of learning and methods of testing are relevant to the form of the curve of retention may serve to explain certain results of our experiments. Our results concerning the curve of forgetting may be summed up in the following way: In the case of memorizing, the results were in agreement with the main features of the Ebbinghaus curve. The earlier performances of our subjects were better than their later performances. But learning by understanding brought about different effects—the average performance made several weeks after training was as good as the performance immediately after training. Thus we did not find a rapid decline in the initial stages of the curve. A third (or fourth) performance was as good as, and frequently better than, the second performance. Thus we did not find a regular and smooth curve. The experimental evidence for these statements will be given in the next few pages and in a new experiment to be described later.

In those experiments in which the subjects memorized the solutions of the tasks, the tasks which were taught in the practice period were better recalled in the test than in the retest. With a lapse of time the score decreased in the card-trick experiment from 42 to 32 percent, in match Experiment A from 42 to 33 percent, and in Experiment C, where different groups of subjects were tested after shorter and longer intervals, from 67 to 53 percent. New tasks also were solved better immediately or shortly after the training period than several weeks later. In Experiment C one group attained a score of 25 percent in new tasks one week after training, while another group scored only 14 percent three weeks after training. In Experiment B the average score of the memorizers was 24½ percent for the two new Tasks 9 and 10 immediately after training (Table 6, Chapter IV), but only 13 percent for the equivalent Tasks 4 and 5 four weeks later (Table 8).[5] We find a similar decline by comparing the net scores obtained with new tasks in the tests and retests of Experiment A.

As to the results of learning by understanding, we first refer to the experiment in which the performance of different groups of subjects was compared after intervals of various lengths. In Experiment C, with practiced tasks, one group scored 58 percent a week after and 52 percent three weeks after training, while with new tasks we obtained in both cases a score of 55 percent. There was no significant change between the earlier and the later performances. In the other experiments the same subjects were tested twice. In comparing tests and retests made with practiced tasks, there was in the card experiment a slight improvement, from 44 to 48 percent (when the same task was used in test and in retest), and in Experiment A a slight deterioration, from 46 to 43 percent (when different but comparable tasks were used). More important are the results with new tasks. The net new scores of Groups Und., Ex., and Help in the card experiment and in Experiments A and B were higher in the retest than in the test. This result was best indicated in Experiment B, because in that case two new tasks (Nos. 9 and 10) tested immediately after training may be called equivalent to two new tasks (Nos. 4 and 5) tested four weeks later. In the first case the score was 44 percent; in the second case 48 percent (Tables 6 and 8), although the working time was shorter in the retest than in the test.

By studying the individual scores instead of the group averages of those who learned by understanding, we find in each experiment a few subjects with very extensive differences in their test and retest scores (reductions as well as increases). We find also that

---

[5] The decrease from twenty-five to fourteen, and so forth, may appear small, but it must be remembered that the scores fell almost to the point of "no learning," since the retest scores were about equal to the control scores.

with very few exceptions the subjects who had the highest test scores scored high in the retest. Improvement in the averages was caused by the subjects whose performance was mediocre in the test; most of them improved their score in the retest.

Many other individual experiments were made to determine the difference in the performance of the subjects after a lapse of time. Only a few of these experiments, however, can be considered reliable.[6] When we take into account only those experiments in which uncontrolled practice between the tests can be excluded with reasonable certainty, the number of our comparable records becomes rather small. Still we can draw certain general inferences from these records.

I. In this experiment the tests were made at monthly intervals. Three subjects who were taught individually by the method of help and who obtained high scores with three new tasks immediately after the training, stated on every later occasion that they did not think of the tasks between the experiments. "I know the tasks anyway," said one subject. The scores in the immediate test were about 80 percent of the maximum possible scores: about a month after training every one of the three subjects, tested with three new tasks, had somewhat higher scores; two months after training the scores were again around 80 percent; three months after training they were again slightly higher, but not as high as one month after training. New tasks were used in each test. We may say that there was no indication of forgetting during a period of three months, when learning was by understanding and tests were administered in the interval.

II. The scheme of the first experiment was successfully completed with three more subjects. "Successfully" means that the subjects reported at each of the successive tests that they had not thought of the tasks in the interval. One subject, who was taught by Method Mem. (Experiment A) and who obtained a mediocre score in the first test, had a very low score one month after the training and failed completely two and three months later. On the latter occasions she could not solve even the practiced task. The second subject, who was taught by the method of help and who also had an average score immediately after instruction, showed a similar deterioration in her performance. The third subject, with a mediocre score

---

[6] The match tasks are interesting, and many subjects are therefore inclined to think of them and to try them out in the interval between the experiments. Strict prohibition to do so and an appeal to the subjects for assistance in scientific work were not effective in all experiments spread over a long time.

immediately after the instruction with the method of help, improved considerably in the second and third tests. Three months after training she still performed better than in the immediate test, but not as well as in the previous test.

III. Two other subjects who had learned by the method of help were tested again after three months without intermediate tests. Test and retest were comparable, each consisting of four new tasks. The performances were rather good and only slightly lower the second time than on the first occasion. We conclude: retention of well-understood tasks may remain high even without intermediate practice.

In these experiments we found no general confirmation for the Ebbinghaus curve in the case of learning by understanding. Further experiments with a greater number of subjects are in order, especially to explain the frequent level and rising phases of the curve.

Practice versus Forgetting

In reviewing the experiments of Ebbinghaus on forgetting Woodworth stresses the difference between a "practice curve" (or learning curve) and a "curve of forgetting" (112, pp. 53, 90). Ebbinghaus tested the rate of retention of nonsense syllables, learned by rote, after various intervals. He obtained a curve of forgetting by using different lists of syllables for each of the intervals. Had he used the same list for each test of retention, he would have found no deterioration of performance but, on the contrary, he would have found a practice curve. The consecutive tests would have improved the performance. Can this description be applied to other forms of learning as well as to rote learning of nonsense syllables?

In order to answer the question about the relationship of the practice curve and the curve of forgetting, we may devise the following general scheme of experiment.

We must have three comparable groups; the first assumes the role of control group, inasmuch as it has no intermediate tests at all, whereas the form of the intermediate tests differs for the second and third groups. The letters "ABC" and so forth, in the scheme may represent any kind of learning material, for ex-

SCHEME OF EXPERIMENT

	First Group	Second Group	Third Group
First session: training	ABC	ABC	ABC
First session: immediate test	ABC	ABC	ABC
One week later:			
intermediate test	....	DEF	ABC
Two weeks later:			
intermediate test	....	GHI	ABC
Three weeks later:			
intermediate test	....	KLM	ABC
Four weeks later: main test	ABC and XYZ	ABC and XYZ	ABC and XYZ

ample, match tasks (in this case each letter would represent one match task). The third group is tested at weekly intervals with the same materials or tasks which it has used in the training period, while the second group is tested with different materials or tasks in each of the intermediate tests. In order to determine the effect of the various forms of testing, we conclude the experiment by what we call "main test": that is, we test uniformly all three groups with the practiced material (ABC) and with entirely new material (XYZ). The main questions which we try to answer by such an experiment are: Which group will know the most at the end of the experiment? Will the performance be the same in the main test, or will it differ in practiced tasks, in new tasks, or in both? Which group will show the greatest transfer effect?

Experiment E.—The material of the match tasks was selected in order to carry out an experiment corresponding to the scheme just discussed. One specific match task was used in the place of each of the letters in the above scheme. The experiment was administered in comparable classes of the College of the City of New York. The groups were approximately the same with regard to scholastic achievement and the distribution of I.Q. The first experimental session was the same for each of the three learning groups. The training (ten minutes) consisted of slow and careful application of the method of help by presentation of three different tasks one after the other. Thus, according to the results of the previous chapters the training was "good," and there were even more examples used than were used in the experiments described in Chapter IV, in which Group Help was taught by only two examples. The three tasks, we call them "practiced tasks," were given as tests immediately after the conclusion of the training period.

Group I was not interviewed between the first session and the main test. Groups II and III were each tested three times during that interval—Group II with nine different tasks, and Group III three times with the three practiced tasks. In the fourth week, in the main test, which was identical for all the groups, the three practiced tasks and three entirely new tasks were presented in a random order. In the tables containing the results the practiced tasks are separated from the new tasks, but they were presented to the subjects without such designation. A time limit of three minutes was set for each task. At the close of each experimental session the subjects were asked not to think of the tasks, and at the beginning of each session they were asked whether or not they had reviewed the tasks in the meantime. In the tables are used the test papers of only those subjects who answered this question consistently in the negative.

Tasks 3*b*, 1, and 4 served as the practiced tasks—corresponding to the letters "ABC" in the experimental scheme above—and Tasks 6, 5, and 9 served as the new tasks in the main test—corresponding to the letters "XYZ" in the scheme. Each of these groups of tasks contains one easy task (Task 3*b* or Task 6) and two difficult tasks. The two groups of tasks are of about equal difficulty as determined by the scores of a fourth group (the control group), which has had no training. The experimenter tried to make the same arrangement for each of the intermediate tests of Group II, by selecting three tasks for each test, which together were of the same difficulty as the practiced tasks and which consisted of one easy task and two difficult tasks.

In order to present the results of the experiment, performed under the conditions described, the following scoring method is used: two points were given for the solution of the easy task (for example, Task 3b or Task 6), four points each for the perfect solution of a difficult task, and one point for a "probable" solution of a difficult task (if scrutiny of the test papers showed that a subject had probably solved the task even though his drawing was not entirely adequate). If a subject solved all the tasks of a test (the two difficult tasks and the one easy task), he thus obtained a score of ten. This is the highest possible score.[7]

TABLE 14. AVERAGE SCORES OF EXPERIMENT E

	Group I 19 Subjects	Group II 22 Subjects	Group III 21 Subjects	Group Con. 20 Subjects
Immediate test				
Practiced tasks	7.79	7.91	7.90	...
One week later	...	5.14 [a]	7.52 [b]	...
Two weeks later	...	5.59 [a]	8.57 [b]	...
Three weeks later	...	6.00 [a]	9.62 [b]	...
Main test				
Practiced tasks	5.94	6.47	9.81	2.40
New tasks	5.84	6.91	3.86	2.50

[a] New tasks.   [b] Practiced tasks.

---

[7] We find the "percentage of solutions," the measure used for presenting the results of Experiment C in Chapter IV, if we multiply the scores of Table 14 by ten: an average score of 7.90 means that the group obtained 79 percent of the maximum score. The weighting of the observed values, which consists in attributing to the easy task one-half the score attributed to the difficult tasks, is necessary because of the fact that most of the subjects of Group III when tested with the new tasks and most of the subjects of the control group solved only the easy task and failed to solve the two difficult tasks. The absolute values of the perfect solutions obtained in the main test shall be presented here in order to enable the reader to pass judgment on the scoring method used:

NUMBER OF SUBJECTS SOLVING THE INDIVIDUAL TASKS OF THE MAIN TEST

	Group I 19 Subjects	Group II 22 Subjects	Group III 21 Subjects	Group Con. 20 Subjects
Practiced tasks				
Task 3b	14	20	21	11
Task 1	10	12	20	3
Task 4	11	13	21	3
New tasks				
Task 6	16	19	16	11
Task 5	10	13	7	3
Task 9	9	15	5	4

We obtain a second significant measure of the respective performances if we determine how many subjects of each group solved all the tasks and thus received the highest possible score of ten in each test.

TABLE 15. NUMBER OF SUBJECTS WITH PERFECT SCORES

	Group I	*Group II*	*Group III*
Immediate test: practiced tasks	11	12	12
Main test: practiced tasks	5	8	20
Main test: new tasks	6	8	2

The results [8] of the experiment will be discussed first by studying separately the performance of each group.

Group I. The experiment performed with this group is analogous to that performed with Group Help in Experiment C3. The results constitute a confirmation of what was previously established. A good method of learning resulted four weeks later, without intervening practice, in the ability to solve both the practiced tasks and the new tasks with the same ease. Four subjects had a "transfer effect" of 100 percent, while seven subjects solved the new tasks better than the practiced tasks and eight subjects the practiced tasks better than the new tasks (cf. Table 30 in Appendix 2). The rate of forgetting can be studied with this group only with regard to the practiced tasks. They were solved better immediately after training than they were four weeks later.

Group II. In the main test this group, too, showed about the same results for practiced and for new tasks. There were eight subjects with a 100 percent "transfer effect," eight with a higher, and six with a lower effect. The same ease in solving old and new tasks is, however, not the result which we want to stress here.[9] The decline in the practiced-task scores from 7.91 to 6.47 likewise does not need much explanation in view of the perform-

---

[8] The reliability of the results is discussed in Appendix 2 (p. 279).

[9] From the data of Group II alone it is not possible to disprove an alternative explanation for the similarity of the scores obtained for the practiced tasks and the new tasks in the main test. The similarity may be due to the circumstance that the nine intermediate tasks contained recurring elements which contributed to the same extent to all tasks of the main test. But this explanation cannot be applied to the performance of Group I or to Group Help in Experiment C.

ance of Group I, although it is worth mentioning that this decline was smaller with Group II than with Group I. It is more important, first, that with new tasks in the main test the performance of Group II was the best of all the groups. Secondly, there was a steady improvement from one intermediate test to the next. By testing the performance at various intervals, each time with different tasks, we obtained, not a curve of forgetting, but a practice curve.

Group III. By reviewing the performance of this group solely with the practiced tasks we find a perfect example for a practice curve. In the first intermediate test a slightly lower score was obtained than in the immediate test, but from the first to the fourth week the improvement proceeds in a straight line. In the fifth test (main test) the twenty-one subjects of the group committed only one error in solving the three old tasks; the group average was almost equal to the maximum score of ten. Observation of the behavior of the group shows that we have here a performance strictly comparable to the well-known effects of practice by drill. As is described in Chapter V, the subjects who had learned by understanding adopted a problem-solving attitude in the tests reported there. Except for the first intermediate test nothing like this was observed with members of Group III. The test paper was opened—and the subjects drew the design required for the solution. There was no "solving" of a problem, but rather a recall of well-learned data. Here we find reproduction instead of reconstruction.[10]

Turning our attention to the performance in the new tasks, we find that the ultimate performance of Group III was worse than that of Group I, which had had no intermediate practice at all. If we consider the intermediate tests as additional practice, we are confronted with the following fact: The additional practice made

[10] A similar case has been clearly stated by Breslich as the result of investigations on learning algebra: "Simplified, routinized processes are sometimes the outcomes of earlier understandings that have been reduced to formulas which are merely held in memory . . . When a process takes on the form of the routine procedure, it is often difficult to determine whether or not the pupil ever understood it" (in Judd, 38, p. 85).

Group III expert in solving practiced tasks, but made it distinctly inferior in solving new tasks. Routine practice, or stereotyping the performance, obliterated the effects of "good" instruction. The way in which Group III learned originally would have permitted application of the knowledge to all kinds of tasks after a long interval—as proved by the performance of Group I, which obtained the same instruction as Group III. But additional training, which consisted in several routine repetitions of the specific solutions, altered the subjects' knowledge of the match tasks. After four weeks the group's achievement was such as would have been obtained with a group which had memorized the solutions of the practiced tasks by drill procedure—that is, practiced tasks were solved much better than new tasks.[11]

The curve of forgetting.—Before we continue to study the different effects of the two forms of intermediate practice, we must return to the discussion of the curve of retention. We shall first examine the curve for the tests in which new tasks were solved at various intervals. Fig. 20 contains the results obtained under these circumstances in Experiment E and also the main results of Experiments B and C, described in Chapter IV.

Each point in the graph represents tests made with tasks which were never seen before by the subjects (either in the practice period or in a previous test). In Experiment E, in which all three groups learned by understanding, we did not make an immediate test with new tasks. Therefore the test of the new tasks made one week after training (first intermediate test of Group II, score 51 percent) forms our starting point for the discussion of this experiment. Since all three groups had learned in the same way and since the groups were equivalent, it may be assumed that the score of 51 percent would have been the score of each of the three groups, had they been tested at that time with new tasks. Therefore the point 51 in the graph may be connected with the later scores of all three groups. Group E I, which was not given in-

[11] Cf. Koffka, 50, p. 547: "Drill will no doubt make the traces more and more available for one kind of activity, but it may at the same time narrow down the *range* of availability."

termediate tests, achieved a score of 58 percent four weeks after training: the curve ascends slightly. The curve of Group E II, which had several opportunities to apply its knowledge to other tasks, rises somewhat more and reaches a level of 69 percent. The

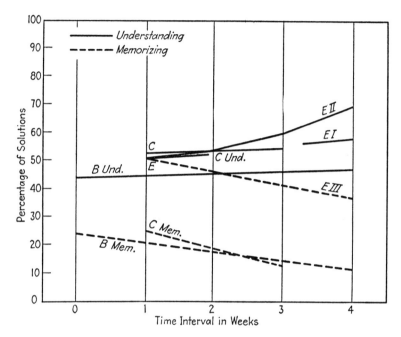

Fig. 20. Retention Curve for New Tasks

curve of Group E III, which because of intermediate training with the same tasks reverted to routine manipulations, has a descending form and ends at 38 percent four weeks after training.

Let us now compare these curves with those obtained in the other experiments. With the passage of time the scores of the groups which had learned by understanding rose in Experiment B from 44 percent to 48 percent (p. 142), and remained in Experiment C at 55 percent. Thus, we obtain a good correspondence with the result of Group E I: when the match tasks are understood, the performance of new tasks remains at approximately the same level, whether we test the accomplishment immediately after training and four weeks later or one and three weeks after training or one and four weeks after training.

By inserting in the graph the curves of the groups which learned by memorizing in Experiments B and C we obtain curves which are similar to the curve of Group III in Experiment E. The accomplishment of Group Mem. with new tasks deteriorated from 24½ percent to 13 percent in Experiment B and from 25 percent to 14 percent in Experiment C (cf. p. 142 above).

A slight change in these curves of retention is indicated when we consider the forgetting of practiced tasks. In this case, too, the rate of retention falls off more sharply after memorizing than after understanding (cf. the results of Experiment C), but even after understanding the curves are descending. When the practiced tasks were submitted to tests, the two "understanding groups" of Experiment E, Groups I and II, scored lower four weeks after training than immediately after training. In the case of understanding we obtained slightly falling curves with practiced tasks and level or slowly rising curves with new tasks. The probable explanation for this divergence is that the starting point of the curves for practiced tasks is raised to an unduly high level by an extraneous factor: immediately after training the solution of practiced tasks is facilitated by the recall of specific solutions.[12]

In order to arrive at a comprehensive knowledge of the influence of the methods of learning on the form of the curve of forgetting, many further experiments are required. But the experiments just summarized as well as the individual experiments described previously and the literature referred to make it probable that the following propositions are valid.

Curve of forgetting without intermediate practice: the accomplishment due to mechanical memorization deteriorates in time, most quickly in the initial stages. The accomplishment due to

---

[12] We made this assumption in the previous chapter (p. 131) and may now confirm it by referring to an important investigation concerning the curve of forgetting. After training animals to choose the brighter or larger of two objects, Köhler found that absolute data were forgotten more quickly than were structural relations (43, cf. 289, below). The remembering of the practiced solutions may therefore be no longer available at a later date, when the integrated knowledge of the principle is applied exclusively to both the practiced and the new tasks.

learning by understanding stays at about the same level for the first few weeks after training, which means that slightly ascending curves are to be expected as frequently as slightly descending curves. If we measure the accomplishment with practiced tasks, or with tasks having elements similar to the practiced tasks, the descending type of curve is more probable than in the other case, in which we use variations of the task to test our knowledge.[13]

The effects of intermediate practice.—How do the various forms of intermediate practice affect the curve of retention? It is possible to distinguish six different conditions under which this question may be studied. They are shown again in a "scheme of experiment," because the different conditions are of general interest and do not apply solely to experimentation with match tasks. The letters in the scheme may represent any learning material.

SCHEME OF EXPERIMENT

METHOD OF LEARNING	FORM OF TRAINING	FORM OF TESTS *Intervals after Training*			
		One Week	*Two Weeks*	*Three Weeks*	*Four Weeks*
Learning by memorizing (*a*)	A B	A B	A B	A B	A B
Learning by memorizing (*b*)	A B	X Y	X Y	X Y	X Y
Learning by memorizing (*c*)	A B	X Y	D E	F G	H I
Learning by understanding (*d*)	A B	A B	A B	A B	A B
Learning by understanding (*e*)	A B	X Y	X Y	X Y	X Y
Learning by understanding (*f*)	A B	X Y	D E	F G	H I

Under the conditions *a* and *d* we learn AB, and it is the same AB which we are asked to do in all later tests. Under the conditions *b* and *e* the tests are again identical, but the learning material is not repeated. Under conditions *c* and *f* each test differs from the other as well as from the learning material. On the basis of the match-task

[13] These statements refer to the form of the curve of forgetting. Concerning the rate of retention we have not arrived at a general thesis. On the basis of our experiments it cannot generally be said that we retain longer what we have understood than what we have memorized, since practiced tasks were frequently solved as well by the memorizing as by the understanding groups after the lapse of several weeks. But the form of the curves makes it probable that appropriate continuation of the experiments over a longer time or the exclusion of overlearning in the case of memorization would prove that understanding is superior even in that respect.

experiments we can indicate the level at which the various curves start. In Experiment C1 the test made one week after training has been administered under all six conditions of the scheme, but the later tests of the scheme have not been investigated in that experiment. According to Table 10 the score 67 percent was obtained for condition *a*, 25 percent for conditions *b* and *c*, 58 percent for condition *d*, and 55 percent for conditions *e* and *f*, one week after training.

The possibilities *a*, *b*, *d*, and *e* may be taken together, because they represent what is commonly called "practice." The tests have the same form in each case. On the other hand, the possibilities *c* and *f* refer to instances of a different kind: no two tests are the same. We have not made experiments with each of the six possibilities. The set-up of Group III corresponds to case *d*. However, the starting point of its curve had a higher position than the curve for Experiment C (75 percent in contrast to 58 percent) because the group used three examples in the learning period (instead of two, as in Experiment C) and its knowledge of these examples was tested immediately after training (in Experiment C no immediate test was made). But we are not concerned here with the level at which the curve starts. We are interested in the later development insofar as it is attributable to subsequent practice. In case *d* the curve rises slightly but continuously: the score of Group III with the practiced tasks was 7.52 one week after training; 8.57 two weeks later; 9.62 three weeks later, and 9.81 four weeks later. A curve of this form may presumably apply to cases *a*, *b*, and *e*, too, although under some of the latter conditions the starting points would be much lower. When we try to solve the same task on several occasions, our accomplishment improves whether or not the original practice consisted of meaningful learning or senseless learning.

In the four possibilities just discussed the intermediate tests represent practice in the sense of doing the same thing more than once. We encounter here a situation similar to that to which we called attention at the beginning of this section: if the same poem or the same list of nonsense syllables were used to test a subject at weekly intervals and the tests were made by measuring the saving in relearning, we would obtain a practice curve. But—and this is a significant result of Experiment E—the curve of Group II runs parallel to the practice curve of Group III. It rises from 5.14 (one week after training) to 5.59, 6.00, and 6.91 (four weeks after training), although different tasks were used for each test. Tests consisting of new tasks each time may therefore also constitute good practice. Group II was investigated under the conditions represented by *f* in our schematic table: the group learned by understanding and faced different tasks at each consecutive test. The "different tasks" were similar, inasmuch as they all contained similar structural features.

Groups II and III practiced the material intermediately. Which kind of practice was better? The answer may be found by inquiring about the applicability of the knowledge acquired by the two methods of practice. We have done this in the main test and have obtained the following result: after the intermediate practice, Group II scored 6.91 and Group III scored 3.86 with entirely new tasks. We may therefore state that intermediate practice consisting of *different* tests (Group II) brings about an improvement in the ability to apply knowledge to new tasks, while intermediate practice consisting of *identical* tests (Group III) interferes with the applicability of knowledge.

We have just studied the effect of several intermediate tests. But in the experiments reported in Chapter IV we used only one intermediate test, since our experimental set-up included only a test and a retest. In a discussion of the testing of new tasks we may distinguish two possibilities: (*a*) learning AB, testing XY, retesting XY, and (*b*) learning AB, testing XY, and retesting ZU. The first possibility was examined in Experiment B, where two "tested tasks" were included in the retest (four weeks after training and test). They were better solved on the later occasion than on the earlier occasion—a result which held both in senseless and in meaningful learning. The second possibility was examined in Experiments A and B: there was a marked improvement in the retest over the test in the case of meaningful learning, but a deterioration of the performance was evident in the case of senseless learning. Thus it holds true only of learning by understanding that its results can be improved by a single test or review which consists of the solution of various tasks.

The Concept of Repetition

The term "repetition" can be applied to the intermediate tests of Experiment E, the results of which we just discussed. Should "repetition" be defined as the frequent occurrence of the same material and the same response, we would face a paradoxical situation. Measuring the learning effect by the ability to solve new tasks, we would have to state that repetition resulted in deterioration of knowledge. But the term "repetition" is ambiguous.

A short survey of the different usages of the term "repetition" will show that in everyday life and in discussing psychological experiments we use the word "repetition" under circumstances in which it does not mean a reoccurrence of the same, unchanged material or response. We memorize a poem by repetition. What is the actual procedure as used by an actor who knows how to learn by heart or by a subject who knows of the results of psychological research? Every repetition may somewhat differ from the previous one. The actor and the subject will resort very soon, often at the instance of the second reading, to recitation. They will avoid looking at the poem except when necessary and by covering the page they will change the stimuli. The reading and reciting will improve, the performance will become smoother and better with each successive repetition—which means that the responses do not remain identical.

When a rat learns by frequent repetitions how to arrive at the food compartment in a maze, it encounters the same surroundings at each trial. Whether the stimuli remain the same, we do not know. But the responses do change every time. They change not only in that errors like entries in blind alleys are eliminated but also insofar as hesitations and oscillations at turning points are successively omitted. The performance becomes smoother and better (and therefore quicker). It is, of course, well known that at its sixth trial the rat does not copy what it did in its fifth or its first trial.

The learning of skills by human beings may serve as another very clear example. Professor Wertheimer uses the learning of dancing (or of skating, cycling, and so forth) to illustrate this. The teacher shows me a new dance step. I "repeat" it. My first repetition does not at all resemble the one perfect step which the teacher showed me. I repeat the step again; I do not take the same step that I took the first time, but my performance is better. Each successive repetition may differ from all others. After ten repetitions I may know the dance step; my last "perfect" movement is entirely different from my first trial. There was a development from step 1 to step 10. I learned by each different step—but nevertheless I learned to dance by "repetition."—Suppose this description does not hold true for subject X, who repeats the dance step each time exactly as he did it the first time—then he does not learn to dance. Identical repetitions do not lead to the acquisition of mastery in dancing.

In view of these different usages of the term "repetition" [14] we may say with the same justification that Groups II and III learned by repetition. The first group dealt repeatedly with match tasks that contained identical structural features, while the latter group repeated specific solutions of certain tasks. The results of these repetitions differed in the two cases. Therefore it is not sufficient to state that a learner acquired knowledge by repetition —it must be known whether the repeating was done in a stereotyped mechanical fashion or in a way which we may call "gradual meaningful learning."

In the course of this investigation we had occasion frequently to emphasize that learning by understanding may occur without repetition. When the number series 5 8 1 2 1 5 and so forth was understood, repetition was not needed for knowing the series in

[14] Repeating nonsense syllables will be discussed in the next chapter; repetition as a part of direct practice in our experiments was mentioned on p. 109. With respect to the extensive literature on the effects of repetition we need only quote the summary of Woodworth concerning the learning of skills: "Repetition of a performance by a well motivated subject gives progressive improvement" (112, p. 164).

contrast to the memorizing of the same series. The principle of performing card tricks did not have to be repeated, because the subjects were able to understand and to apply it after one presentation. When the good methods of teaching were employed in the match tasks, no example or help was shown twice. These examples prove that learning by understanding is possible without repetition. But must we assume that it occurs only without repetition? Are we to distinguish between memorization, or drill, on the one side, and learning by understanding, on the other, by characterizing the first as a gradual step-by-step process and the second as an instantaneous grasp, or flash of insight?

In literature we find a tendency to answer this question in the affirmative. In the opinion of Thorndike, to quote just one author, suddenness of change from total inability to mastery might be the most satisfactory criterion of ideational learning, which is often contrasted with associative learning (93, p. 135). Probably he has in mind that Koffka (49, p. 182) demonstrated that sudden improvement rather than gradual improvement is the typical occurrence in many animal experiments which were usually explained by trial and error.[15] Adherents of gestalt theory had every reason to call attention to the frequent occurrence of a sudden change in the learning curve: it often happened that after many trials which brought about no progress the animals or the children suddenly changed their behavior; wrong movements or choices were suddenly eliminated, and correct responses became predominant. It was necessary to stress that quality of the learning process which did not fit into a theory of forming arbitrary, or blind, connections.

The relation between the concepts of repetition and of insight has been analyzed by Adams: "One thing at least is finally established by the mere occurrence of insight (which Köhler forced upon our attention), and that is that learning is *not* caused by repetition." "There is no real or necessary or causal relation between learning and repetition or frequency of repetition" (4,

---

[15] Among others N. R. F. Maier (66 and 67) stresses that the type of behavioral integration called insight consists of sudden experiencing of new relations.

p. 157). "Learning occurs without repetition and repetition occurs without learning" (p. 155).

On the other hand, it was not denied by gestalt psychologists that learning is very often a gradual process. In the same book to which we have just referred Koffka uses maturation as a central concept. In his more recent book he expressly states: "Insightful behavior is not necessarily a behavior in which the full solution occurs at once" (50, p. 631). Wheeler (109) asserts that the learner grows to a better performance in the interval between the repetitions; learning, then, rests upon a given degree of maturation. We conclude that the process of gradual organization, the slow transition from a worse to a better state of affairs, from a bad to a good gestalt, is just as important for the psychology of meaningful learning as is the flash of insight.

We need the concept of gradual meaningful learning to understand the learning process in the experiments reported in Chapter IV and in those discussed in this chapter. The thesis that a single exposure is sufficient, that repetition is not required, cannot be justly applied to learning by examples or help. Only if we falsely define "repetition" as the repeated occurrence of the identical contents A,B,C,D and their apperception in an unchanged form at several successive presentations, may we say that repetition cannot occur in meaningful learning. But by using the term in a different sense the successive steps in the method of examples may be said to constitute repetitions. The subjects did not first learn an A, then a different B, then a different C in order that they might finally know the principle X, but gradually developed X by observing first A, then B, then C (cf. pp. 116 f.). Of course, this description of the learning process implies the acceptance of the fact that a single presentation is sufficient to bring about improvement. Yet the repeated presentation of "examples" brought about still more improvement.

Group II in Experiment E repeated the match tasks on three different occasions, which we called intermediate tests. The result of that experiment, the straight ascending line connecting the consecutive tests, proves that understanding can develop and can be perfected by gradual learning. Each repetition contributed to the crystallization of knowledge of the geometrical problems. Each consecutive example broadened and deepened the understanding of the principle.

Repetition in these cases, as in skill-acquiring situations, is not repetition of one set of identical elements, rather it is a gradual development of structural features. One does not do the same thing over and over. On the contrary, one is always passing on to a more advanced performance.

The effect of learning, the advanced performance in contrast to the earlier performance, should here be characterized only briefly as a smoother process of greater unity and better organization. A movement consisting of six different and independent components is learned and can be performed when the pieces lose their identity and organize themselves as parts of a consistent whole.[16] "Repetition" sometimes brings about that change, often step by step instead of by sudden transition. In the summary of the second chapter we spoke of sudden understanding, which constituted the learning process, and of regrouping and organizing the material which made sudden discovery of the inherent relations (of a principle) possible. Now we know that organizing and discovery may have, and often do have, the form of development: the better understanding of a principle is then attained step by step. The result of the development is not merely information, but it is, as with skills, well organized and articulated knowledge, which will not soon be forgotten and which can be applied under various circumstances.[17]

[16] The statement that learning results in better organization is not in contradiction to our analysis of the match tasks, in which we have pointed out that the task often required the breaking up of a structurally good figure (cf. the definition of the structurally difficult tasks on p. 69). A well-organized figure—for example, a big square divided into four smaller squares—when presented with the demand to transform it into another figure, becomes part of an unsatisfactory situation. The situation now contains a gap, an unsolved problem. At the end of the learning period, however, there is a better organization of the whole situation (although not of the figure viewed alone).

[17] Can we describe the gradual development of a principle as the formation and verification of a hypothesis? In describing their experiences in learning the match tasks a few subjects reported that after the first or the second help they gained

Learning does not end with the training period. In describing the tests of the experiments with card tricks, we had to refer constantly to the change in the subjects' solutions, to abbreviations, additions, and alterations. Such changes are due to the development of knowledge. Knowledge of the principle continues to develop at each successive test, because learning is not restricted to unchanged circumstances. The same was the case with the match tasks: the first task in a test often caused greater difficulty than the last—not because it was more difficult but because the knowledge of the principle was less complete at the beginning of the test than later. The performance due to understanding of the principle, even when achieved by a sudden discovery, can still be perfected gradually in the course of later tests.

Experiment E, which resulted in a practice curve due to intermediate tests of different form, shows how extraneous and unimportant is the distinction between the training period and the testing period. In both periods the subjects endeavor to understand and to apply the principle of the tasks. We may describe the entire process from the beginning of the training period to the last test

---

a "notion" of the principle or formed a "hypothesis" (a theory) about the principle. At the next example they proceeded to ascertain whether or not their notion or hypothesis was correct. In some cases the notion was very definite, but not quite correct, at the beginning and had to be altered in the following steps. In other cases it was rudimentary and was enlarged and developed in the course of the learning process.

However, the conscious formation of a hypothesis does not appear to be the only form or the main form of gradual meaningful learning. Probably there is one type of learner especially inclined to form hypotheses, while another is of a more passive or receptive spirit. The second type of subject understands something without generalizing it consciously and builds up the notion of the principle gradually—the notion may remain unformulated even after the knowledge has been acquired. In these cases, too, it is possible to speak of forming a hypothesis, but then the concept will be identical with that of developing a principle, whereas in the few cases described above it meant specific active guesswork and testing (ascertaining the correctness of the hypothesis). Therefore it is more appropriate to consider the formation of hypotheses as an important special case of developing a principle.

It is difficult to decide how far our usage of the term "hypothesis" is related to that of Krechevsky and of Tolman. The latter recently summarized his theory as follows: "Learning consists in the formation of new sign-gestalt-expectations—hypotheses" (97, p. 195). Tolman explains these expectations as "some set in the organism which is adjusted to the fact that a given spatially and temporarily immediate stimulus object is going to lead to a spatially and temporarily more distant object."

by stating that to find the principle and to solve an individual task was very difficult at the beginning and became gradually easier. Constructive processes thus characterize learning (when they may be called "organizing") as well as remembering (when we speak of "reconstruction"). Gradual meaningful learning, we may add, is a never-ending process of assimilating and incorporating a principle into the learner's wealth of knowledge.[18]

That practice and testing have common characteristics holds true for the acquisition of skills as well as for learning by understanding. When does learning to dance end? Certainly not with the last visit to the dancing class. The process is continuous also in learning to play bridge and to understand a theory of physics. With each application, with each test or recall, the knowledge may be further developed and enriched. This follows from the concept of learning by examples.

We may now recapitulate our discussion of the curve of forgetting. The evidence of the match-task tests confirmed the validity of the Ebbinghaus curve in the case of direct practice. But the principle acquired by understanding could be applied in most cases as readily on one occasion as on another. A possible explanation for a "retention curve" which has the form of a straight horizontal line for extensive periods or which comprises ascending as well as descending phases, can be derived from our concept of gradual learning. Let us suppose that Task A is learned and understood. After an interval a test is made with four different tasks, and after another interval Task A is tested again. In such a case forgetting will not be the sole effective force, because the intermediate tests constitute a review which may improve the ability to solve Task A. But when the solution of Task A is memorized in a mechanical way, intermediate tests with different material will have only a small effect on the later performance. Review in the form of similar tasks or examples undoubtedly occurs more frequently than review in the form of identical repetitions. If

[18] The learning process "never ends," at least as long as remembering revives certain knowledge. The problems of complete forgetting and of 100 percent knowledge, which are involved in the expression "never," need further investigation.

knowledge is acquired by understanding in situations which are much more significant for the learner than are the match tasks, then forgetting may not occur for a long time. A student of mathematics who has understood the main points of a new hypothesis may have the hypothesis at his command several months later, even though he may not have thought of it in the meantime. Such a performance is not necessarily due to overlearning; it may be due to the acquisition during the interval of knowledge which is different and yet related. Additional practice of a different kind may strengthen an integrated knowledge by enriching it and by widening its scope. The reverse of that statement also holds true: understanding is that form of learning which can be perfected by different kinds of application.

A second possible explanation of the apparent absence of forgetting in our experiments with learning by understanding is to be found in the method of testing. If recall takes the form of reconstruction instead of reproduction, the occurrence of the Ebbinghaus curve is less probable.

Are these two explanatory principles sufficient to account for the differences which we found in the curves of forgetting of the match tasks? The experimental evidence is too meager to permit a positive answer. A slower rate of decay of the traces formed by learning by understanding than of the traces formed by memorizing may also be assumed. We shall discuss this problem in later chapters.

Chapter VII

GROUPING AND LEARNING

HAVING STUDIED LEARNING BY UNDERSTANDING and its results, we must return to the investigation of the process of memorizing. Apparently there was a gap between the two processes of learning with respect to the transfer effect and the curve of forgetting. In order to determine whether or not it is fair to assume that there is a dividing line, we must reverse the starting point of our inquiry. Instead of continuing the study of experiments in which meaningful methods of learning can be applied, we shall study the classic material used in investigating the memory, that is, rote learning of nonsense syllables.

Artificial Grouping

There can be no doubt that lasting scientific achievements have been made by investigating rote learning. In the history of psychology a great many problems were first attacked with nonsense syllables as the tool. The investigation of these problems accomplished much. With nonsense syllables the curves of practice, retention, and forgetting were first established; the effects of the various numbers of repetitions, of overlearning, and of barely learning were determined; the roles of the length of the material, the difference between massed and distributed practice, and between the whole and the part method were studied. In addition, the mechanism of association was explored: direct and indirect associations and remote and backward associations were defined, and various types of associative and reproductive inhibitions experimentally established. Finally, by means of nonsense syllables a vast amount of knowledge concerning individual differences among various types of learners was assembled. All these accomplishments would be no less valuable if it should become apparent that some laws or rules established with nonsense syllables must be understood as part of a greater law or as valid for only certain forms of learning.

There are good reasons why scientific research of memory started with investigating nonsense syllables. The nonsense syllables, first used by Ebbinghaus in the eighties of the last century, are meaningless combinations of three letters—one consonant, one vowel, and another consonant—such as "kem" or "fap." The guiding idea of Ebbinghaus was to eliminate the influence of previous associations and to equalize the differences among the various materials of learning. He believed that in studying the laws of memory as they apply in learning by heart poetry or any other meaningful material we cannot eliminate the fact that a learner may be more familiar with or may find greater difficulties in various parts of the material. Uncontrolled individual differences and learning material which varied in difficulty would prohibit a comparison of the results of two subjects and even of the same subject learning different materials. The justified aim to control the stimuli and to obtain constancy of conditions seemed to many scholars to demand the use of a completely new material, for they believed that only by material which had never before come into the experience of the subjects involved could the laws of experience be demonstrated.

Some investigators of learning nonsense syllables, however, knew of problems caused by the tendency to oversimplify the learning material. Unfortunately such problems are usually treated very sketchily in the textbooks, which are generally preoccupied with reviewing the achievements. In reality these difficulties are of prime importance, since they reveal the differences and the similarities between learning nonsense syllables and learning other kinds of material.

As long ago as in the nineties of the last century exact experiments showed that Ebbinghaus had neglected to study one important form of inequality in his series of syllables.[1] The syllables were learned by being read aloud, but it is hardly possible to read a long series of syllables without using a rhythm. Even if the

[1] Mueller and Schumann (70).

time interval between consecutive syllables were always the same, there would appear an unavoidable accentuation. The next step in research was, naturally, to control the rhythm by prescribing which syllables are to be accentuated. The introduction of accents, however, brought about a division or articulation of the material, disturbing the presupposed uniform regularity of a long series of nonsense syllables. Not being concerned here with the history of psychology and the development of concepts, we shall give only a short description of the experiments performed. They led some investigators in that field to the opinion that articulation of the material definitely influences the learning process.

In the first experiments, performed more than forty years ago, the subjects were asked to read long series of nonsense syllables with a trochaic rhythm, that is, to accentuate the first, third, fifth, and so forth, syllables: kém fap zít yev pím zun (and so forth). A day after such a series was learned a new series was formed, which consisted of the same syllables rearranged in a new order. The amount of time saved in relearning derived series was an exact measurement of the influence of a change in the order of the syllables. If in a new series the accents were changed—that is, if the formerly unaccentuated syllables were accentuated and vice versa—the syllables were relearned with greater difficulty than were syllables with unchanged accents. These and many similar experiments were explained by theories concerning the shifting of attention. But additional theories had to be formed because of further experiments, which showed great difficulty in relearning derived series of accentuated nonsense syllables, even though the accents were not changed. We give here a schematic description of experiments first performed by Mueller and Schumann.

Suppose a series of sixteen syllables is learned the first day, together with other series. The first, the third, the fifth (and so forth) syllables were accentuated: í 2 3́ 4 5́ 6 . . . 1́5 16; each number representing a syllable. Thus uneven numbers represent syllables originally accentuated, and even numbers syllables originally not accentuated. On the second day one-half the subjects learned Series I, and one-half learned Series II.

Series I: X́ 2 3́ 8 9́ 12 1́3   6 7́ Y
Series II: X́ Y 3́ 4 9́ 10 1́3 14 7́ 8

X and Y represent new syllables, whereas the numbers represent syllables learned in the original series.

Series II was much easier to learn (it was learned with greater saving of time) than was Series I, although the accents remained unchanged and the number of consecutive original syllables was the same in both derived series. In order to explain this result, it was assumed that the accents create measures, or groups. If we rewrite the items of the experiment in the following manner, the difference between Series I and II becomes obvious:

Original Series: 1 2 | 3 4 | 5 6 | 7 8 | 9 10 | 11 12 | 13 14 | 15 16 |
Series I: X 2 | 3 8 | 9 12 | 13 6 | 7 Y |
Series II: X Y | 3 4 | 9 10 | 13 14 | 7 8 |

In Series II entire groups of the original series were repeated. In Series I there was the same number of pairs repeated, but the pairs (for example, 2 3) were not taken from original groups. The last member of one group and the first member of the following group were placed in the derived series.

There is another interesting arrangement of the syllables with which the difficulties of relearning have been investigated.[2] After learning the original series, we can construct the following series:

Series III: X 3 | 4 9 | 10 13 | 14 7 | 8 Y |

In this series complete groups of the original series were repeated, the same as in Series II. Syllables belonging to one group in the original series, however, became members of different groups in the new series. The relearning of Series III proved to be more difficult than that of Series II. Witasek even found that Series III was somewhat more difficult than Series I.[3]

[2] Witasek (111).

[3] The paper of Witasek, which also contains a verification under various conditions of Mueller and Schumann's introduction of Series I and II, shows a more profound theoretical understanding of the role of grouping than the paper of Mueller and Schumann written twenty-five years earlier. It is therefore rightly quoted by

Grouping of nonsense syllables was found to be much more general than it was originally assumed to be. It was established by several methods in addition to that of accentuation. In optical presentation and silent reading grouping was achieved if the time interval was increased regularly after certain syllables. Another method was to present each two syllables beside each other instead of one below the other in order to promote the formation of pairs. Moreover, methods of testing seem to have influenced grouping in the learning experiments which followed the first tests. The method of paired associates (called also the "scoring method"), in which during the test the subjects are given every second syllable and are asked to reproduce the syllable which follows the given one, brings about in later learning experiments a grouping in pairs.

Grouping has rules. They were first established in experiments with nonsense syllables, and they hold true for that material, no matter how the grouping originated. In the next section we will discuss to what extent these rules are valid for material other than nonsense syllables.[4]

Rule 1.—Between members of the same group there is a stronger association than between members of different groups.

Rule 2.—Part of a group has the tendency to reproduce the entire group.

Koffka (50, p. 564) as a proof of the necessity of changing the old association concept. Series III is more difficult to interpret than the other series. That accentuated syllables became unaccentuated in Series III is not of major importance. But it should be emphasized again that the same measure was used in all these experiments; should we use the trochaic measure in the original series and the iambic measure in the derived series, we should introduce new factors complicating the results.

[4] The following four rules are to be found in various publications of G. E. Mueller. The systematic presentation given in the text is the author's, since Mueller had never summarized his research on this subject. His concepts developed gradually, and his later books stress the subject of grouping much more than the earlier ones do. Most of the experiments, which will be referred to as arguments supporting the rules, are described in the books published in 1900 and 1917 (71, 74), but the older experiments are explained again in view of newly developed concepts in the books of 1911 and 1924 (72, 75).

Mueller uses the expressions *Komplex* and *Komplexbildung,* not the German equivalent of the word "group." There is one important difference between Mueller's account and the one given in this book. It concerns the origin of the groups (according to Mueller the groups are formed by collective attention)—not the experimental facts and not the laws of grouping, with which we are solely concerned at the moment.

Rule 3.—Groups have their own associations, which may be different from the associations of their members.

Rule 4.—Grouping facilitates learning.

Appendix 3 contains experimental evidence supporting these four rules. The material discussed there is rather extensive, but it is hard to decide whether or not further evidence is needed in order to prove conclusively the general validity of each of the rules. The most urgent task is, however, not the attempt to find additional evidence for the four rules of grouping nonsense syllables. Two considerations of a more basic nature offer themselves. First, the question arises whether the four rules of grouping are sufficient. Do they fully explain the experimental facts? Or are there any experiments with nonsense syllables which require assumptions in addition to those expressed in the four rules? Secondly, the four rules are unsatisfactory, inasmuch as they were established *ad hoc* because of experimental results, which could not be explained by the usual association theories alone. There is therefore good reason to search for a more general principle from which the facts and the laws of grouping can be deduced.

The author proposes to formulate the following "principle of grouping": in a rote series of nonsense syllables the function of a syllable varies in accordance with the group of which it forms a part.

The principle, although necessary and adequate for the explanation of a large number of experimental results—which we shall endeavor to show presently—is not established for this purpose alone. It constitutes an application of the whole-part relationship to the learning of nonsense syllables, and it is therefore connected with the fundamental propositions of gestalt theory. A more general formulation of the principle makes this evident: each syllable differs according to the group to which it belongs. Or, each syllable is influenced by the group of which it is a part.[5]

---

[5] In order to connect this proposition with the thesis of gestalt theory, we need only cite Wertheimer's formulation: "What happens to a part of the whole, is determined by intrinsic laws inherent in this whole" (the quotation is translated by Koffka, 50, p. 683). The most compact discussion of the concept of a part, in contrast to an independent content, is to be found in Wertheimer, 107.

The last proposition is not restricted to the special case in which a rote series of nonsense syllables is memorized. Instead of the word "syllable" we could write "any material of learning." Of course, part of a group may be influenced by a group in various ways, and it is not to be assumed that the material of learning (whether or not it is nonsense material) plays no role in determining the quality of the influence actually exerted. But at this point we are concerned only with the verification of the principle as stated at first—that the function of a nonsense syllable varies in accordance with the group of which it forms a part.

This principle serves to explain the experiments of Mueller and Schumann cited above. If originally 1 2 | 3 4 | 5 6 | 7 8 | (and so forth) were learned, a new series containing groups such as 3 4 and 7 8 was more easily relearned than a series with groups like 2 3 and 6 7. Syllable 3 has different functions in groups 3 4 and 2 3. The fact that a certain syllable was part of a well-memorized group does not help if in a new series the same syllable is part of another group. The same principle explains the difficulties encountered in relearning Series III in Witasek's experiments to which none of the four rules of grouping can be applied. In that series groups of the type 3 4 and 7 8 were repeated, but they were rearranged into new groups: X 3 | 4 Y. Syllable 3 has not the same function in group 3 4 as in group X 3.

The principle also furnishes the explanation for various old experiments on reproductive inhibitions, which are described in Appendix 3. In experiments with the so-called mediate associations we find another important point of application and verification of the principle. These experiments have been performed for the last forty years with various materials and in various forms. The set-up of these experiments is the following. At first two contents A and B are strongly connected with each other. Then content B is connected with another content, C. The question is whether A will or will not reproduce C. With meaningful material this question was usually answered in the affirmative. When a European boy memorizes that the capital of New York state (A) is Albany (B), and the following day, that Albany is situated on the Hudson River (C), he will in most cases be able to answer promptly and correctly that the capital of New York state is on the banks of the Hudson.

In applying the principle which was formulated for nonsense syllables, this result is not to be expected. Should B as part of group A B be different or have different functions from B as part of group B C, then the correct answer would not be arrived at, because there is no identical intermediate term (or no common member with identical functions). In accordance with this expectation it was found that mediate associations are extremely rare with nonsense syllables. Instead of referring to past experiments, which in some respects are not suitable for our special purposes, we shall discuss experiments performed by the author with the intention of analyzing the conditions in which mediate associations are absent.

In the form described above the experiment cannot be carried out with nonsense syllables alone. If we connect first two nonsense syllables A and B, and afterward syllable B with another syllable, C, we have no way to test whether the presentation of A will or will not produce C. If A is presented and the subject is told to name a syllable, B is the usual answer. Thus, in the following experiments A and B were syllables, and C was a number between ten and ninety-nine. Suppose we learn first "kem fap" in a long series of syllables; then we learn "fap 38" in a new series; finally "kem" is presented and the subject is told to mention a two-digit number. In most cases numbers other than thirty-eight will be the response. The explanation is: fap (B) in group "kem fap" (A B) has functions other than those which it has in group fap 38 (B C).

In these experiments care must be taken that the subjects do not suspect the intentions of the experimenter. We are not concerned with whether it is possible by way of adequate instructions or other means to connect A with C through B; on the contrary, we are interested in finding out whether it is possible to establish two connections A B and B C independent of each other. Does the connection A B necessarily spread to B C? To answer this question the following scheme was used:

SERIES I		SERIES II		SERIES III	
First Day		*One Day Later*		*Two Days Later*	
A1	B1	6X and B3 ⎫ C1		6Y and A3 ⎫	"Name a
A2	B2	B5 B7 B8 ⎬ ...		A5 A7 A8 ⎬	number"
..	..	B10 B11 ⎭ C12		A10 A11 ⎭	
A12	B12				

In the first series twelve pairs of syllables were repeated until tests showed that the subjects achieved complete mastery.

In the second series six new syllables (X) and six old syllables (B) in a random order were connected with two-digit numbers represented by the letter C. Again complete mastery was achieved.

On the third day a list consisting of six new syllables (Y) and six old syllables of the type A was presented and the subject was told to give any number between ten and ninety-nine which comes quickest to mind.

Results: Having made the experiment with six subjects and six critical syllables, we had thirty-six opportunities for mediate associations. In fact, there were only four cases of mediate associations, while another number than that "connected" with syllable A through the intermediate syllable B was mentioned thirty-two times by the subjects.

But even the four apparent examples of mediate association should presumably be explained in a different way. In checking the answers given in Series III we find that the twelve numbers learned the day before in Series II were mentioned nineteen times out of a total of seventy-two responses: four times as a response to A syllables in a way which may be called "mediate association," six times as a response to A syllables without having any mediate connections to these syllables, and nine times as a response to new Y syllables. Suppose the syllable "kem" was connected with "fap" in Series I and "fap" with "38" in Series II; then the number "38" was given more frequently in Series III as a response to syllables other than "kem" than it was to "kem." The number appeared "without any connection" more frequently than it should have according to the probabilities of chance. The preference of a number from Series II in Series III may be due to perseveration, which explanation may apply to the A syllables as well as to the Y syllables.

The experiment was performed with eight subjects, whereas we gave the results of only six subjects. The results were omitted in the case of two subjects who did not follow the instructions. In the test with Series III subject No. 7 gave the response "21" to the second syllable and continued after that to respond "22, 23, 24," and so forth, thus excluding the occurrence of mediate associations. Of greater interest are the results of testing subject No. 8, who was also bored by being instructed to say the first number which came to his mind. This subject, a psychiatrist, called the instruction senseless and searched for a meaning in the experiment. Therefore it took him thirty to forty seconds to respond. During his first six answers he could find no meaning; but after repeating syllable A7 aloud several times, he recognized it as part of pair A7 B7. Nevertheless, after almost two minutes the subject responded with a new number. At the next A syllable, however, the subject happily announced his discovery: the A syllable was connected with a B syllable, which in turn was connected with a number; he presumed that the experimenter wanted him to recall that number. Thereupon he gave the number which was required as mediate association.

The experimenter is of the opinion that the achievement of subject No. 8 is a confirmation of the experimental evidence with the other subjects. Both the behavior of subject No. 8 and the responses of the other subjects reveal that under the circumstances of the experiment A B is a connection independent of the connection B C. The situation A–? (number) again presents the syllable A in a different way from its membership in group A B. Subject No. 8 found it rather difficult to overcome the barriers established by grouping and to identify the same syllable when it was a member of two different groups. The results of the other subjects, who had less intellectual curiosity about the experiments, show that the barriers cannot be overcome automatically. The "pathway" does not lead automatically from A by way of B to C, even if both connections are established and item C complies with the requirements of the situation.

The experiments, in addition to showing that syllable B plays a different role in group A B than in group B C, also reveal that there exists specific learning which does not spread. The knowledge about syllable B acquired in Series I was of no use in Series II, in which the same syllable occurred again. In both series connections were formed which retained their specific nature, as the test in Series III proved.

Nothing in our experiments, however, indicates that this result is generally valid. Only with great precautions and careful concealment of the purpose of the experiment was it possible to achieve the result described. With the help of appropriate instructions—or perhaps with different material—it is possible to form "mediate associations." Is this the case, then in Series II not the connection B C is formed, but rather the connection (A B)–C: B belonging to A becomes connected with C. The acquisition of specific data which do not spread is, therefore, dependent on the conditions of training. One of the conditions, a certain kind of grouping, that is, a certain influence exerted on the part by the whole, seems to be of paramount importance. In order to obtain specific learning effects, each member of a group must be considered merely a part of its whole, and no relations to other wholes must be taken into account.[6]

Let us summarize the evidence here assembled with regard to the learning of nonsense syllables. Let us suppose that twenty syllables are presented in a vertical column on a sheet of paper. At first glance it does not look as though there could be any difference in the relationship between the syllables. Now the subject begins to read aloud with the intention to learn. At the first repetition the accents are still rather weak, and the grouping is rudimentary. In later repetitions, however, the second syllable belongs to the first, the fourth to the third, and so forth (if the first, third, fifth, and so forth, syllables were accentuated). The material is then organized, and groups are formed as units which have their own qualities and localization. It appears that learning consists largely of the formation of such groups, in which one part tends

[6] That is the same result which was obtained in investigating direct practice in Chapter V. There we expressed the same idea in stating that in order to obtain direct practice, we must isolate the material of learning (p. 126).

to recall the whole group. Within a group the function of each part is affected by the group to which the part belongs. Thus, the application of the whole-part relationship to the learning of a series of nonsense syllables changes the usual assumption that with this material connections are established between neighboring syllables which are uniform and always of the same strength.[7]

We used the expressions "whole" and "part," which must be explained in greater detail. The entire series of syllables can have the function of the whole, in which case the groups formed in the process of learning can be designated as "sub-wholes" (or "sub-units"). The sub-wholes are divided into real parts—in this case, into syllables. In an optical presentation of the series in pairs the division of the series into sub-wholes and real parts is obvious:

kem	fap
jav	zit
pim	jub
wub	kex

In this series "kem fap" is a sub-whole (a group) and "kem" a real or genuine part of the group. The letter "k" is not a real part of the group, nor is the upper part of the letter "k" a real part of the syllable "kem." Everything said about the role of parts in grouping holds true only for real parts: the letter "k" does not help to recall "kem" or "kem fap," any more than ⌐ tends to recall the capital letter "H" (example given by Köhler).[8] It is the real parts whose connection with each other is stronger than their connection with parts of other groups. The groups which originate in this way have their own qualities, for example, of being the first group or one of the first groups or of having a central position. This description shows that the groups are members

[7] This description holds true for the learning of a series of nonsense syllables in the best and the most efficient way, with which we are mostly concerned. In some cases grouping is less complete and less regular, but here the efficiency of learning diminishes.

[8] Cf. the following discussion of Köhler: "The expression units and groups (as applied to gestalt phenomena) is used to indicate that some segregated wholes are continua, others, the groups, possess discrete members. The former sometimes, and the latter always, contain genuine parts" (44a, XI, 203; translation by Ellis, 18).

of a larger whole (the entire series) and are influenced by it.[9]

It is probable that further research will reveal still other ways in which the syllables are influenced by the groups, and the groups by the whole series. The pronunciation of a nonsense syllable at the first reading is hardly influenced by its neighbors, but it is at least possible that in the course of learning the pronunciation is altered by the formation of groups. Suppose the syllables "yad" and "zen" are neighbors in a series of nonsense syllables. When the well-established group "yad zen" is formed, the pronunciation has probably undergone a change. Should groups "kem yad | zen fap" be formed, the pronunciation of the same syllables will probably again be different.[10]

The grouping in which nonsense syllables are involved when learned is a grouping of a special kind, from which other kinds of grouping must be differentiated. We have had no occasion so far to speak of the properties of parts or of the quality of the relationship between the parts and the whole. The quality of the part appears to have no influence on the form of grouping. Moreover, a series of syllables can be divided into a large or a small number of groups, since it can be learned in groups of two, three, or four syllables (groups of more syllables are unusual). With which kind of grouping one proceeds is arbitrary. The groups created are artificial products of an arbitrary procedure on the part of the learner. Grouping of this kind we shall call "arbitrary," or "artificial," grouping.

Grouping According to an Arrangement

Does grouping play a role in learning other materials than nonsense syllables? If it does, is the grouping the same for both senseless and meaningful material?

[9] Here is an additional factor which contributes to the result of our experiment on mediate associations. The pair "kem fap," learned the first day, belongs to a different whole (the first series) than the pair "fap 38," learned the second day, because that pair is a member of Series II.

[10] New investigations of E. B. Newman, discussed by him at the meeting of the Eastern Psychological Association in April, 1939, indicate still other changes in the qualities of nonsense syllables, which are due to organization and which influence learning.

The memorizing of long series of numbers has been studied extensively. In many cases it revealed the same form of grouping which has been described with regard to nonsense syllables. Suppose the following series of numbers is memorized: 8 9 5 3 2 9 1 6 7 3 7 4 . . . In order to learn such a series of twenty numbers, for example, sooner or later everyone resorts to grouping. Grouping may be effected by commas or lines supplied by the learner himself after every third or fourth number; it may consist of rhythmical accentuation (8́ 9 | 5́ 3 | . . .); it may be the result of reading "eighthundredninetyfive," and so forth; or it may be a combination of these and various other methods. The size of the groups is chosen arbitrarily. We find here an example of artificial grouping for which the experimenter or teacher may prescribe the order.

In certain experiments the subjects were advised to learn the series in groups of threes by stressing aloud every third number; that is, the subjects had to say: eíght, nine, five; thrée, two, nine; and so forth. Many subjects proceeded in this way throughout the series, but a few changed their method of grouping on various occasions. They learned 895 | 329 and then suddenly 16 | 73 74 . . . These subjects declared that it seemed to them bad procedure to divide the numbers 73 and 74, which would be easy to learn, in groups 167 and 374. It has been found that these learners made quicker progress than those who under all circumstances grouped the material in the same way.

In the last example the learner changed the size of the groups according to the content of the material. We may state that it is no longer an order of the experimenter or chance which determines the grouping, but the material itself is the decisive factor. Does the determination of grouping by the material represent a new principle, or does the same thing occur with nonsense syllables? The answer is that grouping may be influenced by a given material in several ways, which must be distinguished from each other. Some of these ways, in which what we may call external qualities of the arrangement are decisive, will be revealed as only slightly different from the grouping of nonsense syllables.

Frequently a square consisting of five rows of five-digit numbers has been used to study the laws of memory.[11] Such a square is learned in five groups consisting of five numbers each, and the strong effect of this grouping is revealed if the subjects are required to recite the numbers in an order different from the order used in the learning period. To recite the numbers backward or in vertical columns (from top to bottom) takes considerably longer than to repeat them forward. Both with visual and with nonvisual learners according to Mueller (74, pp. 570 ff.), it takes on the average four times as long to recite the numbers from top to bottom as to recite them from left to right. Similarly, the usual (forward) memorizing exercises only a small transfer effect on the memorization of the same square in a different order. After the square was completely mastered in "forward order" an average saving of less than 20 percent occurred when it was necessary to relearn it from top to bottom.

The grouping of number squares does not differ fundamentally from certain forms of grouping of nonsense syllables. If pairs of nonsense syllables are presented in rows, or if groups of nonsense syllables are printed in different colors, the arrangement of the material is found to limit the size of the groups. In the number square the arrangement brought about groups of five. The experiments on mediate associations of nonsense syllables revealed the varying functions of identical members of different groups; similarly, the same digits learned in different groups (once in horizontal lines and once in vertical columns) appear to have different functions. By dividing the numbers into certain groups a specific knowledge results which is of very little value when the grouping is changed.

If the material of learning is not uniform, there are many cases which show great similarity to the number squares. If nonsense

[11] Cf. Binet (9), Mueller (74), Ogden (77). The following is an example of such a square which is learned by reading "one, seven, two, eight, four," and so forth.

```
1  7  2  8  4
5  4  6  1  9
4  4  7  6  3
9  3  4  8  6
2  8  5  3  7
```

syllables and numbers, or words and numbers, or words and pictures are memorized, the grouping is determined by the order in which the various materials are presented. If the different kinds of materials follow each other in a regular way, grouping is determined involuntarily by the form of presentation, and arbitrary changes of the grouping are very difficult. A list made up of two words, two two-digit numbers, two words, two two-digit numbers, and so forth, is grouped according to the division of the material, whereas a list made up of one word, one number, one word, one number, and so forth, can be learned either by relating the number to the preceding word, or the word to the preceding number. This holds true, of course, only if words and numbers are presented one at a time—not in pairs. The latter arrangement was used in extensive experiments performed by Thorndike.

In these experiments [12] a long series of pairs, each time a word and a number ("bread 29, wall 16, Texas 78," and so forth), was read once to the subjects. Certain sequences, both words-numbers and numbers-words, were often included in the series (twenty-one and twenty-four times). The tests were made by asking the subject what comes after "bread" or what comes after "16." Comparison was made of the tests in which the number followed the word less frequently than the word followed the number. Nevertheless, many subjects answered correctly, when asked what number followed a word, while correct responses to questions as to which word followed a number were not more frequent than the probabilities of chance guessing. Thorndike states: "The nature of the instructions, the way in which the pairs were read, and the habits of life in general, led the subjects to consider each word as belonging to the number that followed it, and each number as belonging to the word that preceded it" (93, p. 24; 94, p. 70).

One of the findings referred to in the previous section has a strong resemblance to Thorndike's experiments. We reported that the excitatory tendency from the last member of a group to the first member of the next group is much smaller than from the first to the second member of the same group—the first rule of artificial

[12] E. L. Thorndike (93, pp. 16–30, and 94, pp. 64–77).

grouping. Let us test this rule again in the following small experiment. A list of nine pairs of nonsense syllables was written in the following way and was read aloud eight times by the subjects:

Series A

kem	lap
fan	zit
pim	jub

After the learning period the subjects were asked to name the syllable which followed various syllables presented by the experimenter. The number of correct answers following syllables of the kem and fan type was compared with the number of correct answers following syllables of the lap and zit type. In a second experiment we replaced the nonsense syllables by words and numbers of the type used by Thorndike.

Series B

house	51
flower	26
weather	17

Again a series of nine pairs was presented to the subjects, who were permitted to read it four times. The number of correct answers following words (for example, "house" or "flower") was compared with the number of correct answers following numbers (for example, 51 or 26).[13]

Among twenty-four subjects there were two who gave no more correct answers following the presentation of the first member of a group than following the presentation of the last member of a

---

[13] The number of repetitions used in these experiments was carefully determined by means of preliminary tests. The intention was that the subjects should fail to answer a number of questions. Sixteen questions were asked, the first and the last of the eighteen items not being used in the test. The number of correct answers was, on the average, seven in each series. Grouping was aided by accentuating the syllable, word, or number on the left side. Moreover, the scoring method was used generally (that is, all the tests had the form: what follows after . . .) and at no time were the subjects asked to recite the whole series. The testing method has, as is well known, a very strong effect on subsequent learning. The first test of Series B, in which the question "what follows after 51" is used, may alter the results of all the following learning experiments by artificially changing the grouping. The experiments, therefore, were performed with subjects, each of whom learned just one series of each type (after some preliminary training).

group. The number of correct "intra-group" responses of all subjects exceeded the number of correct "extra-group" responses 3.3 times in Series A and 3.2 times in Series B.

The experiment shows that the first rule of artificial grouping applies to involuntary groups as well. For groups consisting of nonsense syllables and those consisting of words and numbers the rule appears to operate similarly. But the rule applies only if learning does not result in complete mastery. Otherwise, localization of the items in the series and intentional strengthening of the weak connections may compensate for the differences.

That the results of Series A and Series B are similar is easy to understand, because in both cases we are confronted with comparatively weak grouping effects. Grouping in Series B, which was based on the experiments of Thorndike, obviously does not furnish the real counterpart of arbitrary grouping of nonsense syllables. Therefore the experiments were continued by presenting to different subjects Series C, consisting of nine pairs to be read four times.

Series C

house	flower
51	26
weather	moon
17	83

In Series C the correct intra-group responses (the responses to "house" or to "51") were 4.9 times more frequent than were correct extra-group responses (the responses to "flower" or to "26"). This result indicates that the barriers between the different groups following each other are presumably stronger in Series C than in the other two series.

Suppose the words and numbers of Series C are printed in a column and the experimenter instructs the subjects to form groups of three by stressing every fourth word (or number). It is difficult for the subjects to do this, whereas with nonsense syllables it would be easy. We can begin to learn "house flower 51," then "26 weather moon," then "17 83 tree," and so forth, but very soon we would change more-or-less automatically to another grouping. Those who do not change the grouping would make a special effort, and their learning would be less efficient.

The grouping generally resorted to in the last example will be called "grouping according to an arrangement." The following principles apply to this kind of grouping, in contrast to the artificial grouping prevailing with nonsense syllables: (1) Grouping according to an arrangement occurs sooner than arbitrary grouping. Usually several repetitions are needed before artificial groups are formed and firmly established, while the other type of grouping sets in with the very first reading—or at least with the second reading. (2) Grouping according to an arrangement creates stronger boundaries than does arbitrary grouping. The excitatory tendency from the last member of the first kind of group to the first member of the next group is usually very weak. To enable one to recite a series consisting of several such groups, the transitions from one group to the next must be repeated and stressed. (3) Groups formed according to an arrangement cannot be discarded or altered as easily as can artificial groups.

Except for these differences the rules of grouping as established in the previous section appear to be the same for both types of groups.

The rules of grouping seem to account for most of the facts referred to by Thorndike when he established the concept of "belonging." In one of his experiments many sentences of the following type were read several times:

"Alfred Dukes and his sister worked sadly. Edward Davis and his brother argued rarely. Barney Croft and his father watched earnestly," and so forth.

After the training, questions such as the following were asked: what word followed immediately after "sadly" (or "rarely")? Frequency had scarcely any effect on recall. After ten repetitions the correct answer for a sequence from the end of one sentence to the beginning of the next was 2.75 percent, while for a sequence from the first to the second word in the same sentence (from the first to the last name) was 21.5 percent.[14] Thorndike therefore assumes that repeatedly experiencing A and B in succession without any awareness that B after A is right and proper or that B belongs with A has only very slight influence; mere sequence or repetition is influential only if the response belongs to the situation.

If Thorndike's concept of belonging had been derived solely from the experiments involving the memorizing of sentences, we could assume that this concept implies various factors of meaningful organization. But belonging appears to be the same in the sentences and in the previously-reported experiments on memorizing lists such as "bread 29, wall 16," in which there is no understandable relation between the number "belonging" to the word.[15] In order to understand the experimental results referred to by Thorndike, the rules of grouping as discussed heretofore appear to be sufficient. The sentence "Alfred Dukes . . . sadly," being entirely unrelated to its neighbors, forms a group with firm boundaries, just as the words "house flower" form a group when preceded and followed by numbers. A member of such a group has a much stronger tendency to recall the whole group (Rule 2 of grouping), or other members of the same group (Rule 1 of grouping), than to recall a member of the next group.

There is one of Thorndike's experiments which may lead us further, beyond the three rules of grouping according to an arrangement. We mentioned that there were scarcely any correct answers to questions of the type "what comes next after 'sadly'?" The excitatory tendency of words like "Alfred" (and so forth) was stronger, but still better results were obtained with questions of

---

[14] The excitatory tendency from the last member of a group to the first member of the next group is extremely weak here, much weaker than in our experiments described above. Köhler (48, p. 107) remarked that the weakness of the associations in Thorndike's experiments is due partly to the accumulation of similar sentences in a very long series. In the next few pages we shall discuss Köhler's concept of accumulation.

[15] Thorndike expressly states that "belonging" should not imply a logical or essential connection. "The belonging . . . need not be more than the least which the word implies . . . Any 'this goes with that' will suffice. Each nonsense syllable in a series belongs to the one before it in the series. 1492 belongs to Mr. Jones as his telephone number as truly as to Christopher Columbus" (94, p. 72).

the type "what comes after 'worked'?" (and so forth). Thorndike explains this result with a brief reference to the "degree of belonging" and the "contrast between little and much belonging," [16] without describing what constitutes more or less belonging. Nor does he use this concept in his later theories. One may assume that a long group is divided into sub-groups. "Worked sadly" may be a sub-group in contrast to the preceding five words, for example. One should expect the connection between members of a sub-group to be strong, especially strong if the sub-group consists of only two members.

These statements imply two questions. First, is it true that grouping according to an arrangement is for certain parts more advantageous than for other parts? Secondly, what determines the formation of such groups and sub-groups? We shall study these questions with the help of ingenious experiments made by Köhler and Restorff (47). They presented their material systematically in various arangements in order to discover the effect of the arrangement on reproduction and recognition. After preliminary experiments they arrived at the following scheme, which represents three extreme arrangements for one kind of material:

Series 1: A A A A X A A A A
Series 2: X X X X A X X X X
Series 3: X Y Z W A V U T S

The configuration of A in Series 1 is called "accumulation" and in Series 2 "isolation." In Series 3 we have only isolated members. The letters A, X, Y, and so forth can represent any material. Suppose A represents nonsense syllables, X numbers, and the other letters miscellaneous material—small geometrical drawings, words, and so forth. This set-up can be used in experiments on recognition when each series is presented just once, in order to test whether on a later occasion the fourth syllable in the first series or the fifth in the second and the third series is better recognized. The set-up is also suitable for the application of the scoring method. In this case each of the letters represents a pair, A a pair of non-

[16] 93, p. 23; 94, p. 68.

sense syllables, X a pair of numbers, Y a pair of drawings, and so forth. After three repetitions the first member of each pair is presented, and the subject must respond with the following syllable, number, or drawing. Again it is possible to decide which of the three arrangements is best for the learning of a pair of nonsense syllables (A).

Restorff obtained unequivocal results in various experiments. The recall, reconstruction, and recognition of A was best in Series 2, not quite as good in Series 3, and least good in Series 1. Isolation appears to be more favorable for learning than is monotonous accumulation, and isolation appears best when the isolated object is surrounded by uniform objects.

Our concept of grouping according to an arrangement can be applied to these experiments. In learning the first two series grouping occurs much sooner and with stronger boundaries than in the case of artificial grouping. The first four members of the series form the first group, the fifth member the second group, and the last four members the last group. This division of the series provides an advantage for the fifth member, which is a group in itself. In the third series no cue exists for grouping (provided that each material differs sufficiently from the other), and learning must proceed by forming groups artificially.

But why is item A in the first series at a disadvantage as compared with A in the third series? Restorff's experiments prove not only that forming a group in itself is advantageous for learning but also that belonging to a monotonous group formed by members of the same kind is disadvantageous for learning. Restorff explains this result by demonstrating the analogy between the principles of memory and perception. Perceived objects are organized according to well-established laws. An object which is surrounded by many different objects, which are all similar, naturally becomes the center of our visual field as the one independent figure commanding over a monotonous ground. On the other hand, one of a great number of similar objects not characterized by distinguishing traits remains an inconspicuous part of our perception. Between these two extreme cases we find the analogy to the third series. In a perception consisting of parts which all differ from each other none will have the advantage of isolation and none will have the disadvantage of accumulation.

The reference to the laws of perception is more than a picturesque analogy. In Restorff's experiments on recognition the series was presented only once. This means that "learning" consisted of a perception and was, of course, determined by the rules of perception. But even in the memory experiments (recall of pairs) the organization of the material was, as usual in grouping according to an arrangement, completed or almost completed with the first presentation. Thus it follows that the rules for the articulation of perceptions, the laws of equality, nearness, and so on, determine the size and content of the groups. Perceptual rules explain how the groups arise in the case of a series like "house flower 51 26 weather moon . . ." Similar parts, such as the sequence of numbers, belong to the same group. In memorizing sentences the rules of auditive perception—accents, time intervals, and so forth—and in certain cases also the effects of past experience play their role in determining the different forms of grouping.

The experiments of Restorff illuminate the difficulty of learning an inarticulated series of nonsense syllables. Such a series is the best example for monotonous accumulation, which has been found to be disadvantageous for learning. The same idea can also be expressed in the following way: it takes a long time and great effort to learn a series of nonsense syllables, because of the impossibility of other than arbitrary grouping. Grouping according to an arrangement helps learning to a greater extent than the forming of artificial groups: certain groups of the first type have, because of differentiation in emphasis, outstanding advantages over the artificial groups.

The "arrangement" which determines that a series consisting of two words, two numbers, and two words is grouped differently from a series of three words, one number, and three words is a quality of the entire series. Grouping therefore is dependent on features of organization, which are expressed by principles such as equality, nearness, and spatial and temporal distribution. The relation of a part to the other parts and to the whole determines whether the part becomes a member of one group or the other. It follows that these kinds of series can be grouped according to or against their arrangement: we may speak of good or of natural grouping in the first case, and of bad, unnatural, or irrational grouping in the second case. As an example of the first case we may refer to the formation of homogeneous groups in a series which consists of three words, two numbers, three words, and two numbers, whereas the grouping of the same series into five groups of two items each would be an example of "bad" grouping.

This distinction may lead us to assume that there is a great difference between arbitrary grouping and grouping according to an arrangement. But we must bear in mind that in all the forms of grouping discussed up to this time it is only the belonging of a part to its group which is affected by the whole-principle. This is still a rather external effect of grouping, because the quality and the content of the part are not determined by the whole.

Different Forms of Grouping

The principles of grouping discussed above are essential for the process of mechanical memorizing. But we know from the preliminary experiment on "Federal Expenditures," which we described in the first chapter of this book, that they are not the only possible forms of grouping. In order to understand the interrelation of the various forms of grouping and to compare the results obtained by different ways of grouping, we shall again discuss the various methods of learning number series.

A quantitative experiment performed with the material of the "Federal Expenditures" differed in several respects from the preliminary experiment reported in Chapter I. There our aim was to show that grouping occurs and has different forms. Therefore we attempted to have identical material learned in different ways. In this second experiment, however, since we are now aware that the identity of the material is not preserved in the different methods of learning, we shall present the same number series in four different ways. In the preliminary experiment the instructor always began by asking the subjects to learn a series of numbers. Now we differentiate between classes which were asked to learn (memorizers) and others whose task was to understand the subject matter presented. Further changes of the experimental set-up were these: the second time twenty-four numerals were used (instead of twelve); the test was made half an hour after the learning period (instead of immediately); the retest was made three weeks later (instead of one week later). Four comparable undergraduate classes were used.

The material of the experiment was:

2 9 3 3 3 6 4 0 4 3 4 7
5 8 1 2 1 5 1 9 2 2 2 6

Class I.— The numbers were written on the blackboard as above. The subjects were told: "The numbers are not in random order. They have a principle. Try to find it. I shall give you one cue: both rows have the same principle." The subjects had three minutes to study the series. (The principle is that 5 plus three is 8; 8 plus four is 12; 12 plus three is 15 . . . 26 plus three is 29 . . .)

Class II.—"I want you to learn the following series by heart." Then the following numbers were written on the blackboard:

293   336   404   347
581   215   192   226

"In memorizing the best method to use is rhythmical grouping. Therefore you should learn: two nine three; three three six; and so forth." The numbers were read aloud five times.

Class III.—"For the sake of a psychological experiment I want you to learn a few facts on Government finance. The expenditures of the Federal Government have recently increased rapidly. The amounts are given on the blackboard." Then the following numbers were written on the blackboard.

$2,933,364,043.47 in 1929
$5,812,151,922.26 in 1936

"Please repeat the numbers aloud five times in order to know the exact amounts of the Federal expenditures in 1929 and in 1936."

Class IV.—"I shall now give you a short lecture on Government finances. Please listen carefully. In recent years the expenditures of the Federal Government have risen rapidly." A five-minute lecture followed on expenditures, indebtedness, the causes for their changes, and so forth. In the course of the lecture the following data were written on the blackboard:

$2,933 million	$15,192,226,000
$5,812 million	$36,404,347,000

The figures on the left were explained and frequently referred to as the annual expenditures; those on the right as the total indebtedness in the years 1929 and 1936.

In the test and later in the retest the subjects were asked to write down as exactly as possible all the figures which were on the blackboard during the instruction period ("at the time when I discussed Government finances," or "when you memorized the amount of Federal expenditures," and so forth). The results of the tests will be evaluated first according to the number of correctly reproduced items. Each class was asked to reproduce twenty-four digits (we disregard the zeros used with Class IV). Table 16 shows how many subjects reproduced the digits correctly and how many subjects made mistakes.

TABLE 16. REPRODUCTION TESTS WITH NUMBER SERIES

| | Number of Subjects | PERCENTAGE OF SUBJECTS WHO MADE | | | |
		Correct Reproduction	1 to 6 Mistakes	7 to 18 Mistakes	19 to 24 Mistakes
Class I					
Test	29	38	27	25	10
Retest	26	23	23	39	15
Class II					
Test	30	33	20	40	7
Retest	23	0	0	26	74
Class III					
Test	30	20	17	43	20
Retest	21	0	0	38	62
Class IV					
Test	23	0	9	69	22
Retest	17	0	0	42	58

In the test Class I (who discovered a principle) was somewhat superior to Class II (who memorized numbers) and to Class III (who memorized economical data); the performance of Class IV was rather unsatisfactory. In the retest given three weeks later the performance of three classes (II, III, and IV) was unsatisfactory, but Class IV was slightly superior to the two memorization classes. This kind of evaluation of the results discloses, however, only a part of the story.

Eleven of the twenty-nine subjects in Class I gave perfect reproductions in the test. By studying the test papers it became evident that thirteen other subjects had discovered the principle, but had made mistakes in reproducing the series, because they transposed some or all the numbers. The performance of that class in the retest was only slightly inferior to that in the test: six perfect reproductions and twelve reproductions containing transpositions were obtained from twenty-six subjects. The rate of forgetting proved to be rather small.

Class II and Class III show a very sharp deterioration of the performance from test to retest. The best performance in the retest was ten correct figures. Most subjects put only three or four figures down in the retest and complained that it was impossible to comply with the instruction.

Class IV failed in the test, when the performance was measured by the number of reproduced items, because most subjects only remembered the figures 2, 5, 15, and 36. But in the retest those figures were again recalled by several subjects, and thus the performance did not differ very much on the two occasions. In addition many subjects recalled that the numbers 2, 5, and so forth referred to billions—which knowledge was not evaluated at all in the table.

We may compare the results of the three latter classes by determining the number of groups correctly reproduced instead of the number of items. Such measurement is, however, not quite fair to Class II. We had two one-digit groups and two two-digit groups in the cases of Class III and Class IV; the other groups consisted of three digits each. All the groups learned by Class II consisted, however, of three digits. Again we do not score the reproduction of the groups consisting of zeros alone.

TABLE 17. AVERAGE NUMBER OF GROUPS RECALLED CORRECTLY

	Number of Groups Presented	Test	Retest
Class II	8	5.13	0.52
Class III	10	5.63	1.62
Class IV	10	2.74	1.88

Table 17 confirms what was said of the differences in the rate of forgetting. Only in the case of memorizing (Class II and Class III) do we find rapid initial loss. The difference between the performance of these two classes is more qualitative than quantitative: Class II most frequently reproduced the group 336 in the retest, while with Class III groups 2, 5, and 26 had the distinction of being most often recalled.[17]

Reviewing the experiment in a superficial way, one might be inclined to classify the subjects according to the materials presented to them. Class III and Class IV would then belong together: in both cases economical data, that is, meaningful materials, were learned. On the other side, Class I and Class II learned number series devoid of meaning. But the results of the experiment contradict such a classification. The amount of retention and the curve of forgetting were very similar for Classes II and III which proceeded by memorizing. The method of learning determines the performance to a much higher degree than the classification of the learning materials. Arbitrary grouping, resorted to by Class II because of an arbitrary order of the experimenter, should not be separated from grouping according to an arrangement applied by Class III, because of the habit of grouping amounts of money in a certain way. When we memorize either senseless or sensible material, a similar type of grouping occurs.

[17] Appreciable qualitative changes in the contents remembered result if the method of memorization is not prescribed in detail. If the material of Class II is presented to the subjects and they are not compelled to start to read rhythmically right after seeing the numbers, then learning usually begins with a scrutiny of the whole material. In this case, certain regularities (the second group is larger than the first and the third is larger than the second) are noticed and retained for a long time to come. In the material used for Class III, the relation between the two amounts of expenditures is usually noticed first and is also retained for the longest time.

With Classes I and IV, which were not asked to memorize, we found similarities in the curve of retention. Transpositions also occurred in both classes: some members of Class IV reproduced incorrect amounts in the retest, but the relation of these amounts was substantially correct. Yet the achievement of the two classes was by no means similar. A learning process of the type described when the understanding of the match tasks was discussed has been found only with Class I, which grouped the material according to a principle. In this case the subjects were able to reconstruct the individual items, because the latter could be derived from a whole-quality or a principle which formed the real object of learning. Class IV also learned by grasping and understanding various facts and occurrences of fiscal history. But the test, the verbatim or item-for-item reproduction of the amounts, was not commensurate with the whole-qualities acquired. Undoubtedly Class IV was taught by a meaningful method, but that method could not be applied to all individual items given in the series.

We shall continue the discussion of the interrelation between principles and facts, whole-qualities and individual items, in Chapter IX. For the moment we are interested mainly in the qualities common to the learning process. There is a common feature in arbitrary groups and groups that are formed according to an arrangement on one side and in groups that are understood in part because of their context and groups understood fully because they are learned in terms of a principle on the other side. Learning proceeds in all these cases by the organization of the material. Organization in efficient learning is as complete as the material permits. If there are no intrinsic relations between the parts and the whole, memorizing by means of grouping appears to be a profitable way of learning, inasmuch as it brings about a quick and accurate retention of individual items, at least for a short time after the learning period. How the groups are formed in the memorizing process is not irrelevant. Grouping should emphasize the most important items of the material, which items therefore are learned more quickly and retained longer than the other items.

Chapter VIII

MEMORY TRACES

IN THIS ATTEMPT to understand the process of learning I propose to go a step further and to resort for a short while to what is often called speculation. I propose to discuss the following questions: What takes place between the learning period and the recall? What is the nature of the occurrences in that interval? This discussion ought to be of help in gaining a clearer understanding of the nature of learning and in predicting certain characteristics of remembering, which should be tested by experiment.

Since our arguments concerning the nature of the traces will lead to new experiments, the contents of the following pages may be considered hypothetical statements. In this sense this chapter could have appeared considerably earlier in our investigation. Some of the experiments reported in the preceding chapters were devised to test and to clarify certain ideas and notions which will be presented shortly. Thus, the following statements will have the form not only of hypotheses but also of a summary of certain results gained from experiments with the card tricks and match tasks.

I meet a man for the first time (event A). A week later I meet him again and recognize him (event B). Or, a week later someone mentions his name, and I recall his features (event B1). It is generally agreed that events A and B (or A and B1) are somehow connected with each other. One widely held assumption is that event A left a trace (or a bundle of traces) which was reëxcited on the later occasion. The new situation plus the effects of the reëxcitation, or the new situation as influenced by the trace, led to event B (or B1). The word trace in this sentence may stand for a definite concept which assumes memory to be the function of a bundle of rigid, unchanging traces. Each event is then supposed to leave a trace behind which is conceived as a true picture or a true copy of the event itself. It is usually further assumed that these traces are stored in definite locations until they fade or become blurred with the passing of time. But the word trace need not imply such a theory, which cannot be maintained in the light of newer research. The concept of traces has been used and can be used in the sense of an aftereffect which is in dynamic interaction with older traces, new processes, and new traces.

In the following discussion the word "trace" should indicate nothing else than the carrier of the connection between events A and B (or B1). Should an event having the same characteristics as B or B1 occur, we would assert that a previous event had left a trace. The traces need not be thought of as automatic effects of every mental process. A process of the type A may or may not leave a trace; we believe that the mere fact that such a process occurred does not prove anything about the trace. The qualities of the traces will not be derived from the processes in which they originated—only from their effects. The manner in which processes of the type B are influenced by effects of previous experience will be taken as the starting point for the investigation of traces.

In our experiments we have studied a great many instances of remembering, reproduction, reconstruction. From these experiments are derived four propositions characterizing the qualities and laws of traces which are assumed to be responsible for the various forms and qualities of recall. These propositions we shall submit in the form of hypotheses: we shall endeavor to test them in further experiments. It should be noted that they are not interdependent; one or the other statement may prove to be false, while others may be correct.

Hypothesis I: Traces referring to specific items of past experience and those connected with and derived from the whole-character of a process can be distinguished from each other. We shall call the first "individual traces," the latter "structural traces."

Hypothesis II: Individual traces are characterized by a certain degree of fixation and rigidity, while structural traces are more readily adaptable and flexible.

Hypothesis III: The formation of individual traces is usually a long and strenuous process, while under certain conditions understanding may lead quickly and with less effort to the formation of structural traces.

Hypothesis IV: Structural traces persist longer than individual traces, which vanish soon unless reinforced.

Structural Traces

Someone listens to the explanation of the card tricks in the experiments described in Chapter II. By tests made several weeks later it is ascertained that he understood in a general way the procedure required to perform the trick, but that the actual words heard and even the individual steps performed did not remain in his memory. In reformulating that statement we may say that the single presentation of the explanation resulted in a structural trace: a general trace embracing the entire explanation was formed. It is possible, of course, to learn the whole explanation by heart—to form individual traces for each of the sentences. But that takes much longer than the formation of a structural trace—the understanding of the principle—and requires greater effort and diligence. It is a different process with different results.

Since the concept of traces is derived from their effect, the only proof of the existence of a trace is that remembering was found to be a reconstruction, not a pure construction. Thus, according to the results of the card-trick tests we are not entitled to assume that individual traces of the various specific parts of the explanation were left behind by the process of meaningful learning. The results indicate only that a structural trace was formed containing the essential features of the process but not the particular details presented to the subjects. It was different when the subjects memorized the correct order of the cards. In this method of learning individual traces of a specific sequence of the cards were formed; they were fixed and rigid, but not durable. The structural trace of the procedure, on the other hand, was adapted to many situations and persisted in this way for a long period of time.

A possible misunderstanding must be avoided. The structural traces should not be thought of as the counterpart of vague and hazy ideas. The distinction between clear-cut and indistinct images is not at all analogous to that between individual and structural traces. A picture may be observed for a very short time, so that the observer gains only a vague idea of its contents. That is not what we mean when we speak of a structural trace. The latter is the carrier of as clear a knowledge as an individual trace but of a different kind. I memorize a random series of digits: we may assume that many individual traces were formed. I understand a story: structural traces resulted, conveying a very clear and definite idea of certain events, being centered in a distinct way and with outstanding points. Nevertheless, these structural traces must be assumed as flexible because every time I retell the story I do it differently: with different words; in a changed order; with stress on different points—all according to the situation, the listeners, my own position, and so forth. In spite of all changes it is the same story, which means that the same structural trace has contributed to it.

Further assumptions are possible, which will be tested later by experiments. The order of the various parts in a structural trace is determined by the meaning of the whole, not necessarily by the original sequence in time; the time sequence is superseded by a more important form of organization. The meaningful order of structural traces implies the work of a selective principle similar to that operative in perceptions. We know that sensory experiences do not follow the properties of all the local stimulations that reach our sense organs at a given moment.[1] The perception is a whole, centered in a certain way; therefore it is a selection to which certain stimuli contribute extensively and

[1] Cf. chap. iii of Köhler's *Gestalt Psychology* (45) and the investigations quoted there.

others hardly at all.[2] Just as a perception can be called a unified, centered, and condensed result of the stimuli, a structural trace can be called a unified and condensed result of a perception. The perceptions are not summative copies of the external world, and the traces are not copies of the perceptions. The process of organization begins in perceiving and continues in learning, that is, in the formation of the traces and their changes.

Organization may involve omissions, alterations, and even additions, but what we must stress at the outset of our discussion on the formation of the traces is that by the process of organizing the emphasis becomes more strongly marked and the hierarchy of the parts becomes clearer and simpler. Due to this process the structural traces may be called the condensed meaning of the events. (It seems better to coördinate traces and events than traces and perceptions.) A person hears a story, the explanation of a theory, or he acts in a certain way, takes a walk—these are examples of events of which structural traces are often formed. We assume that only meaningful events yield such traces, and it is the center, the main point, the leading idea of the events around which the trace is focused, often by intensification of the emphasis or shift in the emphasis. Thus, the structural trace will frequently have a higher form of organization than a perception has. "Higher form of organization" means more unity, greater dependence of the parts on the central point, greater coherence, and better structure.

The main point which compels us to differentiate between vague ideas and traces is as follows. Suppose, as happened a few times, that a subject taught by the method of help did not understand the essential points in the match tasks and had only a vague idea about holes and squares. In the tests his performance was far below average. Since the concept of traces is derived

---

[2] Cf. chap. iii, above, where Wertheimer's investigations on the articulation of perceptions are discussed. Perceiving in contrast to the sum of the effects of the stimuli was studied extensively by investigating the phenomena of perceptual constancy. There the dependence of the perceived part (e. g., the size or color of an object seen) on the articulation, constellation, and organization of the total process instead of on the properties of the various stimuli could be demonstrated. Cf. Katona (40, 41), Gelb (22).

from observable effects—the form of recall or later performance —we must say that this subject had no structural trace of the principle of the match tasks. He might have obtained an individual trace of the word "hole" or even a structural trace of some part of the explanation which he had understood. But the structural trace of the principle which brings about applications because it can be adapted to new situations appears to require understanding of the problem. Understanding is required to form a structural trace.[3] As the effect of understanding the meaning, not some incidental point, is preserved. The meaning persists because the center of a structural trace is stable (not rigid), while the details or items are modifiable and flexible. But a structural trace enables reconstruction of its parts, because meaningful processes in contrast to senseless processes can be reconstructed.[4]

Now we can understand the "flexibility" of the structural traces. The trace constantly adapts itself to the needs and requirements of the situation by which it is resurrected. This appears to be the essence of application of knowledge, of its use under changed circumstances. On the other hand, a series of words or digits memorized, which is not understood, does not leave an adaptable structural trace. The flexibility of structural traces means therefore adaptability to situations, not everlasting senseless change. The structure, or certain whole-qualities, is stable and remains preserved even if all the individual items are changed according to the new situation.

The concept of structural traces helps us to understand the results of the match-task experiments. We said that by the method of examples, or help, the subjects acquired, not knowledge of a few specific solutions, but integrated knowledge about increasing or decreasing the number of squares. To such knowl-

---

[3] The understanding required to form a structural trace need not always be correct understanding, it can also be a misunderstanding which is not "not-understanding." In such a case the trace cannot represent the true meaning of the event, but it does represent some kind of meaning.

[4] In chap. i we have shown that there is no way to reconstruct a senseless series of numbers even if we remember most of the individual items.

edge, more-or-less independent of the actual content of the specific examples, corresponds a structural trace. Its revival at the presentation of new tasks helps in solving these tasks. Thus, solving a new task is construction; nevertheless it differs from unassisted problem solving. It is remembering, because a trace contributed to it, even though the task was new. And the trace was useful as a help, because it was, not a trace of a different specific task, but a general trace derived from at least one, usually from several, examples.

In Chapter V we spoke of the application of general principles. The word "application" suggests a conscious utilization of a principle which is well known to the subject. That is so in some cases, but not in all. A trace can be effective even if the principle is not consciously formulated. The structural trace is not "applied," it fuses with the new process and contributes to it.

There are instances in which the structural trace results from one presentation. If with match tasks acquaintance with the arithmetical principle enabled a few subjects to solve all future tasks, it must be assumed that such traces have a sudden origin. Often, however, "repetition" is necessary, because the first presentation or the first example yields only a vague, indistinct idea, not a structural trace. The distinct, well-centered form of the trace must develop. This may happen by a process of perceptual reorganization or by a crystallization of the traces.

Individual Traces

Memory does not function always by constantly adapting itself to new situations. Fixation also occurs, and there is such a thing as a rigid, never-changing recollection. The rigidity in memory functions might be considered sometimes an exception—even a pathological exception: when certain events of our life, like visual or verbal images, again and again return in an identical form, we may assume that it is an abnormal functioning of memory. But fixation occurs also as a result of memorizing. I know a series of historical events and data. I know a few poems, proverbs, and lists of names which I learned many years ago.

I can recite these poems and lists almost automatically, when I am tired and sleepy, as well as when I am fresh and fully awake, and I notice that my voice, intonation, rhythm, and form of speech are very similar each time I recite the same text.

Most members of the groups who memorized one solution of one match task were helpless when asked to solve a new task. When the practiced task was given in a test, they reproduced the practiced solution, not other equally satisfactory solutions. The subjects who had learned by memorization and had not understood the principle of the match tasks had acquired traces which could be resuscitated only by one kind of stimulus (the practiced task) and which brought about just one kind of response (the learned form of solution).

These facts may lead us to the assumption that in addition to general traces there also exist fixed and unchanging traces of individual data. They are not formed suddenly by insight or gradually by adequate organization of a material, but are the results of a slow, patient, and laborious method—memorizing. Countless presentations by the advertisers have hammered in our minds a large number of individual trade names. We know the names of a few tooth pastes, cigarettes, automobiles, and so forth, because we repeated them a thousand times voluntarily and involuntarily, in visual perception (in the subway, on the highways), in auditive perception (at the radio), and when reading newspapers and periodicals. Suppose a new brand of cigarettes is manufactured and advertised in a nation-wide campaign. It has a new senseless name; we never heard the name before. A few weeks later the name of the new cigarette may become one of the familiar, well-known names which constitute a part of our knowledge. A possible explanation for this process is that an individual trace of the new name was formed. Usually it is formed by a great number of repetitions, in a different way from that in which most structural traces are formed. We assume further that the individual traces obey different laws of retention and forgetting than do the structural traces. The initial rate of forgetting is very great in the case of the individual traces, and it seems that most of them lapse completely if they are not reinforced again and again by new repetition. The structural traces can be effective after a long interval when an apparently new solution is found to be a reconstruction. But there is no reconstruction on the basis of individual traces. I have forgotten the names of most cigarette brands in Germany, although a few years ago they were as familiar to me as "Camels," and "Chesterfields" are at present. No reasoning and no meaningful process can revive these names.[5]

The rigidity or fixation of individual traces emphasized in contrast to the qualities of structural traces must not be misunderstood. Even these traces are not exact copies of the perceptions and even they persist only in dynamic interaction with other traces. We call the word "Chesterfield" or the group "kem lap fon," consisting of three parts and repeated often, material of which individual traces are formed, notwithstanding the fact that we perceive the word "Chesterfield" in a great many ways; sometimes we hear it, sometimes we see it in small letters on a package of cigarettes and sometimes in large print on a billboard. We need not assume that there is a very large number of memory traces for every single word because of the different pitches of sound and qualities of voice in which the word was heard. Likewise, nonsense syllables can be memorized even though each repetition is different. In our experiments an individual trace of a specific solution of a single match task was formed by presenting that task every time in a different form (Group Mem. in Experiment A). The tests revealed traces, not of each side line and its change, but of the transformation of one specific situation into another specific situation. Thus, the object or perception which left the trace behind is not assumed to be rigid, but the form of remembering indicates that a content survived specifically. The existence of individual traces is assumed, not because we know something about specific qualities of the traces, but because specific recall occurs.

Are the two types of trace unrelated to each other? Various observations prompt us to assume that there is a relation between

---

[5] Nevertheless, the names may not be completely forgotten: relearning may show savings as compared to the original learning.

individual and structural traces. It is inconceivable that they are formed only on different occasions and in different ways. For there are transitions between general and specific remembering. The knowledge of a principle usually carries with it the knowledge of certain details, and the recollection of specific events is most reliable and most enduring if these events fit into a general concept.

Let us return to our experiments. The understanding of the card tricks led to the solution of various tasks because it involved knowledge of a principle. Yet certain words used in the explanation, such as "second row" and "alternation," were remembered together with or in addition to the integrated knowledge. Are we to assume that in these cases individual traces of these words were formed without repetition? The words remembered were not random recollections, arbitrarily chosen from the more than one hundred words heard by the subject. To remember arbitrarily selected words, memorizing is required. But it seems that the knowledge of the principle may carry with it a certain amount of specific knowledge. The center, the lasting kernel of the flexible general trace, may be some knowledge or meaning inexpressible in words or images, but it also may be one or a number of details, words, and images. The match tasks furnish examples of both types. It happens that specific words, such as "double function," and "hole," become the center of the knowledge of a principle. Outstanding details, names, and titles can thus survive specifically in spite of lack of memorization, because they represent the general principle, the main point, understood and acquired by organization of the material.

Specific details carried by the structural trace are one important form of transition or connection between the two kinds of trace. By investigating the formation of individual traces we also arrive at transitions. Perhaps it is possible to memorize successfully a small number of unconnected items and to recall them without the situation in which they have been presented and without any indication of an organization affecting the items, connecting them with their environment and with former experiences. But memorization even of a series of nonsense syllables has been shown to utilize at least rudimentary processes of grouping. There is only one proof of the formation of individual traces, namely, specific survival in recall. We found that in order to recall individual items, such as nonsense syllables, words, and numbers, they must become parts of a whole process which creates at least an arbitrary organization and exerts influence on the parts and their mutual relations. Recall of individual items, explained by the formation and survival of individual traces, does not mean remembering in a piecemeal way.

There are many stages of transition from individual to structural traces. A single item may retain its individuality because it is a genuine part of an artificial whole (for example, the syllable "kem" in the series "kem fap zit yev"). Or one item may survive individually because it is singled out by the whole-process (that was the case with the syllable "kem" when it was surrounded by numbers in the experiments of Köhler and Restorff). Or an individual item survives because it is artificially fitted into a whole-process. If we memorize the arrangement of cards which is required to perform a specific trick or the changes required to solve a specific match task, we form individual traces grouped artificially, but always as a part of a larger context. We have meaningful learning if the item fits naturally into the whole and if we understand the process of fitting in: then a structural trace of the process can be formed. We have senseless learning if the connection between the part and the whole is created artificially and the causes of the connection are not understood. But nevertheless there is an organization: we recall the senseless order "two red cards, one black card . . ." as a part of the situation "black and red cards should be arranged in such a way that at first a red card should be placed on the table . . ."

Structural traces may also show higher and lower types of organization. If whole-qualities of a process are retained and if individual items are transposed, we may assume that a structural trace is functioning. But the experiment with the number series, in which the alternation of differences of three and four was remembered, shows that a structural trace must not be far removed from the specificity of the contents. The structural content of "periodicity" may, of course, be separated from the content "differences of three and four," as some transpositions indicate (cf. p. 12). In the next chapter we shall attempt to study structural traces of a more logical type and their relation to specific contents.

These considerations suggest the assumption that the various types of trace belong in one continuous series. We can recognize certain outstanding points in this series. One extreme consists of individual traces of loosely connected pieces, the laws of which we have studied in the preceding chapter. Somewhat further in the series we may recognize individual items fitted into a whole process which, however, is not understood as a meaningful whole. A structural trace in which many individual items survive because they are carried by the principle, is an instance further down on the list. At the other extreme is the structural trace of a well-understood meaningful whole which is detached from specific contents.

Essentially the various parts of this series differ in the quality of the organization. The third and fourth hypotheses on memory traces contain certain assertions concerning the relationship between the quality of the organization and the functioning of the traces. Apparently there is a correlation between ease of learning and strength of organization; with better organization, learning becomes easier. Hypothesis III on the formation of traces may be used to explain that correlation, but its validity must first be tested by experiment. Hypothesis IV asserts that there is a correlation between the grade of organization and the duration of retention. A month or more after the training period in various experiments with numbers, cards, and matches individual traces could not be revived, while structural traces of the principle were still effective. The persistence of the principle as compared with that of specific details requires further investigation, as does the relationship between better organization and the ease of learning. The experiments to be described in the next chapter were designed for that purpose and should therefore serve to test the various hypotheses which have been offered in the preceding pages.[6]

[6] In Appendix 4 several important investigations on memory traces are reviewed. We discuss there the similarities and differences between our ideas and those of various authors.

Chapter IX

RETENTION OF PRINCIPLES AND FACTS

THE EFFECTS of memorizing and understanding on the rate and the curve of forgetting were discussed in Chapter VI. Since retention is a function of memory traces, the results of our earlier investigation must now be connected with the qualities and laws of the traces.

Forgetting and the Qualities of the Traces

Experiment E, in which the effects of different forms of repetition were analyzed, may be viewed as a contribution to the study of "the dynamic interaction of organized traces and new processes" (50, p. 566), an expression which is borrowed from Koffka, who in his investigation of the various forms of forgetting differentiates between transformation of traces "through communication with a new process" and "through communication with other traces," and the "autonomous destruction of traces" (50, p. 524). For the moment our interest is mainly in finding out whether there is a difference between the effects of memorizing and those of understanding, with regard to the autonomous decay which occurs with the passing of time. According to Koffka the autonomous destruction of traces is due to "lack of cohesion" (p. 524). "Traces of chaotic processes have a much lower survival value than traces of well-organized processes" (p. 507). "Preservation of a trace is a function of its own stability" (p. 507). We must distinguish between the effects of various grades of organization: "The process corresponding to the apprehension of meaningful material must be better organized than that corresponding to a nonsense series, and hence the trace of the former must be more stable than the trace of the latter" (p. 569). Greater stability involves greater survival value.

This theory is presented in connection with experiments of Wulf (113) and his followers, who studied mainly the transformation of slightly organized unstable traces of senseless material.[1] The question in which we are interested is different. In the experiments with match tasks the process of organization, or at least most of it, was completed when understanding resulted from a "good" method of learning. Therefore the question arises about the factors instrumental for the preservation or destruction of traces of well-organized processes. Suppose a certain material is learned in a meaningful way; its essential points are understood because of appropriate organization. What will be retained and what will be forgotten in such a case? Will the quality of retention resulting from understanding differ from that which follows mechanical memorizing?

Hypothesis IV on memory traces, as formulated in the previous chapter, may be assumed to be connected with Koffka's thesis that the survival value of traces depends on the grade of their organization and their stability. "Stability," as the term is used by Koffka, does not involve rigid, unchanging preservation, but a stable core (formed by a whole-quality, such as symmetry in some of Wulf's drawings) around which many less important details may be constantly changing. This description applies to the structural traces, which according to Hypothesis IV are supposed to have a higher survival value than the individual traces (provided, of course, that they are the result of learning processes of equal strength and recency).

The contention that structural traces, in contrast to individual traces, are the carriers of long-range remembering, may also be expressed in less technical language. The individual traces may be translated into every-day language as the knowledge of more-or-less unconnected facts, while the knowledge of laws and principles, of meaning and significance, of the setting and general forms, is

[1] Wulf used two-dimensional drawings without meaning, which the subjects observed for five or ten seconds with the intention to reproduce them later. Reproductions made after various intervals showed changes, most of which were in the direction of increased regularity, more stabilized forms, better balanced patterns—that is, toward greater "pregnance" of the figure.

the equivalent of structural traces. Thus a definite question arises, the answer to which should prove or disprove the hypothesis formulated. Is it true that principles and meanings are retained for a longer time than individual facts?

In these considerations the different qualities of traces were stressed. If all structural traces have better survival value than all individual traces, then the quality of the material alone would determine the course of forgetting. But there is also another possibility to which we have frequently referred—namely, to differentiate between the two methods of producing traces. We may assume that the method by which knowledge is acquired determines whether a trace is stable or not. Long-range retention with an irregular curve would then result from meaningful methods of learning—in which case we could again refer to Koffka's thesis that the grade of organization affects the survival value of the traces. Everything learned by a meaningful method—individual facts as well as principles, data as well as rules—may have, according to this assumption, a retention curve different from the rapidly declining curve of classical theory.

The experiments which will be described in the following pages are intended to answer this question: Do long-range remembering and an irregular curve of forgetting apply to specific details as well as to principles? We shall study the persistence of knowledge that is well understood, in contrast to fundamental changes in recollection or to a modification of recall which proceeds in a certain direction.

Experiments on the Differences in Retention

In the experiments reported and discussed in this book the process of learning was studied by means of nonsense syllables and lists of numbers and words, numbers grouped according to a principle, and tasks performed with cards and matches. In these experiments meaningful and senseless materials and meaningful and senseless methods of learning were used, but perhaps the learning process which the layman would call the "higher mental process" has not yet been investigated. For the new experiment on forgetting the author intended to select a learning material and a learning method that would justify that description. It has just been explained why material organized in the best possible way should serve as the tool for studying retention. It is now time to inquire about the history of traces formed by meaningful learning, in the true sense of the word.

In contrast to the experiments previously reported, the selection of the learning material for the new experiments was not determined by the intention to compare traces formed by understanding with those formed by memorizing. Quantitative experiments concerning different results of the two processes of learning will therefore not be reported here. Nevertheless we shall again compare the qualitative differences between the contents which are retained and those which are forgotten as the consequence of the two kinds of learning.

Subject matter belonging to a scientific field was chosen as the material for the experiment, and adults accustomed to study scientific texts were chosen as the subjects. In order that the results of testing various subjects might be comparable, material unfamiliar to all subjects was needed. Since psychologists, physicians, and mathematicians were used in the experiment, the learning material had to be selected from a field outside their specialties, but, nevertheless, it had to awaken their interest. If the subjects were to acquire full understanding of the material, they had to be interested in it, especially since the author wanted to carry out the experiment without the usual more-or-less artificial atmosphere of a psychological test. If the subjects had been told that experiments on learning were to be performed, a special and unnatural situation would have arisen.[2] If adult subjects had been asked to learn a text in order to remember its content or meaning for a few weeks, they would probably have consented merely out of kindness, but they would hardly have brought about the best possible organization of the material. Therefore the experiment was concealed in a scientific discussion about the interesting economic problems of pros-

---

[2] College students were not chosen as subjects except in a group experiment which will be reported on p. 218.

perity and depression. The procedure used in the experiment is explained in the footnote.[3]

In the course of the discussion on prosperity and depression the subjects studied a scientific text for the purpose of finding out whether or not the text furnishes a satisfactory explanation for the periodic occurrence of business cycles. The text was an extract from the book *Prosperity and Depression,* by G. von Haberler, published by the League of Nations in 1937. A theory contributing to the explanation of business cycles, called "acceleration principle" and explained on pages 81–87 in that book, was condensed to six hundred words. All subjects were familiar with the main facts of the business cycle and were generally interested in them, but the specific theory expounded in the text was new. The text contained the following table, which was thoroughly explained in the text

---

[3] The experiment had the following form. When the author met a prospective subject, he began a discussion by asking: "Are you interested in economics?" Whatever the answer was, this question followed: "In your opinion is scientific procedure possible in economics?" Usually a short discussion followed, the experimenter concluding with the following suggestion: "I want your unbiased opinion about the question of scientific procedure in economics. Here is a typewritten text given me by an economist as an example of a scientific approach to a law in social sciences. He also asserted that economics is different from natural science insofar as intelligent adults are able to understand it without special preparation. I should like to test these statements. Would you be good enough to study the text carefully and then tell me whether you agree with it and whether you consider it a good example of scientific procedure."

A typewritten text containing a table was then presented to the subject. The experimenter waited in an adjoining room until the subject finished studying the text. Ten to seventeen minutes elapsed before the subject called the experimenter, who greeted him with the question: "Do you agree with what you have just read?" Thus a discussion started which must be considered part of the practice period. During the discussion the experimenter made sure that the subject understood the text and remembered the main points immediately after studying. Most subjects expressed some criticism of the text, while the experimenter pointed to the logically correct thought process as especially indicated in the table. When the discussion was closed, the subjects did not realize that the performance remained unfinished.

Approximately four weeks later the experimenter met the subjects again in order to administer the test. Now the atmosphere characteristic of a psychological experiment could not be avoided. Each subject was told: "When I saw you the last time you read a text on economics. Now I want to ask you to tell me everything you remember about that text as exactly as possible. For the purpose of an experiment on remembering I should like to hear everything you remember. Keep as strictly as possible to the original form of the text." After the subjects had complied with this instruction, several questions to be discussed later were asked. A few subjects were tested a second time about two months after the first session.

and which served to exemplify the essential points of the ideas expressed in the text.[4]

YEAR	NUMBER OF SHOES PRODUCED (PAIRS)	NUMBER OF MACHINES REQUIRED	PRODUCED
I	1,000,000	500	50
II	1,100,000	550	100 [a]
III	1,150,000	575	80 [b]

[a] 50 + 50. [b] 55 + 25.

Four weeks after the "scientific discussion on economics," in a second experimental session, a psychological test was made to determine which parts of text and table the subjects remembered and which they had forgotten. Since the results of these tests can be made clearer by comparison with certain experiments on memorizing, the latter will be discussed first. In the memorizing experiments the table reprinted above served as material—the table alone, and not as in the "understanding" experiments, the table as a part of the text. From a certain point of view it may be said that the identical material—the same words and the same numbers—was presented to those who learned by understanding and to those who were memorizers. Yet in the first case, when the table was a part in a text and exemplified a principle, it was studied in a different way than in the second case, when the table was presented without any explanation. The memorizers read the table thoroughly with the intention of learning it—the minimum number of repetitions was six—while most meaningful learners read the table just once or

[4] To explain this table, instead of reprinting the whole text it will suffice to point out that the acceleration principle was explained in two examples—the demand for shoes and the construction of apartments. According to the principle slight changes in the demand for consumers goods produce violent variations in the demand for producers goods. A 10 percent increase in the demand for shoes may bring about a 100 percent increase in the output of equipment required to produce the shoes. That is the case if prior to the increase in the demand one million pairs of shoes were produced by five hundred machines, of which 10 percent must be replaced each year (cf. the table: in the second year fifty machines are produced for replacement purposes and fifty machines to permit an increase in the shoe output). The third line of the table indicates that the rate of operation at the factories producing shoe machinery may fall, even though the demand for the finished product continues to grow at a slower rate.

twice but turned to it briefly a few times when they read the text.[5]

The subjects who participated in the memorization experiment, likewise professional people comparable to the subjects of the "understanding" experiment, were tested about four weeks after the learning period. The subjects were asked to write down everything they remembered about the table. It proved to be rather difficult to make the subjects understand what the experimenter wanted them to do. Two of the six subjects professed that they had entirely forgotten the subject matter of the first experiment, and they could not be induced to try to reproduce the table. In the test papers produced by the other subjects some details, such as the words "shoes" and "year," as well as a few numbers, were recalled correctly, but the meaning of the table was not to be found in the reproduced material. Not one subject presented a table which could have been used as an illustration of the acceleration principle. The following tables are examples of reproduction after memorization:

REPRODUCTION OF SUBJECT M [a]

(27 Days after Learning)

QUARTER	NUMBER OF PAIRS OF SHOES	
	Produced	*Sold*
I	50 000	45 000
II	25 000	15 000
III		
IV		

[a] The subject finally crossed out the word "quarter," stating that it must be a mistake. Then she remarked: "I am very uncertain about all the figures; the figures on the right must have been much lower; I have forgotten the whole thing."

---

[5] Despite the fact that the elements presented in the two experiments were identical, the material of the two experiments was, of course, different. It was possible to learn how to perform the card and match tasks by memorizing the result and also by understanding the principle; but the economic theory was unsuitable for memorizing. No subjects could have been found who would learn the six hundred words by heart; and even if the text could have been memorized verbatim, understanding of the text could not have been avoided. But the table could be easily memorized. The subjects of the experiment on memory had to repeat the table until they knew it by heart. When they declared that they knew the table, they had to reproduce it in writing from memory. Learning was continued until the subjects presented a perfect reproduction (including both the words and the figures of the table). The frequent questions about the meaning of the table were left unanswered. The subjects were not told that they were to be tested again; they believed that the experiment was finished when they achieved their first correct reproduction.

In contrast to Subject M, who obviously tried to bring order and meaning to her table, we show below another type of reproduction.

REPRODUCTION OF SUBJECT V [a]

(26 Days after Learning)

Number of	Number of	Number of
1 000 000	1 100 000	
50 + 50	25 + 50	50 + 75

[a] The subject commented, "following the words 'number of' there were two words, different each time, but I can't recall them."

We find in these tests, as well as in a similar group experiment administered to a college class,[6] that grouping processes such as we have described in Chapter VII play a role in memorizing. But the recall of one part does not cause the reconstruction of another missing part, and the reproductions do not contain any examples of sensible transpositions.

Of the results of the experiments in which the subjects learned by understanding, the facts referring to the recall of the table will be reported first. The subjects who learned by understanding were asked four weeks after their reading of the text: "Was there a table in the text?" Regardless of the answer to this question, the experimenter asked them to reconstruct the table which they had seen on the second page of the text. Three of the twelve subjects refused to comply with that demand and insisted that they knew of no such table. One subject constructed a table which resembled those produced by most memorizers: it did not fit into the context of the acceleration principle. But the remaining eight subjects constructed tables which were in one respect satisfactory: they gave correct pictures of the function of the acceleration principle

[6] The performance of college students who memorized the table after the completion of a match experiment was somewhat better than that of the subjects who were tested individually. The test was made again four weeks after the learning period. In a class of nineteen the test papers of six subjects were blank, or they contained no correct reproductions; eight papers contained many uncoördinated details similar to those given above as examples; two papers were almost perfect; and three papers contained correct reproductions. Only the three perfect reproductions could serve as an illustration of the "acceleration principle," in all other reproductions the essential relationships were not preserved.

in increasing the output of equipment to a disproportionally larger degree than would have corresponded to the increase in the demand for consumers goods. Thus the relation given in the first two lines

FIRST TEST OF SUBJECT B
(32 Days after Learning)

	Machines Produced Each Year
500 000 shoes produced with 500 machines	50
550 000 " " " 550 "	100
10% increase	100% increase

SECOND TEST OF SUBJECT B
(56 Days after Learning)

	Machines Produced Each Year
500 pairs of shoes produced with 50 machines	
Life of machines 10 years	5
Demand for shoes increases 10% to 550 pairs of shoes	10
10% increase from 500 to 550 pairs	100% increase in machine production

FIRST TEST OF SUBJECT K [a]
(24 Days after Learning)

PAIRS OF SHOES PRODUCED	SHOE MACHINES REQUIRED	SHOE MACHINES To be Replaced	To Be Produced
100 000	100	10	0
110 000	110	11	10
50 000	50		

[a] After having written the figure "50," the subject crossed out the last line, remarking: "A third line showed that a 10 percent decline in shoe production brings about a very sharp decline in the production of shoe machinery, but I do not remember the exact figures."

FIRST TEST OF SUBJECT L
(28 Days after Learning)

INCREASE IN PRODUCTION

Consumers Goods	Producers Goods
By 10 000 tons of soap or 10%	By 10 machines or 100% [a]
" 20 000 " " " " 20%	" 20 " " 200%

[a] "Ten machines produced for replacement and ten machines produced for additional demand."

of the original table—the relation of the first to the second year—was preserved. The relationship of the further increase in the demand for consumers goods to the decrease in the production of producers goods (third line, or transition from the second to the third year) was reconstructed correctly by only two subjects.

Correct reconstruction of an essential relationship does not mean that the tables constructed by the subjects were identical with or similar to the original table. The tables on page 213 are examples of what the subjects did. These tables show correct recollection of the first relationship (first two lines); the second relationship was omitted.

The last table contains none of the words and numbers in the original table. Nevertheless, it can serve as an illustration for the acceleration principle, just as the original table does. Moreover, it is, not sheer invention on the part of the subject, but the result of his remembering. The distinction between consumers and producers goods was of paramount importance in the whole text, but by accident, we may say, this distinction was not included in the original table. In the subject's recollection shoes were changed into soap, in accordance with the fact that shoes were mentioned only as an example in the text and everything told about shoes might have applied equally well to soap.

In such cases it is possible to speak of "sensible transposition," since the main relationship between the items was preserved, but the individual items were changed. In view of the behavior of the subjects, however, the constructive characteristics of reproduction should be emphasized. By studying and understanding the text the subjects acquired some knowledge about the content and the functioning of the acceleration principle. When asked to reproduce the table, they were able to reconstruct it with the help of their general knowledge. The formal principle, which they remembered, assisted them to construct specific details, which differed from the original, but whose relations were determined by the function of the whole.

This description of recall as a consequence of meaningful learning must be changed to some extent. Several subjects reproduced also a few specific details which were not relevant to the principle and which, therefore, could not have been constructed because of the knowledge of the latter alone. We reprinted the table presented by Subject B: he changed the numbers referring to the shoe production, but remembered correctly the numbers "500" and "50" referring to machines, although these numbers, too, could have been changed into other numbers of similar relationship, as was done by Subject L. Most subjects remembered the words "shoes" and "machines," and several subjects remembered also the number "80." The reconstruction of a relationship with the help of formal principles remembered may be expressed in terms of structural traces alone. But in the instances just referred to, the survival of individual traces must also be assumed. It appears that meaningful learning in forming one or several interconnected, well-organized structural traces of high survival value permits also the persistence of a few individual traces in a rather rigid form.

The result of the experiment concerning the high survival value of a few individual traces as a consequence of learning by understanding involves a slight modification of Hypothesis IV given in the preceding chapter. The words "shoe production," "machine," "machines produced" were recalled by most subjects who learned meaningfully, while only one or two memorizers could retain some of these words, although the memorizers learned by means of a much greater number of repetitions and with the intention of learning. But it appears that in the meaningful learners the will to learn and the intention to remember were successfully supplanted by interest in the material. Comparison of the tables constructed by the students of the text on economics with those constructed by the memorizers shows that senseless learning may be at a disadvantage even with regard to the recall of specific details —if the recall is tested several weeks after the learning period. The question is: which persists longer—words and numbers memorized by frequent repetition or the same material as a well-understood part of a meaningful whole? Experimental evidence points to the second alternative.

The main effect of learning by understanding is, of course, not the persistence of a few specific details, but the persistence of the general form and meaning. The function of the structural traces should be clarified by a report of the rest of the experiment.

Most subjects who about four weeks earlier studied the text of the acceleration principle were completely surprised when the experimenter asked them to recall the text. They replied promptly "I have forgotten it all." At the experimenter's insistence they started slowly to give reports in which they inserted many apologies and ironical remarks about their faulty and poor recollection. Nevertheless, some of them took as much time to give the report as they needed for studying the text. Twelve subjects spoke for an average of nine minutes each, while the learning took them fourteen minutes. In describing the text seven subjects began where the text began—by explaining the distinction between consumers and producers goods and its importance for the understanding of business cycles. (In many cases the exact terms "consumers goods" and "producers goods" were not recalled.) Otherwise, however, there was no exact correspondence between the reports made by the subjects and the original text. Certain thoughts expressed at the end of the text were given at the beginning, and vice versa; long discussions which did not form part of the original text were interpolated several times. These additions consisted to a considerable extent of the subjects' reactions to the text, some of which had been expressed to the experimenter following the learning period. Counterarguments and viewpoints restricting the validity of the principle were discussed in detail, although they had no foundation in the original text. Moreover, the argument of the text was developed and extended by eight subjects in the same direction. The text explained the principle only with regard to an increase in the demand for consumers goods; however, in recalling the text eight subjects dealt also with the decrease in demand and tried to explain the occurrence of economic depressions (which was a pressing problem in the spring and summer of 1938, when the experiments were made). Finally, a few subjects included in their reports new details which were entirely irrelevant to the principle, such as the price of the shoes and the shoe machinery.

Is it possible to summarize these and many other considerable differences between the original text and what was remembered by asserting that memory falsified the text? The changes show a certain trend, for many reproductions reflected the skepticism of those subjects who had at the end of the learning period denied the possibility of scientific progress in economics, and they indicated that other subjects had accepted what they read without criticism. But apart from this significant transformation of the material the main argument was preserved without any falsification. The statements by the subjects about the role and functioning of the principle gave in most cases a good account of the original text, in spite of the fact that the subjects used different words and changed the order of the arguments. Three of the twelve subjects failed. Their recollections of the text, which were stenographed by an assistant during the test, were not rational accounts of the principle. But when the reports of the other nine subjects were read to students who did not know the original text, the students were able to understand the essential idea of the acceleration principle. The reports contained not only the scheme and the setting but also the major points of the principle, and they were suitable for conveying knowledge of it.[7]

While recollection of the table and of the main thesis of the text was in the majority of cases rather satisfactory, most of the subjects failed in answering certain specific questions. The answers to such questions as "How many examples were given for the functioning of the principle?" "Which example was the first?" "What was the title of the text?" and so forth were incorrect in

---

[7] The difference between this result and that of famous old experiments on "errors of memory," like those of Binet, Whipple, and so forth, lies in the material, the method of learning, and also in the evaluation of the results. There the number of distinct ideas contained in the text was counted, and it was ascertained how many ideas were omitted, inserted, and altered in the reproduction. In order to obtain a quantitative result stories were chosen for materials of the experiments which contained many descriptive details, that is, were similar to a senseless material insofar as both contained enumerations (lists of events or objects).

most cases. Many details were entirely forgotten. Thus in addition to the main points of the text, only certain individual traces persisted.

A group experiment was carried out with the material of the "acceleration principle" to test the effect of certain variations. It was an exploratory experiment rather than one leading to quantitative measurements. The general scheme of the experiment was changed as follows, since it had to be adapted to classroom conditions: (1) in the "learning period" the students knew that a psychological experiment was in progress (they were told that the experiment was being made in order to discover whether or not they understood a complicated economic text); and (2) in the test the subjects were not asked to reproduce the contents of the entire text. The test made four weeks after the training consisted of a few specific questions and two tasks. The subjects were asked to "explain in a few words [in writing] the functioning of the principle" and then to reproduce the table from memory.

Three comparable classes of undergraduates were used. To the members of Class I were given mimeographed copies of the same text used in the individual experiments. We shall call these papers "good text and good table," meaning that both text and table were logically clear and that the table fitted organically into the text. Class II studied the same text, but with a table inserted containing the actual changes in the shoe output and the shoe-machinery output in a European country. This table, too, contained relationships which could be explained with the help of the acceleration principle, but the table did not form an organic part of the text. Moreover, the table contained no round numbers, and the relations among the numbers were not simple. We shall in this case speak of "good text and bad table," using the word "bad" in the sense of greater difficulty in remembering. The material of the study of Class III we shall call "bad text and good table." The same table was used as for Class I, but the text was changed; the new text lacked the logical clarity of the "good text," and it contained three examples of the functioning of the principle which were not made clear with the help of tables. Nevertheless, this text also was understood by the subjects, as was revealed when the subjects were questioned at the close of the learning period.

We present the results of the test [8] on the basis of a rather strict evaluation. The accounts given of the principle and the reproductions of the table were evaluated by studying whether the relationships essential for the functioning of the acceleration principle were preserved or not. We thus differentiate between (1) the test papers which contained a good account of the principle and (2) those which did not. Furthermore, we differentiate between (3) the papers which contained a table suitable to illustrate the principle's function and (4) those which did not. In cases 1 and 3 we awarded a score of one; while in cases 2 and 4 we did not award a score. There were several test papers to which a score of one-half was given (Table 18), because the experimenter could not readily determine whether they belonged to the first or to the second group.[9] In Table 19 the results are recapitulated by summarizing the scores and expressing them in percentages of the total number of subjects.

The material used in the individual experiments was the same as that used in Class I in the group experiments. Yet satisfactory

[8] The test papers of the few students who knew of the principle before the experiment and who admitted that they had thought of it between training and test were not scored.

[9] The tables scored as "good" recollections contained transpositions, in addition to those which were more-or-less-exact reproductions. The following tables illustrate our scoring method:

Year	Number of Machines Used	Number of Machines Produced
1	500	50
2	550	100
3	575	80

The above table was given the score one, although it was less complete than most other tables receiving that score. The following table is an example for a score of one-half.

	Number of Machines	Machine Replacements	Production in Heavy Industry
First year	1000	50	50
Second "	1050	55	150
Third "		80	200

TABLE 18. EVALUATION OF THE TEST PAPERS IN THE
ACCELERATION-PRINCIPLE EXPERIMENT

	PRINCIPLE			TABLE		
	Good State-ment	Score of One-half	Bad State-ment or No State-ment	Good State-ment	Score of One-half	Bad State-ment or No State-ment
Class I (26 subjects)	10	7	9	7	7	12
Class II (24 subjects)	11	6	7	2	1	21
Class III (27 subjects)	6	9	12	3	5	19

TABLE 19. SCORES IN THE ACCELERATION-PRINCIPLE EXPERIMENT

	PRINCIPLE		TABLE	
	Absolute Score	Percentage Score	Absolute Score	Percentage Score
Class I	$13\frac{1}{2}$	52	$10\frac{1}{2}$	40
Class II	14	58	$2\frac{1}{2}$	10
Class III	$10\frac{1}{2}$	39	$5\frac{1}{2}$	20
Twelve individual subjects	9	75	8	67

accounts of principle and table were given more frequently in the
first case than in the second case. The difference is probably due
to the difference between the individual and the group situations
and also to the method of selecting the subjects. The circumstances under which the group experiment was made were not
conducive to a high degree of retention, especially with regard to
the recall of the table. Nevertheless, our former conclusions concerning the role of persistent structural traces brought about by
understanding are confirmed by the group experiment.

The differences in the results of the three classes contribute to
our knowledge concerning the important question: how does the
structure of a whole affect the survival value of the parts? Class
I had the highest scores. (The difference between the "principle
scores" of Classes I and II is not reliable.) Especially for the recall of the table the role played by the table in the text appears to
be of great importance. The difficult table presented to Class II

did not obstruct the understanding of the text, but the recollection of the table by this class was very poor. The performance of Class III was inferior to that of Class I. The "bad" text used by Class III had a greater effect on the recollection of the table than on the reports dealing with the principle. The results of the group experiment should not be analyzed further, because this experiment represents only a first attempt to investigate a problem, not a crucial test from which definite answers may be derived. Nevertheless, both the individual and the group experiments may serve as useful aids in describing the functioning of memory.

Availability and Embeddedness

The results of this investigation concerning retention of knowledge acquired by understanding are still rather indefinite. It was established that general principles, including a few specific details but excluding many others, are retained; but no rule of selection has been found that would indicate the contents to be retained and those to be forgotten.

In terms of traces our problem can be clearly stated. The first question is: which processes leave traces behind? The second question deals with the survival value of the traces. The third asks: what determines whether a new process is or is not able to resuscitate a trace?

In summarizing the factors responsible for the connection between certain situations and certain responses, Thorndike mentions in addition to other more important factors the two factors "identifiability of the situation and availability of the response" (93, p. 101). In his larger book it is stated that "much of learning consists in changes in the identifiability of the situations" and "in making certain responses more available" (94, pp. 344, 347). The concepts "identifiability" and "availability" appear to this author to be only loosely connected with the fundamental ideas of Thorndike's connectionism. Identifiability and availability are not just factors strengthening arbitrary connections between two contents, such as frequency or the aftereffect consisting of the word "right" of the teacher, but they are also the conditions of the learning and the results of the learning process. In both cases these concepts may have their place in any theory of traces. Thus, Koffka speaks of "availability and unavailability of traces" (50, p. 522 ff.) when he analyzes the circumstances of forgetting.

Köhler's extensive experimental investigations on certain aspects of reproduction concern the problem of identifiability.[10] Let us assume that a process A left a trace behind; let us further assume that the trace survived until the moment when process A1 occurred. Köhler then asks: On what does the communication of A1 with the trace of A depend? The same question can be expressed as follows in terms of association psychology: If A was associated with X and if later a somewhat different A1 was able to reproduce X, then A1 must have somehow resuscitated the trace of A. Reproduction is possible only when that trace is available and also identifiable with A1. We are concerned here with factors which constitute conditions for reproduction.

Communication between the process A1 and the trace of process A implies, according to Köhler, the formation of a pair A1–A. Two parts of a perception form a pair if they are sufficiently alike. That means that among parts of an entirely different kind two slightly similar parts may form a pair, whereas in a field consisting only of resembling parts the two parts must be very close to each other in their relevant qualities in order to form a pair. Köhler was able to prove that the same conditions hold for reproduction as for perceptual organization in pairs. In order to communicate with the trace of the older process A, the process A1 must be similar to the former. The grade of similarity required depends on the processes occurring in the time elapsing between A and A1. In Köhler's experiments we find the two cases A B1 B2 B3 B4 B5 A1 and A A2 A3 A4 A5 A6 A1 (the letters indicate events or items succeeding each other). In the first case, when several processes occurred between A and A1 which were not similar to these processes, A1 communicated with the trace of A, which

---

[10] Cf. Köhler and Restorff, 48, and also the papers of Köhler's pupils Bartel, Mueller, and Ortner in *Psychologische Forschung*, Vol. XXII.

means that the identifiability of the situation caused no difficulties. But in the second case, when seven successive processes similar to each other took place, no communication resulted. In the first case process X, strongly connected with A, was recalled after and because of the occurrence of process A1; while in the second case it was not recalled. In various experiments Köhler tried to determine how the nature of the occurrences in the interval between A and A1 (*Zwischenfeld*) facilitates or hampers reproduction. He showed that the communication of a new process with a former trace and also the survival of a trace are less probable when the first process which left the trace is followed by several similar processes than if it is followed by processes without resemblance to it (theory of reproductive inhibition).

The theory of the effects of the interval on the availability and identifiability of traces may be extended in various directions. Of these we are most interested in the circumstances that may be favorable or unfavorable for the formation of traces. Moreover, the question arises as to the effects of the interval on structural traces, because in the main experiments of Köhler specific processes, such as the recollection of a senseless word or a certain measurement in building with architectural blocks, formed the investigated processes A and A1.

In the experiment with the acceleration principle we find a set-up which at the first glance appears entirely different from the one in Köhler's experiments. In the latter we have first a distinct process A, then a comparatively short interval filled with a few processes well known to the experimenter and changed by him according to a plan, and finally another distinct process A1. In our experiments we have a rather complex situation at the beginning (learning), a very long interval about which nothing is known, and lastly the complex situation of the test. Can the theory just described be applied to such a situation?

Köhler's statement that the communication between a process and a trace is the function of emerging as a pair from the environment may be taken as the point of departure for our discussion of the formation of traces. The table on shoe production was a part of the learning situation. Whether the table will prove to be a salient part depends on the other parts preceding and following the table, which determine the structural role of the table in the text. For Classes II and III in the group experiment the table was not the outstanding part of the text, because the preceding and following parts did not point to it. The tests showed that in this case persisting traces of the table were less often available than in another case in which the table emerged as the conspicuous central theme of the learning material.

The main concepts to be used in discussing what is retained and what is forgotten are therefore "outstanding features" insuring availability of traces and "embeddedness" of traces. In this respect also we are in agreement with Koffka, who speaks of the superiority of the "traces which were organic sub-systems of a larger trace system" (50, p. 624) and who states that "a trace strongly embedded in a trace system is less available for a new process than a trace loosely embedded" (50, p. 623).[11]

In our experiments learning consisted of the long and complicated process of studying the text of the "acceleration principle." This process involved organization of the material. Groups were formed, not according to some arbitrary standard, but according to the meaning of the whole. Often the learner had a preliminary group dealing with the difference between consumers and producers goods. This group formed a whole consistent in itself, but it was, nevertheless, intimately connected with the other groups; the distinction was significant for the theory of business cycles. The main part of the organization was not divided into several equivalent groups succeeding each other, as it might have been if the text had consisted of the enumeration of a series of slightly connected facts, but it consisted of a "radix" in which many thought processes ("groups") participated in different degrees and on which they depended for their meaning and even for their existence. Auxiliary processes can be reconstructed—that is,

---

[11] This concept of embeddedness was used before by Harrower (28), who has shown that the correct answer to a question may be so embedded in a text that the subjects, even after having read the correct answer, cannot answer the question. Cf. also Maier (66).

they can be made to exist again—by starting from the center; but they are destroyed if the central process cannot be resuscitated. The tests on remembering the text showed that for most individual subjects the central theme of the text was the consistent and definite idea that a marked increase in production of machinery would result from a small increase in the demand and the output of consumers goods. Thus the radix consisted of the process which was exemplified by the first two lines of the table.[12]

The alterations, additions, and omissions which occurred in the memory test may serve as further indications of the center, or radix, of the organization achieved by the subjects. We know that the flexible structural trace permits application under altered circumstances. The answers given by the subjects to questions asked by the experimenter revealed that most of them believed that they had read also about the effects of depression: the principle which tells about the spurt in the machinery output could be applied to a precipitate decline in the case of reversed conditions. The fact that the principle persisted in some cases without any of the specific details by which it was presented (cf. the reproduction of the table by Subject L on p. 213) is another indication that the ideas expressed in the table formed the center of the organization.

If we know about the center, we have some means of ascertaining which parts will not be remembered. Parts blurred because of embeddedness in a well-organized whole are not those which are completely unrelated to the center. The unrelated parts may form a coördinated group, which, if well organized, may have a fairly good survival value. But if parts are unnecessary, they will suffer

---

[12] In writing the text of the acceleration principle the author intended to make that part the center of the theme so that the remembering of the specific details in the table when learned in a meaningful way may be compared with remembering when learned in a senseless way—but an author, of course, does not always succeed in his intention. The organization which the reader makes may or may not be determined by the author's intention. The only way to know about the actual organization is to ask the reader to retell the text or to discuss the matter in question. If the account of the reader does not indicate any organization, although it shows the recollection of many details, then it may serve as proof that the reading was not "meaningful learning." The latter may be the case because the material was senseless or because the reader failed.

from embeddedness even if they were read several times. The statement about the apartments, seven lines in the text, was forgotten by almost everyone because it did not contain any new factor after the statement concerning the shoes had brought about understanding of the principle. The fact that the principle was first exemplified by shoes was forgotten by those who grasped the idea that it was of value only as one of many possible arbitrary examples (while for some other subjects the whole text dealt essentially with the production of shoes).

Embeddedness of a part may result also from its proximity to important neighbors. A part may be suppressed by neighbors that capture all the attention for themselves. That seems to be the best explanation of the fact that the idea expressed by the third line of the table on shoe production was forgotten by most subjects. The idea of a decrease in machinery output as a consequence of a reduced rate of increase in consumers' demand was interesting and important enough to persist if it had been presented in a different context. But that theme was embedded in the main thought process of the text, which dominated the situation.

Finally, we find examples of that kind of embeddedness which is analogous to the situation investigated by Köhler. Embeddedness may be the consequence of too many similar neighbors. Being a part among many other resembling parts leads to obliteration, and no conspicuousness results. Moreover, a series of equivalent resembling elements is not appropriate material for meaningful learning; we proceed by memorizing arbitrary groups, if we want to fix each element of a series in our memory. The forgetting of the technical terms used in the text may be an example of that kind of embeddedness, because the first part of the text contained several of them, such as "producers goods," "consumers goods," and "monetary and technological theory of the business cycle."

In contrast to the embeddedness of a detail we spoke of salient features. Of course, it is, not a detail, but the radix or central theme of the whole event which constitutes the main example of conspicuous features emerging from a context. But recalling the persistent words and figures mentioned above, we must assume that in addition to the knowledge of the main point certain details can also be carried by the principle. These details usually depend on the center or can be derived from it. They are not the ones most often repeated, but those which are not obliterated by the dominance of the radix or by many surrounding similar parts. There were very few numbers in the text, but numbers appeared in the table, which was not superfluous. Therefore, the main relations and also some details of the table had a strong survival value.

So far we have described the process of understanding the scientific text used in our experiment. With regard to the theory we assume that traces of the various parts of the text are formed according to the principles described. The organization of the traces corresponds to the organization of the perceptual material. We obtain thus a structural trace of the radix, a more-or-less complete structural trace of each consistent group, and individual traces of outstanding details. But many specific details, as well as general ideas which are embedded in a context, do not leave traces behind and are therefore not available on a later occasion. The following diagram is an attempt to express these ideas.

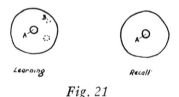

Learning   Recall

Fig. 21

A persistent trace will be formed by the radix, indicated by the small circle in the figure, and also by the outstanding detail A which is carried by the principle, but no persistent trace will be formed by the detail B, because the latter is repressed by its environment. The diagram shows what we have achieved so far and what we have neglected to discuss. We have heretofore merely described the occurrences in the learning process by trying to answer the first of our three questions concerning the origin of traces. We omitted the discussion of the interval and the situation on the occasion of the test or recall.[13]

As to the possible effects of the environment in which the test was given, the experiments we made with matches and the acceleration principle do not contribute to our knowledge. We were compelled to identify the tasks assigned to the subjects as completely as possible, and it never happened that a subject who had learned in a meaningful way failed because he did not recognize that the experimenter's question would lead to knowledge previously acquired. But the experiments of Köhler make it seem probable that the figure at the right in the diagram must be constructed similarly to the one at the left. It may happen that a process is unable to communicate with an existent trace because the process, embedded in a different context, is not apprehended in the right way.

The role of the interval is of greater interest for us. The detrimental effect of similar intervening processes, discussed above, is not a complete answer to our second question, which is concerned with the survival of a trace in the interval between its origin and its ultimate effect. We are less interested in adding further factors explaining the unavailability of traces than in knowing the reasons for their persistence without decay and for the occasional improvement of remembering with the passage of time. The experiments with match tasks indicated that occurrence of several examples was one main factor contributing to the improvement and development of structural traces. Examples are, of course, processes resembling each other which serve to build up an integrated knowledge. We thus arrive at two contradictory effects of similar processes occurring in the interval between learning and test. But the contradiction is apparent rather than real. We must distinguish between the submergence of a trace into similar processes, which causes its extinction, and its incorporation into a trace system, which gives it more solidity because it forms the center of the

[13] We also restricted our description to the occurrence of one single learning process, whereas the division of learning into several units, each separated by an interval from the next, frequently occurs; however, that omission does not appear to be fundamental.

system. Individual traces appear to be involved in the first process, and structural traces in the second.

As Koffka said, the unavailability of the traces may be due to autonomous factors, or it may be caused by communication with other traces and processes. Communication with similar processes which absorb the trace and destruction by interfering processes seem to be important special cases of forgetting.[14] Availability of traces after a long interval, that is, lasting retention without apparent decay, has been established in both structural traces and individual traces as a result of meaningful methods of learning. We found that these methods yield an organization which by shifting the emphasis and selecting what is retained makes it possible to reconstruct the material after long periods of time. We may therefore conclude that it depends on the method of learning and the method of testing whether or not we will remember, and it depends on the surroundings of process A and its trace, during the practice, the interval, and the testing situation, whether item A will or will not be remembered. The theory of retention necessitates a complete discussion of the circumstances of learning, the occurrences during the interval, and the environment of the test or recall, but fortunately in actual investigations we may assume that some of these factors were indifferent or constant, and therefore we may restrict our investigation to the remaining factor or factors.

Summary.—The following principles of the formation and persistence of traces, which are based on the researches described in this chapter, constitute a modification of the hypotheses formulated at the outset of our study of memory traces. We called the carriers of relatively inflexible remembering individual traces, which refer to specific items of past experience. Such traces are effective, or, to state it less technically, "raw facts" are retained as such, if the items are: (*a*) reconstructed (that is, if they are derived from an integrated whole); (*b*) carried by the whole as es-

---

[14] Frequently theories were formulated according to which all forgetting is a matter of interference or inhibition, but they do not appear to have been proved.

sential parts; (c) impressed upon the learner by memorization; or (d) impressed upon the learner by affective factors.

Memorizing by frequent repetition results in relatively rigid and specific functioning of memory. In addition, whole-qualities or principles may cause persistence of specific items provided the latter can be derived from the former or if they are essential parts of the former. In such cases the laborious method of memorizing can be dispensed with. But formation of individual traces without repetition also seems to occur under certain conditions not yet analyzed. In Appendix 5 we point to a fourth possibility, fixation due to affective factors. Persistence of individual traces may presumably be due also to the fact that they fit into the personality and the rational and emotional traits of the learner.

This description of specific recall leads to an enumeration of the instances in which integrated knowledge is retained in an adaptable form. Structural traces may be nothing more than the setting or framework of individual traces, or they may be the result of understanding, in which case they have a precise content, well differentiated from other contents and consisting of whole-qualities (or in some cases of whole-qualities and a few specific items).

The question "what do we retain" should not be answered by "raw facts (concrete individual items) and words." We retain either more than facts and words or, as in the case of certain types of learning, something different, namely, whole-qualities representing a structure, a principle, an essence, or combinations of principles, individual items, and words. The whole-qualities may be the results of: (a) perception; (b) insight; (c) development; or (d) crystallization of traces. In the first case we seldom speak of learning; in the second case we usually assume a more-or-less sudden learning, and in the third, a gradual understanding which may probably occur in the region of traces as well as in the region of processes. The organized whole-qualities acquired in such a way are flexible and adaptable to new circumstances, but in their structure and essence they are as definite and precise as any concrete individual content.

If we compare the ways in which the different kinds of trace are formed, we find that it is not generally true that structural traces are formed more quickly than individual traces. Yet learning becomes easier and faster with improved organization,[15] and the primary result of good organization is a structural trace. Also, there are exceptions to the rule that all structural traces are more stable and persist longer than all individual traces, because meaningful methods of learning enhance the survival value of both.

These short statements contain oversimplifications and taken alone may, perhaps, give rise to incorrect interpretation. Therefore we should stress once more the main question of our analysis of memory, which may be expressed as follows: Do we retain individual items and organize them in the course of remembering, or do we retain organized wholes and derive from them the individual items? Postponing the discussion of the first alternative, we may conclude as a result of our investigation that the second plays an important role in learning and in remembering.

[15] Cf. the discussion on pp. 243 f.

Chapter X

THE PROTOTYPE OF LEARNING

"Senseless" and "Meaningful"

THE DIFFERENCE between "senseless" and "meaningful" has played an important role in this investigation. By reviewing the road traversed we are now in position to analyze the relationship between these concepts. We can apply the distinction between senseless and meaningful to contents, connections, and learning processes. The first possible distinction is between two kinds of content, for example, between nonsense syllables (kem, fap, zit) and meaningful words (house, gasoline, paper). We are not concerned with that distinction, because meaning or lack of meaning of the contents does not determine whether the connection between various parts of the learning material is meaningful or senseless. That connection, or the relationship between two or more items, can also have two forms. Both meaningful and senseless contents can be connected in a senseless way as well as in a meaningful way. Examples of senseless connections are:

	kem		fap
Telephone number of John		[is]	3705

Wertheimer described in 1921 the main features of this type of connection. He stated (104, p. 49) that in such cases the kind of connection we make is arbitrary, inasmuch as the properties of the contents play no part whatever in determining the connection. The connection is a neutral bond which may be superimposed on any content, a purely existential and external relationship between any events. The connection cannot be understood—it is summative and mechanical. It does not make any difference whether the telephone number is 3705 or 9274; the form of the connection remains the same. There is no way of deriving the telephone number from the name or the character of John. Mechanical memorization is in this instance the way to learn—provided learning is required.

If we reverse these formulations describing senseless connections we obtain the main qualities of the meaningful connections. In contrast to the incidental summation of arbitrary contents, we can refer to the material of meaningful learning. To make the contrast clearer, we can also find "connections" of a simple form which do not conform to the statements given above.

$$275 - 275 = 0$$
$$(a + b)^2 = a^2 + 2ab + b^2$$

It is possible to memorize these equations (as is often done with the second), but they also can be understood. If one content is presented, the second can be derived from it, because these contents are not arbitrarily juxtaposed but are connected in a meaningful way.[1]

I do not propose to characterize the meaningful connections in greater detail, since our aim is to state the differences, not between senseless and meaningful connections, but between senseless and meaningful learning processes. Not all meaningful connections are learned in a meaningful way. The relationship is more complicated, as can be seen from the following scheme:

THE SCOPE OF MEMORIZATION AND OF LEARNING BY UNDERSTANDING

Senseless connections	Meaningful connections	
Memorization		
	Learning by understanding	
A	*B*	*C*

There is a threefold division: Section A contains senseless connections which can only be memorized; Section B contains meaningful connections which can be learned either by memorizing or by understanding; and Section C contains meaningful connections

---

[1] The definition of "meaningful" on which our use of that term is based is to be found in Wertheimer (104, p. 57). He states that meaningful behavior, meaningful completion, meaningful prediction, and so forth, require a unity in which the place of each part is not arbitrarily formed, but in which existence and quality of the parts are determined by the structure of the whole.

which can be learned only by understanding, and not by memorizing.

The concept memorization is used here in the sense of fixation of rigid traces by repetition. It is mechanical memorizing, the formation and strengthening of either senseless or meaningful connections that are not understood (p. 52). Learning by understanding is used here to mean the result of that organization of the material which is appropriate to its inherent structure. Only meaningful connections can be organized in a way that yields understanding.

It may be that the above scheme is inaccurate inasmuch as the lines in Section A should have been drawn shorter than those in the other sections. Fortunately, material which cannot be learned by understanding but only by memorizing is rather limited (except in psychological experiments). Later in this chapter we shall show that enumeration of specific data (facts, information), such as the birth dates of poets and the altitude of mountains, do not form always and necessarily "senseless connections which can only be memorized." The learning of most raw facts belongs to Section B, because it is due only to the lack of adequate organization that the connection between a battle and its date appears to be as senseless as the connection between a man and his telephone number.[2]

[2] However, there is a method frequently employed as an aid to memorizing data and facts, which consists of artificial formation of intrinsically senseless connections. We refer to certain mnemonic devices. There are mnemonic aids which make use of logical relations or make use of rhythm and rhymes and thus facilitate grouping, but some others represent extraneous associations superimposed over two contents without regard to the inherent properties of the contents. Such mnemonic devices belong in Section A, since they exclude real understanding.

Very often such mnemonic devices do not help at all, because they themselves are forgotten quickly. Often the mnemonic devices lead to "stupid mistakes," because they may be recalled in just the opposite way from what was intended (which is not the case with meaningful relations). In some instances the mnemonic aids are remembered *after* the response is given; they help then to increase the assurance of the response (cf. the example "golem" on p. 285). But in other instances senseless mnemonic devices do help us to remember. In the opinion of the author that is only the case if we use them very seldom. One or two mnemonic aids may form stable individual traces because of their strange or amusing form (that is an example of the strengthening of individual traces by affective factors) and because of overlearning.

Our investigation was concerned mainly with Section B. In the experiments with card and match tasks we were able to contrast the results of memorization with those of understanding. Much school teaching and many vocational studies are to be regarded as belonging to Section B. However, it is possible to define the concept of learning in a way which would restrict B considerably and enlarge C. If temporary acquisition of specific data were not considered learning and if the term were defined as a means of changing a reaction, of becoming able to perform an activity with competence, and of not being helpless in new situations—then we would have to admit that memorization hardly brings about such results. Section C is defined as an object of study for which memorization is not sufficient. Here we find, of course, the so-called higher mental activities. Memorizing a ten-page description of the theory of relativity will not produce a knowledge of that theory. We can also refer to the experiments with the "acceleration principle." For those experiments we carefully selected subjects who had scientific training and who after reading the text understood it, because in order to study the consequences of meaningful methods of learning, it had to be made sure that such learning actually occurred. But some subjects in the group experiment failed to understand the principle. The result of their learning process was practically nil. Even the few words and numbers which they recalled immediately after the learning period were quickly forgotten.

The main point exemplified by our scheme should not be obscured by a notion that some instances of learning may belong to Section C instead of Section B. Memorization has a much greater scope than senseless connections. For the intentional formation of individual traces by repetition is possible with many types of meaningful connections. We can learn material that has meaningful relations in a senseless way, that is, without understanding the

---

As an example of extraneous associations used as mnemonic aids we may quote the well-known verse "In fourteen hundred and ninety-two Columbus sailed the Ocean blue," which brought about a false answer on the part of the pupil who remembered "In fourteen hundred and ninety-three Columbus sailed the dark blue sea."

meaningful relations. In some instances memorizing is nothing else than an auxiliary device resorted to because of lack of understanding. If the equation $(a + b)^2$ is not understood, because of a bad method of teaching or other reasons, nothing remains for the pupil to do except to memorize it. Memorizing is, of course, preferable to incorrect or partial understanding. In addition, memorizing may be valuable when a routine performance of only one type is required or when it is sufficient. Memorization is in some cases the quickest way of learning, and it often brings about the shortest reaction time. On the other hand, it was found to be a wrong method when application of knowledge is required, because the results of memorizing are to some degree specific and rigid.

There may be instances in which understanding of meaningful connections may obstruct a required quick reaction. From such cases, as well as from the frequent instances of incomplete understanding, may originate the expression that there is safety in memorizing. On the other hand, the feeling of assurance on the part of the learner is apparently often much greater if he is doing or recalling something which he understands well, than if he is reciting memorized information or performing memorized manipulations (cf. p. 13). Perhaps neither position is entirely correct. In some cases a combination of both methods of learning, understanding followed by the memorizing of certain items, appears to be the most efficient way of achieving certain purposes (mainly quick response). By this combined method a structural trace embracing several individual traces will be formed. Section B in the scheme on p. 233 indicates the field of learning in which it is possible to use such combined methods.[3]

The Role of Past Experience

Are there any additional accomplishments for which memorizing is responsible? Someone may argue that the rigidity of the traces and the unchanging fixed memory enabling literal recall,

[3] Often the joint application of both methods of learning is also called "memorization," e. g., when we say that a musician memorized a composition, in which case we usually mean that after thoroughly understanding the composition the musician learned it by heart.

which we have criticized so often, is an important aim in itself. Literal recall results not only from the learning of nonsense syllables and the learning of poetry by heart, but it is also often considered the necessary result when we begin to study scientific matters. It is said that a first-year student of medicine must memorize many Latin names in his anatomy course, because it is important that he acquire a fixed and ever-ready knowledge of these names. The same holds true for names, formulas, definitions, and laws in mathematics, physics, chemistry, biology, and so forth. It is asserted that these data must become part of the student's knowledge in an unchanging and stable form, so that they may be reproduced quickly even when the student is half asleep, and that therefore they must be memorized. Similarly, learning a foreign language often starts with the memorization of words. It is said that the words must be repeated again and again because individual traces are required.[4]

The argument has still further implications. Those who assert that memorization is a necessary first step in all these studies, often believe that later learning by organization and understanding sets in because of the previous acquisition of a great amount of memorized knowledge. It is admitted that in the beginning the result of memorizing is a bundle of distinct data, words, definitions, and rules. But by increasing the number of connections order is said to be added. If the connections are sufficiently numerous, the knowledge is believed to be no longer piecemeal. For example, Hungarian words are learned by repeating them several times: egy—one; kettö—two; harom—three. That is memorization with the purpose of forming new individual traces. But if someone con-

---

[4] Here we formulated the argument according to which memorizing is required at the beginning stages of the studies of even intelligent adults. A more restricted form of the same argument is often presented by writers who condemn memorizing, but believe that at a certain mental level (or at a certain age) it cannot be avoided. We cite as an example the following passage: "Mechanical memorizing is a perfectly proper method of studying the most elementary, the most fundamental facts which are of frequent application. This is possibly the reason why the teaching is far more effective in the lower grades than later on. In more advanced work the very nature of the subjects makes mere memorizing ineffective" (Schultze, 85, p. 10). But is it a fact that in the lower grades of the school system it is good to memorize?

tinues to study Hungarian for several months, he will reach a stage in which he will not have distinct, quickly fading individual traces of the words "egy, kettö, and harom," but they will be part of his knowledge of that language. He will be able to apply these words in new situations without recalling in every instance the original connection with the corresponding English words. From that example does it follow, as it is widely held, that memorizing is the first step in learning which provides the material of under-standing when we deal later with familiar matter? The example of the Hungarian words is similar to that in the counterargument with which we closed the first chapter (p. 20): we understand the series 1 4 9 16 . . . because at some earlier time we memorized $2 \times 2 = 4$ and $3 \times 3 = 9$. Thus we return to the assertion which is the underlying principle of association research—that mechani-cal memorization is the prototype of all learning.

This book is intended as a challenge to that thesis. One of our principal aims was to show how different are the two processes of learning with regard to both structure and results. But the demon-stration that there are differences between the two processes is not yet sufficient to disprove the assertion of the priority of the process of forming senseless connections. So far we have failed to prove explicitly that the understanding of a meaningful whole is not the result of many arbitrary connections previously formed.

The way we formulated the objection at the end of Chapter I was: 1 4 9 16 . . . is a meaningful series; that is so because of earlier learning. In other words, meaning is due to past experi-ence.[5] But it is not meaning in any of the numerous usages of the term which we have in mind when we speak of meaningful meth-ods of learning. We defined meaningful learning as learning which proceeds by organization appropriate to the inherent structure of

---

[5] Cf. Carr (13, p. 167) "The meaning or significance of an object is dependent upon the indirect and partial arousal of some of the previous experiences con-nected with it." Or Hollingworth (30, pp. 223 and 239) "Meaningful or rational learning is particularly economical since it intrinsically consists in the utilization of learning already accomplished." "Nonsense material is less easily learned than is meaningful material. This follows naturally from the fact that meaningful ma-terial already represents a certain amount of previous learning, since it is *through learning that meaning arises.*"

the material. Therefore we shall not investigate the general statement that "meaning is due to past experience," but our aim is to find out whether or not organization which leads to understanding is the result of earlier senseless experiences. By studying the relationship between organization and past experience we shall try to answer the question, How does experience operate?

While I was writing the last sentence two friends entered my room. Both had been subjects in experiments with match tasks about a month earlier. One of them had memorized the solution of a certain task, while the other had learned by the method of help. On this occasion I presented them with a new task: the first friend was helpless, whereas the second solved the task after a short period of deliberation. For him the task was meaningful. Although he was unable to formulate the principle in exact terms, he understood the task and led by his general understanding of the main points, he found within a short time where to break up the figure, how to make holes out of squares, and so forth. The behavior of this subject differed from his behavior in the earlier experiment, when I first asked him to solve a match problem. At that time he had fumbled blindly and made no progress. Thus it was without doubt the experience of the subject which enabled him on the second occasion to arrive at the correct organization and which made the task meaningful. But a glance at my other friend, who was still vainly trying to find sense in the task, proves that experience does not always operate in the same way. He, too, had had experience with match tasks, but nevertheless the tasks remained senseless to him. Thus we must conclude that it cannot hold true that all past experience has the power to bring about organized wholes.

We contend that only a certain kind of previous experience helps to achieve organization and understanding and thus to create meaning. What is that kind of experience? Our investigation of transfer of training must be recalled at this point. We found that memorization establishes connections whose range of applicability under different circumstances is limited. On the other hand, what is learned in a meaningful way can be applied in various situations. Therefore the effects of the second kind of learning can aid in producing organization. If organization and understanding occurred in the past, then that experience, being applicable to different circumstances, helps to achieve organization and understanding again. We often arrive at meaningful solutions because of previous organization, but not because of any kind of previous learning. Organization is not the consequence of all sorts of experience. On the other hand, we can reverse the last statement and say: we have experience because of organization. My friend who has memorized certain connections in a senseless way has not had any experience which can help him now. My other friend, however, has experience at his disposal because of the previous organization of the material. Experience originates in organization.

Let us examine the first experience of my friends with match tasks in order to determine the role of experience if a certain kind of organization and understanding is achieved for the first time. We have no reason to expect that when confronted with new problems intelligent adult subjects would learn how to solve them without utilizing any prior experiences. Experience no doubt assisted them in organizing the new material, insofar as it was experience of a meaningful and therefore applicable sort. But the vast amount of memorized knowledge with very limited power of transfer with which our subjects were equipped when they first undertook the experiment could not help them in the new situation. The effects of mechanical memorization and drill are restricted to specific materials and therefore do not help to bring about organization of new situations.

The result of this inquiry can be summed up as follows: if we understand the expression "experience" to mean the previous acquisition of senseless connections or the attachment of a response to a stimulus in a mechanical way, then organization which leads to understanding is not due to experience. But experience in the sense of having apprehended meaningful wholes and of having made organization on former occasions, is usually a contributing factor in bringing about new organization.

A shorter way to clarify the role of experience is to refer to traces. Should the statement be true that meaningful organization is the result of earlier senseless connections, then we should have to assume that structural traces are the results of individual traces previously formed. Investigation of the qualities and rules of the traces contradicted that assumption. It was found that in many instances organized traces of organized wholes were formed more quickly than and independent of individual traces which resulted gradually from repeated connections that were not understood. Therefore organization which leaves structural traces cannot be the result of an aggregation of individual traces.[6]

Learning is only in certain not very frequent cases senseless and mechanical memorization. Even if pupils are compelled by a teacher to memorize hundreds of words or to repeat a hundred times $6 + 3 = 9$, $3 + 6 = 9$, $4 + 5 = 9$, $5 + 4 = 9$, and so forth, as human beings with a natural tendency toward organization they will sooner or later organize the material and create meaningful wholes. The merely drilled, but not understood, "knowledge" of $2 \times 2 = 4$ and $3 \times 3 = 9$ is not sufficient to create understanding of the series 1 4 9 16 . . . Fortunately very few human adults are limited to such a drilled knowledge, because at some time in their handling of numerals organization arose.

To a German boy of fourteen who was preparing to emigrate to the United States I sent a *World Almanac*. He was a conscientious boy, who had probably been trained in a certain way in school; in any case, when he arrived in New York several months later, he told me that he knew much about America, the names of the states and the principal cities and rivers. I asked him about the rivers, and he recited promptly in alphabetic order, "Arkansas, 1,460 miles; Colorado, 2,000 miles; Columbia, 1,270 miles," and so forth. With regard to the Ohio River he made a mistake and said "280" instead of "1,280" miles. I asked him which is longer, the Ohio or the Hudson, and after awhile he answered, "the Hudson." Two years later I asked him again the same question. He

[6] Koffka's reference to past experience appears to have a similar bearing: "We had to assume the traces as organized systems, and that presupposes that the processes which produced the traces are organized themselves; their organization can therefore not be a consequence of traces" (50, p. 463).

replied promptly, "the Ohio is longer." "How many miles long is the Ohio?" "I do not know, but at least a thousand miles, while the Hudson is only a few hundred miles long." He had forgotten in the meantime much of his memorized knowledge, but he had acquired with the help of maps and trips a general picture of the country including its main rivers.[7]

In this example understanding and mechanical memorization brought about different answers to the same question. It is therefore not conceivable that the organized whole, the understanding of American geography, was the result of the process of memorizing. The drills $2 \times 2 = 4$, $3 \times 3 = 9$, and the names of the rivers are not the means to understand the number series and the geography of the United States, respectively, but if organization is achieved some memorized knowledge can become part of it and can thereby acquire significance.

The contribution of senseless associations to the acquisition of meaningful connections is often expressed in the following form: meaningful learning is easier than senseless learning because the former only has to strengthen bonds already existent.[8] This explanation is said to account for the fact that it is easier to learn a series of words such as "table, chair, house, garden," than the syllables "kem, lap, zit." In formulating the implication of the "most commonly expressed theory" that "logical learning requires fewer new associations than rote learning of an equivalent amount of material" Lashley (55, p. 555) exposes the improbability of that argument. He says that in logical learning at least a relational framework must be constructed and the elements must be connected with the frame, "a process which would seem to involve more rather than fewer associations" (55, p. 556). The bearing of Köhler's argument is similar. He points out (45, p. 287 f.) that

[7] The *World Almanac* does not contain a map.

[8] We quoted on p. 238 the statement of Hollingworth about meaningful or rational learning, which partly consists in the utilization of previous learning. McGeoch asserts that "the ease of learning seems to vary directly as the meaningfulness of the material," because meaningful (and familiar) material has the advantage of old associations. Such material "is thus already partly learned before the formal learning period begins" (62, pp. 378/9).

pairs of words such as "lake sugar," "pencil gasoline" are easier to learn than nonsense syllables, although we might have thousands of bonds connecting "lake" or "pencil" with other words and scarcely any bonds connecting these words with "sugar" and "gasoline." Organization of those words is, however, so Köhler continues, easier than that of nonsense syllables, and because of the artificially created whole that comprises the two items temporary retention is achieved with less difficulty than in the case of the nonsense syllables. The formation of a whole is still easier with words such as "table chair," and so forth, with which a semblance of an understandable whole may be created. It is, of course, experience upon which depends the difficulty of organization. But experience in this context is not to be understood as "bonds existent," otherwise we shall never arrive at a satisfactory explanation of actual occurrences in view of the multiplicity of competing inhibitions and excitations. But experience in organizing, in forming groups, and in understanding may assist in later learning and explains certain differences in the difficulty of various learning processes.

There is also another reply to the above argument. It is not generally true that meaningful learning is easier than senseless learning. In this book we are not dealing with the results of learning senseless material in contrast to the results of learning meaningful material. To repeat a few times "lake sugar," "pencil gasoline" in order to be able to say "sugar" when the experimenter says "lake" is, of course, not meaningful learning, but memorization. It is not easy to compare the difficulties of memorization with those of meaningful methods of learning, that is, understanding by means of appropriate organization, because the results of the two processes differ. We compared the time required to learn the card tricks in a meaningful way with that required to learn them in a senseless way. If the card trick was simple, or if the goal was the quick performance of one single card trick, senseless learning was quicker and easier. But the quick and easy senseless learning resulted in brief retention of one trick, whereas the slower and more difficult understanding yielded knowledge applicable to many variations of the trick, even after a long period of time. In other instances, such as the learning of a number series like 581215 . . . , understanding proved to be a quicker and easier method of learning than memorization. But it is not permissible to derive a general law from such cases, because adequate organization, such as that required in meaningful methods of learning, must often proceed circuitously by making use of various examples and by detours at first in another direction than that which we intend ultimately to follow (cf. p. 125). In memorizing, and in direct practice in general, we choose the direct road to precisely what we want to know, and still that method is less efficient than a detour method, inasmuch as its results cannot be applied under different circumstances and will, if not often repeated, be quickly forgotten. Because of the great differences in the results of the various methods of learning, it is of hardly any value to compare the ease of learning or the time required for learning in understanding and in memorizing. It is unfortunate that we still read in textbooks of psychology that the main difference between meaningful learning and senseless learning is that the former is easier. Actually, however, the main difference is that meaningful learning is applicable and more lasting.

The conclusion that we do not have organization because of earlier experiences consisting of senseless connections, but that we have experience because of previous organization is not a new discovery. We have tried to establish it for learning, but previously it was established with regard to perceptions. In the psychological laboratories of Wertheimer and Köhler important investigations were carried out to discover how and to what extent experience influences visual perception, how it determines what we see and what we do not see.[9] In many instances there could be found no effect at all of experience that had consisted of a great number of repetitions. The gestalt laws of proximity, equality, closure, pregnance, determined what we saw and how we saw it, while frequent

---

[9] Cf. Wertheimer (105), Gottschaldt (26), Duncker (16), and especially Krolik (53); a very good summary of these experiments in Metzger (69).

previous experiences proved ineffective in determining the new perception. There are, however, cases of this type: a large piece of paper is moved up and down behind a long pencil; it is the pencil which appears to move, not the paper. The "illusion" is usually explained as the result of former experiences of the observer. He has seen pencils moving before a paper much more often than he has seen papers moving behind a pencil. That explanation was apparently confirmed by the first experiments. In a dark room an illuminated picture of a house was moved slowly toward a stationary automobile; the automobile, not the house, appeared to be moving. The same result was achieved, however, with many combinations of a large and a small object. The latter appeared to move, often contrary to habit: in changing the experimental setup in an appropriate way, a small tea cup could be seen to move toward a stationary big bus irrespective of which object was actually moved. Variations of the experiment showed that the arrangement, or constellation, of the objects, their relationship and closure, were the main factors in determining what is seen to move. In these examples it is the surrounded object rather than the surrounding object which we see moving, mostly in accordance with, but in some cases in opposition to, former experiences.

Laws concerning the arrangement or the organization of our perceptions determine what we perceive. Because those laws are operating, experience can develop and become powerful in determining later perceptions. Thus the same rules apply to the functioning of experience in perceiving and in learning. That is not just a coincidence. We had occasion to point out several times that organization plays a similar role in both these mental functions.

The reference to perception may throw light on a question which we have so far not discussed. We have analyzed the origin of organization in the learning process and in recall (by studying the situations in which the subjects learned how to solve the match tasks and in which they were tested on a later occasion). But we have not dealt with the *first* occurrence of organization and understanding. We know that "piecemeal additions of single experiences are not the causes of the organization of reality," to use the words of Wertheimer which refer to perception (105, p. 336). But "our nervous system developed under the conditions of the biological environment" (*loc. cit.*), and thus experience plays a role: [10] the gestalt principles, expressing the rules of organization, originated in interaction with the environment. Our perceptions are organized wholes in the sense that the distribution of the parts within the whole is determined by gestalt factors (Wertheimer 105, p. 349 *n*). What applies to a more or less unintentional organizing in perception also holds true for organizing in intentional learning.

One or Two Kinds of Learning

Memorizing is not the prototype of learning. Does it follow from that statement that there are two independent processes of learning—memorizing and understanding—and that one process cannot be traced back to the other? There is another alternative, because there are three possible assumptions about the original or primary form of learning. 1. Memorizing is the prototype of learning. 2. Understanding organized wholes is the prototype of learning. 3. Memorizing and understanding are distinct and independent learning processes.

The author believes that the second thesis is correct. The objective of this book was to show that the first thesis is not valid. It cannot be proved here that the third thesis is wrong and that the second thesis is right. Such proof would require a detailed analysis of the extensive investigations on association, conditioned reflex, and the acquisition of skills in adults, children, primitives, psychopaths, and animals. It would be necessary to study how the im-

---

[10] The thesis which rejects senseless connections, as assumed by associationism, as a factor bringing about organized wholes and nevertheless does not reject a genetic theory based on experience is expressed by Koffka as follows: "Association has unwittingly assumed a meaning which makes it practically synonymous with experience . . . But association is far from being synonymous with experience. It is *one* way of coping with experience . . . Therefore a criticism of associationism is not a rejection of a genetic theory. There are other, and I believe *better*, ways of treating experience than the concept of association" (50, p. 589).

plications derived from our knowledge of meaningful learning of human adults affect other types of learning processes. That can hardly be accomplished in this limited space. Therefore we shall only show here that good reasons can be given both for the assumption of a common principle governing all kinds of learning activities and against the assumption that the two types of learning are entirely independent of each other. Organization will be shown as that common principle. Under the circumstances most appropriate for learning, adequate organization leads to understanding. Memorizing may be regarded as a case in which organization reaches its "limit"; it is resorted to under circumstances which are not suitable to understanding.

To some extent we have already shown the relationship between the two processes of learning in the chapter on memory traces. Recognition of the occurrence of structural traces and individual traces as two distinct and independent carriers of remembering would correspond to the theory according to which the formation of senseless connections and understanding have nothing in common. However, we had occasion to call attention to transitions between the two kinds of traces which were recognized as two extreme forms of a continuous series. Whether a trace has more or less of the qualities of a structural or an individual trace depends on the form of organization and therefore on one common principle.

Our discussion of grouping was devoted to the demonstration that there are transitions even between rote learning of nonsense syllables and understanding of meaningful connections. By improving the coherence and structure of the organization we proceeded from artificial grouping of arbitrary contents toward the meaningful and understandable principle of a well-organized whole. And we have done more than to establish transitions between the two processes of learning: we have found that memorization of nonsense material has to show at least some qualities of grouping in order that retention and recall may follow. In order to be able to anticipate the consecutive items of a series of nonsense syllables or to reconstruct or recite the series, organization of the material was found to be necessary, at least in the rudimentary form of artificial groups.

We may refer to experiments of Thorndike in order to understand the role of organization in forming senseless connections. In several experiments Thorndike studied the formation of connections under circumstances in which the principle of the connection was hidden from the subjects. The subjects had to make judgments which were pure guesswork at the beginning.[11] By a simple method Thorndike was able to bring about improvement in the accuracy of guessing. The experimenter said "right" or "wrong" when the guesses of the subjects happened to be correct or false, respectively. Thorndike states that satisfying aftereffects (in this case the word "right" spoken by the experimenter) strengthen a connection. We may assume that such a description applies to the learning of hidden, arbitrary arrangements, because the word "right" changed the entire situation. The subjects were no longer confronted by a senseless sum of stimulations, but by a whole, which they could not understand, but could try to organize. The word "right" permitted and stimulated the beginning of grouping processes. In the experiments just described arbitrary groups embracing certain features of the cards were formed, in some cases probably in the form of a notion or hypothesis which was tested by later guesses.[12] Meaningful groups could not be

[11] One of the experiments of Thorndike had the following form (94, pp. 207 ff.). A large number of cards, each containing four straight lines, was presented. The lines were not quite the same length, but the differences were imperceptible. Actually there existed an arbitrary connection between certain features of each card: for example, if there was one thick line on a card, then the third line from the left was the longest. The subjects were not told of that arrangement, but were asked to guess which of the lines was the longest.

[12] But neither verbalization nor conscious understanding of the arrangement is a necessary requirement for the beginning of the grouping processes. Thorndike showed that some improvement in the accuracy of the guesses was achieved even by those subjects who in cross-examination at the end of the experiment admitted that they were ignorant of the construction of the series. He therefore speaks of an "unconscious strengthening of the connections" (94, p. 236, also 95, p. 29). We have found in chap. v, above, that in order that there should be certain learning effects one must not be consciously aware of the factors leading to the reorganization of a learning material and must not be able to verbalize them.

formed, because there was no understandable connection between the situation and the correct answer. The word "right" may operate under certain circumstances in a similar way as an incidental or an intentional discovery of a hidden arrangement. Whatever form the grouping processes have, the situation changes completely when the "and sum" of impressions is transformed into groups; the beginning of organization implies the beginning of learning.

We conclude that organization is a requirement for successful memorization. It must be present in some form in all kinds of learning. In some extreme cases, in which there is, not a lack of organization, but a minimum of organization, the parts (although connected with each other) are called independent units, because a weakly organized group is formed which exerts only a small influence on the parts of the group. Such is the case in memorizing nonsense syllables or telephone numbers.

The traditional laws of association, such as contiguity and frequency (exercise), appear to be valid when the strength of organization reaches its limit. We may employ the term association if we keep in mind that association does not represent the fundamental principle of mental life. As shown by the rules of artificial grouping discussed in the seventh chapter, organization influences even the connections between relatively discrete contents. Uniform bonds of equal strength do not persist among a large number of independent contents. Integration of independent contents into a whole [13] or joining ideas by virtue of their membership in a whole [14] are the more embracing laws of learning, from which, given discrete contents and the special circumstances of memorization, the laws of association can be derived.

Memorizing and organizing are therefore not coördinated concepts. Organization is the more general term of the two. In our experimental work we have contrasted memorization, not with organization, but with understanding. There are two reasons for this differentiation. First, memorization also requires some form

[13] Tolman (96, p. 333).
[14] Ogden (77, p. 186); cf. the formulation of Koffka cited on p. 28.

of organization. Secondly, not all organization is appropriate and understandable organization. The presence of meaningful connections is no assurance that organization such as is required for meaningful learning will ensue. Learning by understanding does not occur every time appropriate material is presented.

Some time ago we postulated that experience originates in organization. Our last discussion of memorizing shows that that statement is valid even in the case of the survival of memorized individual traces. If we find individual traces effective in a specific way, a minimum of organization must have been present, because organization is a necessary condition for retention.[15]

In the closing passage of Chapter IX two formulations were given of the ways of the functioning of memory. Now we see more clearly that the alternative is not whether we retain individual items and organize them later or whether we retain organized wholes and derive from them the individual items. For, it appears that we can hardly retain individual items except as a consequence of a process of organization. That process has several forms. We studied extensively the form in which specific contents were derived from whole-qualities. The second thesis on page 246 expresses the belief of the author that this process, the understanding or dealing with organized wholes, constitutes the prototype of learning. Another lower form of organization of individual items is the result of a special kind of learning, arrived at by isolating the learning material within its setting; this process of memorizing yields more-or-less transitory retention of concrete particulars without understanding.[16]

---

[15] As apparent exceptions to the universal validity of the statement that organization is a necessary condition for retention we may refer first to the phenomena of memory span. Immediate recall of a limited number of items may not show clearly effects of organizing. But does immediate recall without lasting effects deserve the name "experience"? Secondly, affectively or emotionally determined retention of specific items may perhaps occur without clear indication that the individual traces were formed by a process of organizing.

[16] In this connection certain ideas expressed by K. Goldstein are of interest. Goldstein finds (25, pp. 501 ff.) that in drill the acquisition of a performance is unrelated to the nature of the learner. "Drill is achieved by bringing a somehow isolated part of the organism into relationship with a certain part of the environment" (p. 502). We have not the space to discuss how Goldstein explains drill

Thorndike asserts that there is a correlation or correspondence between the amount of knowledge and the degree of intellect, between the number of facts a man knows and the quality of his reasoning.[17] There are important instances contradictory to that thesis, which has been discussed since the time of Aristotle. Of recent investigators Lashley finds that "the capacity to memorize has shown but low correlations with intelligence" (54, p. 14). Judd states that "memorization of facts frequently fails to result in the development of higher mental processes"; in experiments with college students low coefficients of correlation were found between recall of information and the ability to draw inferences from new data (38, p. 17 f.). The relation between memory and reasoning is probably much more complicated than we indicated in these few quotations. We only want to stress one point: should it be true, as Thorndike believes, that in general men of high intellectual ability also know many facts, then that would be an additional important argument for the common origin of the two processes of learning. Organization enables the acquisition and preservation of more-or-less rigid individual traces, and organized trace systems often carry with them a great number of such traces. Therefore command of a large amount of specific information should often be found in the same person who has the ability to organize in the proper way.

The last statement may serve to explain why many educators believe in the value of memorizing. We have referred above to the argument according to which the rigidity of memory traces,

---

in animals as a complex instead of a simple process. Man, according to Goldstein, can undertake drill voluntarily; he must make drill consciously a substitute for real practice in order that it should have lasting effects. "Drill is only effective through insight into, and realization of, its necessity on the part of the learner" (p. 504).—In the last sentences we find probably the explanation for the following result of experiments by Thorndike. "There can be no doubt that our subjects could and did learn facts and skills that were useless and even harmful to them, except for the money rewards and good reports as learners in the eyes of the experimenter and their own consciences" (95, p. 133). The subjects were college students, and the method by which they learned the "harmful" facts was memorization. They did so voluntarily because they realized the "necessity" of drill.

[17] Thorndike's book *Human Learning* (93, p. 171) closes with this thesis which should prove that there is only a quantitative, not a qualitative, difference between learning by trial and success and ideational learning.

that is attained by drill, is an important goal in itself. Now we can state, as a challenge to that argument, that there are many ways to achieve that fixation, which is important when automatic, quick, and never-changing responses are required. One way, which should be applied more frequently, is by meaningful methods of learning, which achieve that goal if the same specific contents are always placed in the center of the organization. Senseless drill of arbitrary connections is another way, which, however, is less frequent and less efficient than a third way, namely, the memorization of data belonging to a general context and understood to belong to a greater scheme. Thus in studying anatomy or geography a skeleton or a map, respectively, are usually presented which facilitate the memorizing (and the grouping) of the names of bones or rivers by forming a general reference system. In most cases it is therefore psychologically false to say that arbitrary connections between senseless names are formed by mere drill, because actually organization (by demonstration and explanation) precedes memorization, and hence the connections formed are no longer entirely arbitrary.

If it is accepted that organizing is the original form of learning and that memorizing is a special form of organization resorted to because the material is comparatively incoherent, then we can understand that the effects of the two processes of learning are apparently not always different. Most of the experiments reported in this book were devised to show the differences between the two processes. But the results of Experiment E made it difficult to determine whether the performance of one group was the outcome of understanding or of drilled habits (cf. p. 149). Real understanding may deteriorate into a routine response which in some cases we cannot distinguish from the results obtained by drill. But in other cases it is possible to determine the origin of a routine response. For real understanding not only makes it possible to perform in a routine manner, but also usually leaves further traces in the organism: it brings about an enrichment of mental life.

We do not advocate a purely monistic theory of learning when we attempt to deduce from the process of understanding organized wholes certain qualities of learning by memorizing. The differences between the two methods of learning and their various intermediate forms are probably of greater significance than the features which they have in common. From a practical point of view it is of paramount importance to determine when, with what material, for what purposes, and to what kind of learner each method should be applied with the greatest hope of success.

Conclusion

EDUCATIONAL IMPLICATIONS

IN VARIOUS experiments we found that knowledge was acquired by a process of learning by understanding. We distinguished that process from memorization. The former is characterized not by the attaching of new contents or responses to old contents or stimuli and the strengthening of the connection between such pairs or series. Rather, the essence of this type of learning is organization or reorganization of the given material by the learner. However, not all kinds of organization are sufficient; organization must be appropriate to the material if it is to yield understanding. Such organization enables the learner to gain understanding by discovering, developing, or creating consistent and inherent relations or whole-qualities. Meaningful organization is not restricted to the immediate learning material; it often proceeds circuitously, utilizing various examples and cues. It results in integrated knowledge of principles rather than in the acquisition of specific information.

Since relations and whole-qualities are not rooted in one specific material, recall of that which has been well understood may take the form of reconstruction. Frequently the whole-qualities alone are preserved, while the individual items are variable and must be reconstructed. This flexibility of the traces formed by understanding results in wide applicability—what has been learned by understanding can be applied under varied circumstances and to new as well as to practiced situations. The results of learning by understanding differ in still another respect from those of memorizing: the knowledge acquired by understanding is retained for long periods of time without substantial deterioration. Its organization can be improved by the use of examples, whereas memorized knowledge can be reinforced only by the repetition of the original situation and the original response.

If memorizing is considered a process of a lower grade, the erroneous notion may arise that memorizing is the original form of learning and that it may be raised to the level of understanding and applications merely by the addition of more associations. On the contrary, mechanical memorization appears to be a limiting case resorted to when a lack of inherent relations in the given material excludes the possibility of understanding. The genuine and good learning process requires appropriate organization.

If the foregoing statements are correct, or to put it in another way, if the psychology of learning developed in this book represents the description of the qualities and the laws of actual processes and occurrences, then our research must yield implications for educational practice. For, psychology of learning and educational psychology are not two independent disciplines; rather, certain important parts of the second represent applications to be derived from the findings of the first. Let us therefore make a very short survey of the relationship between the theories of modern educational practice and the established psychologies of learning. Just three examples will be cited.

W. H. Kilpatrick, in many passages of his book *Foundations of Method* (42), in which he presents the theory and the program of progressive education (especially of the project method), appears to evaluate positively the contribution of psychology to educational practice. He discusses a psychology of learning which consists mainly of the laws of readiness, exercise, and effect as formulated by Thorndike in his *Educational Psychology* (1913). But that psychology of learning is according to Kilpatrick not broad enough to form a basis for the entire scope of educational practice. Kilpatrick distinguishes between a narrow and a wider sense of method:

The narrow sense of method singles out for consideration one specific thing to be learned . . . The wider sense of method knows that in actual life one thing never goes on by itself. This wider method demands that we consider the actual facts, the real world. The narrow sense of method faces always an abstraction, an unreality [42, pp. 10 f.].

The psychology of learning . . . undertakes to answer the first problem [the narrow view of method] [p. 13].

The narrow problem is primarily psychological, the broad problem is rather moral, ethical, philosophical [p. 17].

The narrow problem [of method] concerns itself with how the children shall best learn this or that specific thing, generally named in advance. The wider problem concerns itself with all the responses being made . . . The newer education stresses the wider problem without, however, overlooking the other. In particular the wider problem is much concerned to build attitudes and appreciation [pp. 134 f.].

The psychologist is immediately concerned with laboratory conditions. For him, accordingly, learning largely means acquiring the ability *to give back,* on demand, the skill to do anything when a signal is given . . . But I am concerned with life . . . [p. 189].

These quotations seem to imply that the psychology of learning has a rather limited usefulness for education. But as psychologists we shall not admit that we are not concerned with life. Psychology of learning, in our opinion, has to deal with all the effects of the learning process on the pupil—not only with his learning of a specific thing—otherwise it is a psychology of an abstraction, of an unreality (as Kilpatrick said), and not a psychology of learning.

The relation between educational practice and psychology of learning is expressed in still more negative terms by C. H. Judd. It appears that in his opinion the psychology of learning of the past is not useless but harmful in its effects on education.

The most important reason for inadequate teaching is the general acceptance of a false psychology. . . . There was at one time, not long ago, a wholehearted acceptance of the psychology which regards the process of learning as nothing other than the memorizing of authoritative statements [38, p. 139] [or] the storing of the mind with knowledge [p. 144].

If psychology is to rescue education from the new formalism, . . . if the school subjects are to be taught by some method other than mere drill—there will have to be clear recognition of the difference between the lower and the higher forms of mental activity [p. 165].

Finally, we shall quote an author who has a high opinion of the achievements of the psychology of learning, but believes that the educators have not made sufficient use of it. J. L. Mursell states at the beginning of his *Psychology of Secondary School Teaching:*

Until recent years the secondary school and the college have been relatively static in this respect [in applying psychological principles in teaching]. Psychological knowledge has existed, but it has not been adequately applied at these higher levels [76, p. 1].

All three authors apparently agree that the present relationship between educational practice and psychology of learning is not quite satisfactory. Therefore the attempt to improve the relationship by changing certain fundamental propositions of the established psychologies of learning may be justified. However, the following argument may be raised against the plan of applying the results of our research to educational practice. One may believe that the psychology of learning as discussed in this book and educational practice are separated by a wide gulf, because the former deals with artificial laboratory situations, whereas the latter deals, or at least should deal, with preparation for life. We should teach, as far as possible, what the child and pupil will need in life—so we often read—whereas in this book the solution of "match tasks," a problem that may be called "needless and artificial," was used among others in order to analyze the qualities and laws of the learning process. What is the weight of this objection?

In experimenting with college students we could not use school topics or familiar problems of life as the material of our investigation. Our task was to arrive at certain results by scientific methods, without interference from external and uncontrollable factors. But this restriction of our studies does not imply that we have dealt with problems which are not encountered in school and in life. It could be shown—but we have no space here for the extensive investigation needed for that purpose—that the processes of memorizing and of learning by understanding are both used or may be used or should be used in school and life, and that the different results of these processes, as established in this book, occur also under conditions other than laboratory conditions.

We shall merely illustrate these statements by referring to certain topics of one school discipline, geometry, which we choose because of the geometrical nature of the problem used in our main experiment. In studying the processes of productive thinking, Wertheimer analyzed extensively the various methods by which the theorems of the area of the rectangle and the parallelogram are taught in school.[1] He found that the learning of formulas must be differentiated from the understanding of relations inherent in the problems. We may apply his analysis in devising the following plan of an experiment, which is not easy of administration because of the interference by previously acquired knowledge. Suppose one class memorizes by frequent repetition that the area of the trapezoid equals "half its altitude times the sum of its bases": $\frac{1}{2}h\ (b + b_1)$. In this case most pupils will acquire an "and sum" of various items (of $\frac{1}{2}h$, of $b + b_1$), which are unrelated to the area. Even the usual demonstrations and proofs often do not create real understanding of the relation between "half of the altitude" and the area of the trapezoid. We may predict on the basis of the experimental results obtained in this investigation that the class which had memorized the formula would forget more quickly and would be able to apply its knowledge to a smaller extent than would a class which had learned in a more reasonable way—similar to that which we called "method of examples and help." The problem (what is the area of the trapezoid?), the solution (the formula), and the steps leading from the former to the latter must, then, be organized in a way which yields an understandable whole. Thus it should be possible to use a school topic for studying the different qualities and the different results of memorizing and understanding.

Many similar demonstrations could be made in geometry as well as in other disciplines, in artificial laboratory situations and

[1] With the permission of Professor Wertheimer I refer here to a chapter in his forthcoming book on "productive thinking."

with subject matter taught in school, and in acquiring knowledge in actual situations of life. Real understanding—understanding derived from adequate organization of the material—is not unknown in educational practice. It may be that it is even better known there than in psychological theory. But educational practice may be improved by a progress of the psychology of learning. There is a difference between accidentally hitting upon the right method and choosing it because of a sound theoretical basis. Learning by understanding will take its proper place in the field of education when we appreciate the role of adequate organization and consciously orient our teaching methods according to the requirements of the material. The question is not only how to supplement pure memorizing by the introduction of explanations and demonstrations but also, and more significantly, how and to what extent mechanical memorizing and cramming can be eliminated by means of the adoption of meaningful methods of learning.

Since storing the mind with a great amount of specific data is not the only way and certainly not the best way of acquiring knowledge, we may examine briefly another field of possible application of our results. We have found that it is often not the direct and short road which leads to real understanding; we must resort to structurally clear examples in order to organize a given material adequately. We now ask: is there a connection between the limitations of direct practice in memorization and the tendency toward specializing in school, in professions, and in life in general? May it not be that too much specializing is related to a too-great dependence on short cuts, which bring about routine responses under one set of conditions, but which restrict the applicability of knowledge by preventing the apperception of the greater context, which alone makes specialized manipulations and specialized information meaningful? Some of our results indicate that by learning many different things the knowledge of one subject matter or of one part of a professional activity can be enriched and its usefulness enlarged. Thorough specialized knowledge of one subject matter or one type of activity is a valuable goal, but it may be that present-day society needs also men with a different type of knowledge: men who are able to survey the relationship between several spheres of science, who have acquired understanding of various forms of life, and, most important of all, who have learned how to arrive at understanding itself, how to discover inherent relations—not just how to give back experience in the form in which they had received it.

How, then, shall we characterize the major aim of education if it is not the acquisition of specialized information? Pupils should learn to learn—that is the best that the school can do for them. They should not merely learn to memorize—they should learn to learn by understanding.

APPENDICES

Appendix 1

DETAILS OF EXPERIMENTS

Procedures in the Training Period of the
Card-Trick Experiments

WE SHALL DESCRIBE FIRST the procedure adopted in the case of groups and of individual subjects who learned by memorizing. After the subjects had witnessed the performance of a complicated trick with a large number of cards, they were addressed as follows: "I suppose you would like to know how to perform this trick. I shall teach you the trick with four red and four black cards. We want to arrange these eight cards so that the uppermost card in the deck is red; it is to be placed on the table. The next card should be placed at the bottom of the deck without determining what card it is; then a black card should be placed on the table. This procedure should be continued as long as there are cards in the pack. In order to achieve this goal you must take in your hand: first, two red cards; then, one black card; then, two red cards; and at last three black cards." (The last four sentences were written on a paper or on the blackboard.) "You are to learn this order so as to remember it later. We will, therefore, repeat three times: four red and four black cards are to be arranged as follows: first two red cards, then . . ." (The experimenter pointed to the paper while the subjects read aloud.) In order to learn to perform the trick with thirteen spades, the following arrangement was presented to the subjects: ace, queen, 2, 8, 3, jack, 4, 9, 5, king, 6, 10, 7. The subjects repeated the series until they could recite it twice without a mistake.

In the training period the subjects who learned by understanding used the following procedure. It was exemplified in most experiments with the trick by four red and four black cards alternating.

"We must arrange eight cards. We don't know in what order, therefore we put eight question marks on the blackboard. The first question mark represents the first card; the second question mark the second card; and so forth. The last question mark represents the last card. According to the task, the first card should be a red card. The second card should be placed below the others, we do not know what it is, therefore it is represented by a question mark. The third card must be a black card, while the fourth card is unknown (a question mark)," and so forth. (The letters and the signs reproduced in the second horizontal line of the table below were written on the blackboard while these directions were being given.)

"The four cards which are designated by letters on the blackboard are supposed to be on the table. The four cards designated by question marks are still in my hand. Now we must find out what cards these remaining question marks represent. My two last moves were to put a black card on the table and an unknown card at the bottom of the pack. The next card (that is, the first of the remaining question marks) must, therefore, be a red card. The following card, represented by the following question mark, has to be placed below the others and remains therefore a question mark. Then follows a black card and lastly a question mark." (Compare the third line of the table below.)

"Two question marks remain, that is, I have two unknown cards in my hand. The first one following a black card and a question mark must be a red card, while the next one remains a question mark. This one being the last card, following a red card, must be black.

"Now we are ready to add up our findings. First we have a red card, then another red card . . ."

Scheme to Be Written on the Blackboard

?	?	?	?	?	?	?	?
R	?	Bl	?	R	?	Bl	?
	R		?		Bl		?
			R				?
							Bl
R	R	Bl	R	R	Bl	Bl	Bl

In the above scheme R represents red and Bl represents black.

In a few cases a different card trick was used for demonstration for subjects who learned by understanding. The procedure can be adapted to any one of the card tricks.

Additional Results of the Card-Trick Experiments

The time required to solve the tasks: In the first group experiment there were used as tests practiced tasks, simple variations of practiced tasks, and tasks with a new, previously not-practiced form (p. 38 f.). The first test consisted of the task practiced both by the memorizing and the understanding groups. In this task eight of the nine subjects of the Memorizing Group completed their work before the quickest worker of the Understanding Group did so. The result learned was repeated more quickly than the task could be solved with the help of an understood scheme. However, in the second task, which represented a variation of the principle, five subjects of Group Und. were ready first, and not one made a mistake. Then several subjects of Group Mem. announced that they were ready, but not one of them produced the correct result. The subjects finished their work in a similar succession in Task 3, a difficult variation, while in Task 4 (which will be discussed below) the members of the two groups needed about the same amount of time. Task 5 was a practiced task for Group Mem., but Group Und. had not seen the task before and had to apply the principle in order to solve it. Here Group Mem. worked quicker, six of its members being ready before the quickest worker belonging to Group Und. finished his work.

Behavior of some members of the Memorizing Group: As mentioned in the text, some members of the group which had memorized previously the arrangement required for the solution of two card tricks (Trick A and Trick B) adopted during the tests an attitude which cannot be characterized as a direct effect of the training in the memorization period. When the first task was given, which was a test of the practiced Trick A (correct arrangement: R R Bl R R Bl Bl Bl), there was one among the nine subjects of Group Mem. who was not satisfied with simply putting down the result memorized a short time ago. This subject made calculations in order to find the correct arrangement. She was unable to complete her work within the allotted time, which explains the false result recorded by one member of Group Mem. for Task 1 (cf. Table 1 on p. 39). But the same subject recorded the one correct solution of Group Mem. for Task 2 (here the correct arrangement is: R Bl Bl Bl R R). It was not just a chance solution; the subject discovered the principle during the working time allotted to Tasks 1 and 2. This subject made no mistakes in any of the later tests. Even in Task 5, the test of a memorized trick, this subject chose to solve the problem with the help of a principle rather than to rely on her memory.

The behavior of the other subjects of Group Mem. upon the presentation of the new Task 2, which required the arrangement of six cards, whereas the tasks which had been learned consisted of eight cards, was as follows: Three subjects immediately noticed that the task differed from everything they had learned, and they abstained from repeating any of the arrangements memorized. They tried to solve the new task unassisted by their former training, but they did not succeed in the short time allowed. The other five subjects began by writing down the first six letters of the well-known series of eight cards. Two of these subjects were then satisfied, while one subject wrote the word "false" beneath the result without attempting—at least on paper—a better solution. Two subjects worked hard to correct the obviously false result, but without success.

Upon the presentation of Task 3, which had the entirely new feature of omitting two cards instead of one card, all the subjects of the memorizing group showed signs of perplexity and consternation. Not one copied the well-practiced arrangement, all having noticed that the order must be different if two cards—not one card—are omitted each time. There was only one subject, however, who succeeded this time in solving the problem. The correct arrangement of this task is: R Bl Bl Bl R Bl R R.

In Task 4 two subjects of Group Mem. wrote the results immediately in the correct order; they noticed that they had to use the arrangement memorized for Trick A in spite of the fact that the material given was that with which Trick B was previously learned. The correct arrangement of Task 4 is: E E U E E U U U. E denotes a card with an even number, and U a card with an uneven number; this is the same arrangement as that of Trick A if we write E and U instead of R and Bl. Three other subjects arrived at the correct result after several attempts, while four subjects were unable to apply the well-memorized knowledge under the slightly changed conditions.

Task 5, as a pure memory test of Trick B (arrangement: 1 5 2 7 3 6 4 8), without doubt would have been correctly solved by all nine subjects of the group had it not been for the intervening work with similar material. The recollection of two subjects was falsified by the preceding similar and nevertheless different tasks.

In Task 6 the subjects were asked to arrange four red and four black cards so that at first the four red cards and then the four black cards should be placed on the table and between every two cards placed on the table one card should be put at the bottom of the deck. The solution, R Bl R Bl R Bl R Bl, is found by many persons within a very short time without any previous instruction. Task 6 thus differs structurally from all other tasks, in which unassisted problem solving encounters much greater difficulties. In our experiment, however, this task was preceded by five tests (and a training period) which were all similar in form although not in structure. This *Einstellung,* caused by the immediately preceding experiences, explains the result: only seven of the nine subjects of Group Mem. and only three of the nine subjects of Group Und. recognized Task 6 as an easy task that did not require the application of the previously acquired knowledge; they immediately wrote the correct result on their paper, which did not contain any signs of further calculation. But two subjects of Group Mem. were completely at a loss, as they were when other difficult unlearned problems were presented to them, and six subjects of Group Und. did again what they had done in the previous tasks, namely, they applied the method which they had learned. The application of this method takes much more time and is more troublesome than the simple insight into what is required to solve the easy task. But the habit of using this method was powerful enough to prevent the subjects from noticing that Task 6 could be solved without the use of the learned principle. Applying a well-known principle can thus become a habit which leads to a slower and more laborious reaction than would be possible without such a habit.[1]

Concerning the behavior of the Understanding Group it should be reported only that the new tasks did not cause any consternation or perplexity on the part of the members of this group. When new tasks were presented to them, these subjects manifested an attitude similar to that of the subjects who had no previous practice at all (the members of the control group). The main difference was found in the results: the calculations made by most members of Group Und. yielded correct arrangements, whereas the test papers of the control group contained only two of the possible twenty correct solutions (see the table on p. 39 with respect to the first five tasks).

A few further observations should be mentioned concerning the behavior of the memorizers in the training period. In the experiments, in which the arrangement of thirteen spades was memorized, one subject arrived at the complete mastery of the order in much shorter time than the other subjects. She had to memorize "ace, queen, 2, 8, 3, jack, 4, 9, 5, king, 6, 10, 7." Instead of simply obeying the instruction and reading the series several times, the subject noticed that she need not learn the first, the third, the fifth, and so forth, figure (taking ace as one). Furthermore, she grouped the remaining numbers and cards in the following way: queen, omit three cards, jack, omit three cards, king; then, 8, omit three cards, 9, omit three cards, 10. This method of grouping facilitated the learning process and, as was shown in later tests, improved the reproduction. Yet, when the subject was given new and slightly different tasks, she was unable to solve them. Thus the grouping method, although making use of certain relationships, did not suffice to bring about an understanding of the principle. It may be called an intermediate method, inasmuch as it made use of the fact, connected with the principle, that every second card alternates, or better still, it may be called a not-successful attempt to bring "sense" into the series which the experimenter asked the subjects to memorize.

The experimenter tried to persuade a few subjects to memorize the arrangement required for card tricks with twenty-six or more cards. It is difficult to find subjects who are willing to undertake this task. The order of twenty-six or more cards can only be memorized with the help

---

[1] A. S. Luchins will publish shortly extensive experiments on habit formation of a similar kind; see also Maier (66, p. 141) and Duncker (15).

of various grouping processes similar to that mentioned above, and even so it is a difficult and wearisome process. The subjects are again and again inclined to stop memorizing a meaningless series. Instead of repeating artificial groups, they want to try to achieve an understanding of the principle.

Appendix 2

STATISTICS ON TRANSFER OF TRAINING

The Reliability of the Differences

FIRST WE SHALL PRESENT calculations which were made to determine whether the differences established in the performances of the groups learning in different ways can be considered statistically significant. The average scores of the groups and the standard error of the averages were given in the tables summing up the experimental results in Chapter IV. The standard errors were rather large. That is caused by the frequently mentioned fact that giving the same method of teaching to all members of a group, does not necessarily insure the same method of learning by each individual. We were interested in making the various groups used in the same experiment comparable, but were not concerned with the elimination of individual differences within each group. Thus there may have been differences among the individual subjects of each of our groups, such as various degrees of attentiveness and fatigue in the course of instruction, and various degrees of intelligence. Furthermore, certain subjects may have been content to memorize without question, while others may have speculated about the principles of the tasks in addition to memorizing. Differences in the types of the individual subjects may have also played a part in bringing about different results, as we shall discuss below with special reference to the subjects taught by the arithmetical method. Differences in the past experience of the subjects (such as familiarity or lack of familiarity with geometrical figures) on the other hand, have not been found to influence the learning effects.

Because of the differences just enumerated it was to be expected that the tables containing the distribution of the individual scores of a group will show a rather wide scatter of values. Even after instruction with a "good" method a certain number of low scores was to be expected, while "bad" instruction could not exclude the possibility of a certain number of high scores. That expectation necessarily brought about overlapping in the frequency tables of the groups.

In addition, because of the scoring method used the frequency polygons could not form a regular and smooth curve. The original plan of the experiments, namely, to score only perfect solutions of a task, could not be carried out in all experiments. In each experiment a few test papers were found which could not be classified as correct only because of the omission of minor details and indistinct markings, which were apparently due to lack of time or to inattentiveness or to lack of differentiation between unsuccessful and later successful attempts. It would have been unjust to give a zero-score to such "probable solutions," and therefore we have awarded them a score of one or two. The perfect solution of a task was scored four in all group experiments. An exception to this rule was made with regard to "easy tasks" which were included in Experiments A, B, and E. We call "easy" a task which was solved by a distinctly larger percentage of the control group than were other tasks of the same experiment. The solution of such a task, for example, Tasks 3 and 6, was scored two. The scoring method was, of course, the same for all groups in one experiment. The following distribution of the scores of Experiment A, in which there were two difficult new tasks and one easy new task, should serve to exemplify the scoring method and to indicate the extent of overlapping in the scores.

TABLE 20. FREQUENCY DISTRIBUTION OF EXPERIMENT A, RETEST SCORES WITH THREE NEW TASKS
Range 0–10

Scores	0	1	2	3	4	5	6	7	8	9	10	*Total*
Group Con.	5	2	8	0	2	0	3	0	0	0	0	20
Group Mem.	3	1	8	1	1	0	5	0	0	0	0	19
Group Ex.	0	0	5	1	1	1	4	1	1	0	7	21

Because of the scoring system used, the scores 0, 2, 6, 10 were more frequent than the intermediate scores.

The averages which were given in Table 4 of Chapter IV were computed from the above table. In order to determine the reliability of the differences between these averages, the critical ratios (in terms of sigma) were calculated, with the following results.

TABLE 21. CRITICAL RATIO OF THE DIFFERENCES IN EXPERIMENT A

Groups	*Test*	*Retest*
Ex.—Mem.	4.02	4.14
Ex.—Con.	5.40	4.93
Mem.—Con.	1.97	0.98

According to the generally accepted assumptions the differences obtained between Group Ex. and the other two groups are "very significant," while those between Group Mem. and the control group are statistically not reliable. The experiment thus indicates a considerable learning effect for Group Ex., but does not offer proof of learning by

Group Mem. In Experiment B some of the critical ratios between the learning groups were smaller than in Experiment A.

TABLE 22. CRITICAL RATIO OF THE DIFFERENCES IN EXPERIMENT B

Groups		*Groups*	
Test [a]			
Help—Arith.	0.86	Arith.—Mem.	1.09
Help—Mem.	2.11	Arith.—Con.	2.56
Help—Con.	3.50	Mem.—Con.	1.73
Retest [b]			
Help—Arith.	2.54	Arith.—Mem.	1.37
Help—Mem.	4.33	Arith.—Con.	3.46
Help—Con.	6.40	Mem.—Con.	2.34
[a] Cf. Table 6.		[b] Cf. Table 7.	

There is a significant difference between Group Help and the other three groups in the retest, while in the test the difference between Groups Help and Arith. is unreliable. The difference between Groups Arith. and Mem. is in both cases not significant.

These calculations have no reference to the main result of Experiment B, presented in Table 8. Since in this experiment there were only two tasks in each subdivision of each group, the subjects could obtain three scores: they could solve no task, or one task, or two tasks. We do not have a sufficient number of steps to calculate their deviations. But the frequency distribution given in Table 8 shows clearly that in solving new tasks there was a striking difference in the performance of the various groups: in the fifty test papers of Group Help we found twenty-four solutions of new tasks (48 percent), while in the fifty-four test papers of Group Mem. we found only seven solutions of new tasks (13 percent).

Only the average results of Experiment C were included in Table 10. Further information about the performance of the various groups will be presented here in form of frequency distributions. In this experiment, too, there were only two tasks in each subdivision, but careful examination of the test papers justified the award of a limited number of intermediate scores, as recorded in Table 23.

The relation of the performances of the two groups is shown in a still clearer way in fig. 22. From Table 23 we plotted cumulative frequency polygons, which indicate both for the practiced and for the new tasks the number of subjects who solved two tasks, one task, and no task. More subjects solved one task than solved two tasks, because all subjects who solved two tasks also solved one task, and so forth. Of the eight curves six are almost undistinguishable from each other,

TABLE 23. FREQUENCY DISTRIBUTION OF EXPERIMENTS C1 AND C3
EXPERIMENT C1

TASKS SOLVED	PERCENTAGE OF SOLUTION	NUMBER OF SUBJECTS IN GROUP MEM.		NUMBER OF SUBJECTS IN GROUP HELP	
		Practiced Tasks	*New Tasks*	*Practiced Tasks*	*New Tasks*
2	100	10	2	8	6
	75	2	0	1	2
1	50	11	8	8	8
	25	2	2	0	2
0	0	1	14	5	4
Total		26	26	22	22
Average percentage		67.3	25.0	58.0	54.5

EXPERIMENT C3

TASKS SOLVED	PERCENTAGE OF SOLUTION	*Practiced Tasks*	*New Tasks*	*Practiced Tasks*	*New Tasks*
2	100	8	1	7	8
	75	1	0	1	2
1	50	11	4	12	10
	25	2	4	1	1
0	0	6	19	6	6
Total		28	28	27	27
Average percentage		52.7	14.3	51.8	54.6

while two are of an entirely different shape. Group Mem., in Experiment C1 and in Experiment C3, solved the new tasks in a way distinctly inferior to the way in which it solved the practiced tasks, while in the performance of Group Help there was almost no difference in the solving of new and old tasks. The new-tasks curve of Group Help is much "higher" than the new-tasks curve of Group Mem., indicating that Group Help solved the new tasks much better than did Group Mem. The four curves of Group Help have a form which is very similar to the practiced-tasks curve of Group Mem.: there is no significant difference between six sets of performances. In order to check on the reliability of these results, calculations have been made by means of the chi-square technique. Pearson's P-coefficient is less than .01 for the comparison of Group Mem.'s practiced and new scores (both in Experiment C1 and in C3), indicating a probability of more than 99 percent that the differences are not due to chance. The comparison of Group Help's practiced and new scores yields P-coefficients of .90 and .95, indicating a very high probability that the differences are due to chance.

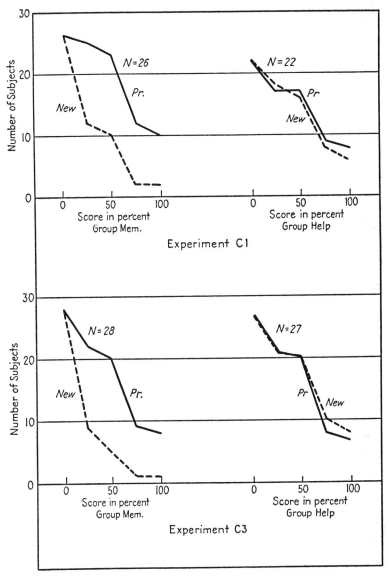

Fig. 22. *Cumulative Frequency Polygons*
Pr = practiced tasks; New = new tasks

Transfer Coefficients

The differences in the performances of the various groups, the reliability of which we have just studied, constitute differences in the transfer effect. The main questions were: to what extent can different groups solve "new tasks" and how significant are the differences in their performance with "new tasks"? With certain groups we have obtained an extensive and with others a very small transfer effect. But as yet we have not measured exactly the extent of that effect.

The measurement of the transfer effect requires the differentiation between direct effect and transfer effect of the same training. Suppose a rat runs a maze A at the beginning of an experiment in sixty seconds (score one in initial Test A according to an arbitrary scoring table) and runs a different maze X also in sixty seconds (score one in initial Test X). The animal then receives practice with maze A ending with a test (last trial) in which he requires ten seconds (score six in Test A); then the rat is placed in maze X and completes a run in, let us say, twenty seconds (score five in Test X). We now call the improvement in running maze A (the practiced maze) the direct effect of the practice, and we call the improvement in running maze X the transfer effect. But the improvement from initial Test X to Test X cannot serve as an exact measure of the transfer effect. We must take into account whether such an improvement is the consequence of a very effective or of a less effective practice period. This we may do by computing the ratio of the two improvements:

(1) Transfer effect of practice $A = \dfrac{\text{Test X} - \text{Initial Test X}}{\text{Test A} - \text{Initial Test A}}$. In the ex-

ample above the transfer effect is equal to $\dfrac{5-1}{6-1} = \dfrac{4}{5} = 80$ percent.[1]

In order to apply the formula to our experiments we must change it in one respect. In our case it was not possible to determine a score for an initial performance. An initial test which could be compared with a final test would itself have constituted in our experiments a great amount of training. Several unassisted trials before the actual practice would

---

[1] The formula given above differs from the most common and most simple formula, according to which the transfer effect of A is measured by the difference between the performances in Test X and initial Test X (when we made first initial Test X, then practiced A, and concluded the experiment with Test X). Abelson (2, pp. 134 ff.) advanced convincing arguments against using this method of measurement, even if it is supplemented by the introduction of a control group. Apart from some further points, Abelson explains that we should not express the transfer effect in percentages of the initial performance. His second transfer pattern is identical with our formula, except that here too he adds a control group.

have exerted a practice effect by themselves. In order to determine the effect of the methods applied in the training period alone, we had to compress the initial test into a very short fore-test. But it is possible to measure the transfer effect without having an initial test score. Just what the initial test was supposed to accomplish—namely, the determination of a score for unassisted trials—was achieved by administering the test to a control group. Assuming that the control group is equivalent to the learning group, we may change formula (1) into: (2)

Transfer effect of Practice A $= \dfrac{\text{Test X} - \text{Control Score X}}{\text{Test A} - \text{Control Score A}}$. Suppose that

A is the ability to solve Tasks 2 and 10, and that X is the ability to solve Tasks 11 and 16 (Experiment C). We practice A but we do not practice X. In order to determine the direct effect of practice A, we test A with the practice group and an equivalent control group and compute the difference between these two tests. The improvement in the unpracticed tasks X must be measured in the same way: the X score of a control group will be deducted from the X score of the group which practiced A. The ratio of the two improvements serves as the measure of the transfer effect. We may write: Transfer Effect $= \dfrac{\text{New(TG)} - \text{New C}}{\text{Old(TG)} - \text{Old C}}$. TG stands for training group, C for control group, "new" for a task, performance, trait, function which was not practiced, and "old" for one which was practiced.

We shall call the above ratio, when expressed in percentages, the transfer coefficient. It expresses the relation of the indirect effect of practice to the direct effect of practice. To explain how the formula was applied to the scores of the experiments, we take first Experiment C, to which we have just referred. Here the control score was 11.7 for both the old and the new tasks. In the test made one week after the practice period Group Mem. had a score of 67.3 for the practiced tasks and 25.0 for the new tasks. The transfer coefficient is equal $\dfrac{25.0 - 11.7}{67.3 - 11.7} = \dfrac{13.3}{55.6} = 24$ percent. To compute the transfer coefficients for Experiment B (retest), we can use the ratios of the net scores given in Table 8.

TABLE 24. TRANSFER COEFFICIENTS

Groups	Percentages in Exp. C1	Percentages in Exp. C3	Percentages in Exp. B
Group Mem.	24	7	− 0.3
Group Help	92	107	89
Group Arith.	..	..	109

In Experiment B we find a small negative transfer effect in case of Group Mem. When we attempt to compute the transfer coefficients for Experiment A, an additional difficulty arises, because here both test and retest included only one old task and three new tasks. An exact determination of the transfer coefficients is not possible, but we may find an approximate value by dividing the net score of the three new tasks by three. The calculation also requires the introduction of scores for the practiced task, which were not included in Table 4. With the help of such expedients we obtain the following results. The four coefficients are comparable with each other, but are perhaps not exactly comparable with the coefficients of the other experiments.

TABLE 25. TRANSFER COEFFICIENTS IN EXPERIMENT A

Groups	Test Percentages	Retest Percentages
Group Mem.	16	21
Group Ex.	63	90

The transfer coefficients [2] are in every case much higher for the Groups Help and Ex. than for Group Mem. For the first-named groups we have generally higher coefficients in later tests than in earlier tests.

Averages and Individuals

The transfer coefficient is a ratio of average scores. The importance of average scores should not be underestimated. While it may be said that individual results may be due to chance, that argument cannot be advanced against the regularity which is evident in all average scores of Experiments A, B, and C. In these experiments there were four groups which obtained "good" instruction (Group Help and Ex. taken together). The 98 subjects in these groups had an average transfer coefficient of almost 90 percent. On the other hand, the 106 subjects belonging to the various Groups Mem. had an average transfer coefficient of 13 percent. This result is of special significance if we want to answer the question posed by educational psychology, namely, how should we teach a class if it is our intention that the class as a whole shall be able to perform new tasks well? Psychological theory, however, is also interested in a

---

[2] The same calculations can also be made for the card-trick experiment, the results of which were reported on p. 47. We compare the scores of one old and one new task: Trick 2 (new) and 3 (old) in the test, and Trick 5 (new) and 3 (old) in the retest. After deducting the control group scores we obtain the following transfer coefficients:

	Test Percentages	Retest Percentages
Group Mem.	15	39
Group Und.	106	112

different problem. We may ask: is it possible that by learning A and B we get to know X and Y as well as or better than A and B? Under what circumstances will that be the case, and under what other circumstances may we arrive at the opposite result, namely, that learning A and B results in nothing but the knowledge of A and B? If we only compute the averages, these questions will not be answered definitely. Group averages may obscure the results. It may be that an average transfer effect of 80 percent is arrived at in spite of a very low transfer effect on the part of a few subjects and a very high one on the part of other subjects.[3]

It is possible to propose a formula for measuring the transfer effect which to some extent is not subject to the objections given above. Instead of computing the average scores for new and for practiced tasks and figuring out the ratio of these averages, we may compute individual transfer ratios by dividing the new-tasks score of each subject by his practiced-tasks score. Then it is possible to compute the average of the individual transfer ratios, to determine its variability, to state the transfer ratio of each quartile, and so forth.[4]

If we want to compute the individual transfer ratios, we encounter the difficulty that we do not have control scores corresponding to each subject's test score. Yet this difficulty is not of great import when the practiced tasks and the new tasks are comparable. In this case, which applies to Experiment C and, to a lesser extent, also to Experiment B (leaving the "tested tasks" out of consideration), we can arrive at significant results by merely dividing the individual new scores by the individual practiced scores. Another method which may be of some value is to deduct the average control score from each subject's test score in order to determine the probable learning effect for each subject.

There is, however, a second difficulty which for the transfer experiments reported in Chapter IV cannot be overcome. It is not possible in these experiments to calculate the averages of the individual transfer ratios. The reason is simple: we have in each experiment a few individual transfer ratios of infinite and of zero. There were subjects who solved one or both new tasks, but not one of the practiced tasks: dividing their new-

---

[3] The same problem recurs in Chapter VI, when the improvement in recall after the lapse of time is studied. In discussing "reminiscence" the statistical difficulty just referred to was clearly stated by G. O. McGeoch (61) and Bunch (12), who speak of the inadequacy of averages as a measure of reminiscence; the percentage of those who have reminiscence is there suggested as a good measure. We follow this lead, because we believe that the same arguments hold true for the transfer effect as for reminiscence.

[4] The ratio of the average scores is different from the average of the individual ratios because $\frac{a + b + c}{a_1 + b_1 + c_1}$ is not equal to $\frac{a}{a_1} + \frac{b}{b_1} + \frac{c}{c_1}$.

tasks scores by the zero-score for practiced tasks we get an infinite transfer ratio. The difficulty is not smaller in the opposite case, in which one or two of the practiced tasks was solved, but none of the new tasks. The transfer ratio of zero may in this case express either a great or a slight superiority of the practiced tasks over the new tasks. We can under these circumstances compute the frequency distribution of the various individual transfer ratios, and this has been done in Table 26, in which the control scores were not taken into account.

TABLE 26. FREQUENCY DISTRIBUTION OF THE INDIVIDUAL TRANSFER RATIOS
EXPERIMENT B, RETEST

TRANSFER EFFECT	NEW SCORE	PRACTICED SCORE	NUMBER OF SUBJECTS *Group Help*	*Group Arith.*	*Group Mem.*
Infinite	Pos. [a]	0	2	3	· 1
Over 100 percent	Pos. >	Pos.	4	3	0
100 percent	Pos. =	Pos.	9	6	1
Under 100 percent	Pos. <	Pos.	3	2	5
Zero	0	Pos.	5	4	10
No value	0	0	2	6	10
Total			25	24	27

EXPERIMENT C

TRANSFER EFFECT	NEW SCORE	PRACTICED SCORE	*Group Help* C1	C3	*Group Mem.* C1	C3
Infinite	Pos.	0	2	3	0	0
Over 100 percent	Pos. >	Pos.	5	5	0	2
100 percent	Pos. =	Pos.	4	8	7	3
Under 100 percent	Pos. <	Pos.	7	5	5	4
Zero	0	Pos.	1	3	13	13
No value	0	0	3	3	1	6
Total			22	27	26	28

[a] Pos. = positive value.

On the basis of this table further statistical calculations could be made. For each fraction of the groups—for example, for subjects who had a transfer effect of more than 100 percent—an average could be computed, and its variability could be stated. We abstain from these calculations. Table 26 suffices to indicate how the groups, taken as a whole, have learned. It indicates also the divergence between teaching and learning: although the teaching was the same for an entire group, there were a few individual subjects in each group whose transfer ratio differs from that which is typical for their group—probably because they learned in a way which was not intended by the method of teaching. The implications of Table 26 are discussed in Chapter V.

Statistics for Experiment E

A comparison of the performances of various groups with regard to practiced tasks and new tasks is offered also by the main test of Experiment E, discussed in Chapter VI. The reliability of the results of this experiment can be computed by means of the standard errors of the averages which are given in Table 27.

TABLE 27. STANDARD ERROR OF THE AVERAGES OF EXPERIMENT E

Tests	Group I	Group II	Group III
Immediate test	.66	.57	.61
First intermediate test	..	.71	.75
Second intermediate test	..	.53	.56
Third intermediate test	..	.71	.26
Main test (practiced tasks)	.71	.66	.11
Main test (new tasks)	.81	.57	.65

The standard errors are of about the same size in all tests, except that they decrease rapidly for Group III, which was tested several times with the practiced tasks. The critical ratio of the differences is of major importance with respect to the results of the main test. The following ratios are obtained.

TABLE 28. CRITICAL RATIO OF THE DIFFERENCES IN EXPERIMENT E

Groups	Practiced Tasks	New Tasks
I– II	0.55	1.09
I–III	5.37	1.92
II–III	4.99	3.54

The performance of Group III differs significantly from the performance of the other two groups. The differences between Groups I and II are statistically not reliable.

Next we may calculate the transfer coefficients according to the formula explained above (new score minus control score divided by old score minus control score).

TABLE 29. TRANSFER COEFFICIENTS IN EXPERIMENT E

Group	Percentage
Group I	94
Group II	108
Group III	18½

The individual transfer ratios, computed in the manner described in the preceding section of this Appendix, show the distribution recorded in Table 30.

TABLE 30. INDIVIDUAL TRANSFER RATIOS IN EXPERIMENT E

TRANSFER EFFECT	NUMBER OF SUBJECTS		
	Group I	*Group II*	*Group III*
Infinite	0	0	0
Over 100 percent	7	8	0
100 percent	4	8	1
Under 100 percent	5	6	16
Zero	3	0	4
No value	0	0	0
Total	19	22	21

From Table 30 it is possible to calculate the averages of the individual transfer ratios, because here we find no "infinite transfer effects" and only a limited number of "zero transfer effects." The averages amount to 103 percent for Group I, 128 percent for Group II, and 38 percent for Group III. These averages are without exception higher than the transfer coefficients computed above. This discrepancy may be due to a large extent to the fact that no control scores were deducted in computing the individual transfer ratios. For our purposes, however, the absolute values of the various transfer measures are not of primary significance. We are here concerned with the differences in the transfer effects of the three groups. The average transfer ratios and the transfer coefficients show the same regularity: the transfer effect is small in the case of Group III, whose performance in the main test was characterized as resulting from routine training with three practiced tasks, whereas it is very substantial in the case of the other two groups, which were taught in a "meaningful way." The average transfer ratio, as well as the transfer coefficient, is higher for Group II than for Group I, which difference indicates a favorable effect of the intermediate training with various tasks.[5]

Equation of Groups

As has been stated several times, the value of the results of the experiments depends on the comparability of the various groups used in the same experiment. If we had selected subjects having superior learning ability as members of Group Help and less ability as members of Group Mem., the results might even have been worthless. We chose a procedure intended to safeguard against such an eventuality. In City College in

[5] The data of Table 30 have been summarized in Table 13, which was discussed in connection with the theory of transfer on p. 130.

New York there are often so many students in one course that they must be divided into several classes. The attendance in each class depends on the student's preference. Such similar classes were used. In addition, without knowing the classes the experimenter decided that the 10 o'clock class, for instance, should form Group Mem.; the 11 o'clock class, Group Help; and so forth. Finally, after the experiment the instructors were asked to rate the classes and to submit scores of comparable college tests, all of which proved that the differences between the classes were rather small. In some cases (Experiment C1) even the average ages and the average intelligence quotients were equal.[6] But there is no need to stress these points. No evidence exists that there is a correlation between the intelligence quotient and the ability to solve such tasks as were given in our experiments, provided that the highest and the lowest brackets of intelligence quotients are not represented in the samples. Moreover, even in case of an exactly identical intelligence-quotient distribution someone may argue that the members of one class were, by chance or because of previous practice, better able to generalize than were those of the other class. We may disprove the validity of such an objection, since we administered some of the experiments by means of a "rotation" technique.

The same classes used in the match experiments served as subjects in other experiments, which, however, also implied some kind of generalization procedure. The experiments were made by using a system of rotation. The 11 o'clock class, which obtained the "best" training in the match experiment, was taught in the "worst" way in a different experiment; while with the 12 o'clock class the order was reversed. We are in a position to show that the accomplishments of the classes with two materials, each learned in different ways, were about equal. The groups, therefore, may be called equivalent.

Match Experiment A was made with the same students as was the quantitative card-trick experiment described in Chapter II. One class formed Group Ex. in the match experiments and Group Mem. in the card experiments, whereas another class formed Group Mem. in the match experiments and Group Und. in the card experiments. In order to compare the accomplishments of the two classes, we refer to the transfer coefficients obtained in the retests: first class, match coefficient 90 plus card coefficient 39, equal to 129; second class, match coefficient 21 plus card coefficient 112, equal to 133.

The classes which formed the various groups of match Experiment B were also used in the experiments on the "acceleration principle," which

[6] The I.Q.'s were almost equal in the classes and were made equal by eliminating two subjects before the experiments. The I.Q. range is comparatively small in the New York City colleges because of the method of selection.

is reported in Chapter IX. One college class formed Group Help in the match experiments and Class II in the later experiments; another formed Group Mem. and Class III; and a third class formed Group Con. and Class I. We recapitulate the scores obtained in the two experiments (cf. Tables 7 and 19).

MATCH EXPERIMENT		ACCELERATION-PRINCIPLE EXPERIMENT	
Group	*Score*	*Class*	*Score*
Help	8.08	II	2½
Mem.	4.41	III	5½
Con.	2.38	I	10½

On the basis of these results the different experimental groups may be considered equivalent.

Appendix 3

GROUPING OF NONSENSE SYLLABLES

IN CHAPTER VII we have formulated four rules referring to the grouping of nonsense syllables (p. 168 f.). The experimental evidence for these rules, gathered mainly from the various books of G. E. Mueller, shall be summarized in the following pages.

Rule 1.—Between members of the same group there is a stronger association than between members of different groups. After reading a few times, but not often enough for complete mastery, long series of nonsense syllables of the type a b / c d / e f . . . (each letter represents a syllable; grouping is caused by accent; the time interval between the syllables is identical), the scoring method was used to obtain knowledge of the strength of the various association bonds. In the test the experimenter asks questions like these: what follows a; f; b; e; etc.? These experiments showed that there is a stronger excitatory tendency from syllable a to syllable b than from b to c. Moreover, the backward associations are stronger from b to a than from c to b.

The rule explains the differences between Series I and Series II in the experiment described on page 167. If from a series a b / c d / e f we transfer pairs, like a b or e f to a new (derived) series, relearning will be easy, because comparatively strong associations must be strengthened. If, however, as in Series I, the derived series contains pairs with weak associations (like b c or f g), relearning will be difficult.

It follows from the rule that adjoining syllables are not necessarily connected by association bonds of identical strength. This holds true also for bonds between syllables remote from each other. The strength of remote excitatory tendencies was studied by constructing new series, such as a c / e g , and so forth, and measuring the time saved in relearning. The associations between two syllables were found to be stronger if both syllables are accentuated than if both are unaccentuated or if one is accentuated and one unaccentuated.

Rule 2.—A part of a group has the tendency to reproduce the entire group. When the syllables were learned in groups of three and every third syllable was accentuated (thus a b c' / d e f' /g h i' . . .) the syllables most readily and most frequently recalled after presenting c, f, and i were a, d, and g, respectively. The backward association from c to a was found to be stronger than that from c to b. This was called the "tendency to initial reproduction." More careful investigations revealed that the response a after presenting c was given only because the experimenter called for one syllable; actually c has the tendency to reproduce a b c, that is, the whole group. It is possible that all backward associations are to be explained by the tendency to reproduce the whole group. If that were true, the syllable b would have a tendency to reproduce a, when a b / c d are learned, because of the tendency of the syllable b to reproduce a b. When groups like a b c / d e f are formed, the tendency to reproduce the whole group will contribute to the empirical fact that a b reproduce c more easily than does b alone.

Rule 3.—Groups have their own associations, which may differ from the associations of their members. This rule explains the fact that a subject is able to proceed from one group to the next when reciting a series, although the last syllable of a group may be more strongly connected with the first syllable of the same group than with the first syllable of the next group. Two consecutive groups are connected with each other. The excitatory value of the whole group appears to be very great; it is often necessary to recall the entire group in order to recall the next group in the series.

Of importance in facilitating the retention and recitation of long series of syllables are the so-called "place-associations." Their strength varies: the first and the last groups are usually associated most strongly with their place in the series, but most of the other groups are also localized to some extent. The existence of place associations of groups—not of individual syllables—was proved by reciting well-learned series in an unfamiliar way. To recite a series backward is usually possible even for nonvisual learners, but it is much more difficult and takes a much longer time than to recite the groups in backward order.[1] In both kinds of recitation we usually proceed in the same manner. We try to remember one group after the other by localizing them in their spatial pattern, but when reciting backward we must, in addition, reverse the syllables within a group. Therefore, backward recitation is most difficult when the syllables are learned in large groups (Mueller, 74, pp. 567 ff.).

Rule 4.—Grouping facilitates learning. When a series of nonsense syllables, printed one below the other, was presented to someone who never before had been a subject in such psychological experiments, and when he was asked to learn the series by heart, he usually had to repeat the series a few times before he could articulate it in stable groups. Subjects who were

---

[1] "Backward recitation" means y x . . . d c b a; "recitation of the groups in backward order," however, means x y . . . c d / a b, when a b / c d . . . x y were learned.

taught how to group syllables have retained after the first few repetitions more than those who did not begin with a grouping procedure. When grouping is facilitated by the arrangement of the material, learning is much faster, especially with subjects who have not had much practice with nonsense syllables; when grouping is disturbed, learning will take much longer.[2] Subjects who were asked to read a series rhythmically, learned it more quickly and after a smaller number of repetitions than did those who while reading the series aloud were forbidden to use rhythm.

If the subject has the intention to learn and if the material is not arranged to facilitate grouping, loud reading will sooner or later automatically become rhythmical, and thus grouping sets in. The result of silent reading is usually the same: grouping arises quickly in case of simultaneous presentation and slowly in case of successive presentation of all syllables belonging to the series. According to Mueller there is only one exception to the rule that we learn series of numbers, consonants, syllables, and so forth, in groups; if there is a long interval (say two or three seconds) between the consecutive syllables, other artificial aids instead of grouping may be resorted to (72, pp. 369 ff.). Often subjects assert, on the basis of introspection, that they have not grouped the syllables, but examination reveals that there were effects of grouping (such as alternating strong and weak connections between the syllables).

When many subjects memorize nonsense syllables, their results vary most in the first few repetitions. Then several subjects are still irregular with their accentuation and grouping and learn, therefore, at a slower pace than other subjects. In general, after a certain amount of initial practice subjects do not improve in learning nonsense syllables. But after considerable practice some subjects show an appreciable improvement in the number of repetitions required. Their special memorizing achievements can usually be traced back to extraordinary grouping ability.[3]

[2] Appropriate methods used to facilitate grouping are to write the first three syllables with red ink, the next three with black ink, the next three with a pencil, and so forth. On the other hand, grouping can be disturbed by using an irregular color scheme (see Mueller, 74, pp. 610 ff.).

[3] Grouping has here been described as *the* general method of memorizing nonsense syllables, whereas certain authors distinguish between mechanized and ingenious learning of the syllables, the latter being characterized as a type of learning different from the grouping process. There are undoubtedly subjects who try to form meaningful words out of the syllables or seek some artificial mnemotechnical help for their learning process. But this kind of transformation of the material is usually discarded as the subject acquires practice in using stable groups. Of course, with certain syllables artificial help is always used; but in general only as a consequence of the grouping process—not as an alternative form of learning. For example, the pair "koh lem" was learned in my experiments by many subjects as "golem" (it was nevertheless spelled and pronounced correctly), whereas

Some of the facts and assumptions described in the foregoing pages are not yet adequately clarified and require further investigation. But the experimental evidence on grouping nonsense syllables is far too extensive to be overlooked. Yet some of the best accounts of the nonsense-syllable research in textbooks omit all references to grouping. As to the role of rhythm, H. A. Carr (13) gives a short paragraph on that subject in which he concludes that "the ease in memorizing any material is proportional to the degree in which it is rhythmized" (p. 230). J. A. McGeoch, in his excellent summary of the "Experimental Studies of Memory" (62) also restricts himself to a brief reference in which he states that "rhythm has been found to be a significant aid to learning" (p. 393). Thus, it is understandable that C. L. Hull (31) formulates his miniature scientific system of learning in opposition to the experimental data referred to in the foregoing pages. His theory presupposes that adjoining syllables in a rote series are connected by bonds of identical strength. This statement is not expressly formulated by Hull, but it is contained in the diagrammatic representation of the excitatory tendencies which forms a part of his definitions (p. 502). All immediate forward excitatory tendencies are represented in the diagram as equally strong; the same holds true for excitatory tendencies between remote but equidistant syllables. The effects of articulation or grouping are not taken into account.

One of the newest textbooks of experimental psychology deals extensively with the question of grouping nonsense syllables. R. S. Woodworth (112) reviews the experiments of Mueller and Schumann and concludes that "Mueller and Schumann proved that, in fact, the grouping is a definite factor in learning a list and in determining what associations are formed" (p. 28). The "summary of the memorization process," as given by Woodworth is a quotation from a mimeographed edition written in 1913. Woodworth states that the conclusions expressed there were based mostly upon the work of G. E. Mueller. The main part of that summary should be quoted in full as a most valuable confirmation on the views expressed in this chapter, which were likewise based on Mueller's work, including his later publications and his lectures. "To look at a list of numbers or nonsense syllables, you would think that the thing to be done was to forge links between the adjacent terms, but the actual learning proceeds largely in quite another way. It does not start with elements and unite these, but it starts with groups, or even with the whole series, and

---

no such help was resorted to when "koh" was the last member of a group and "lem" the first member of the next group. Artificial help, such as associating meaningful words with nonsense syllables, is of greater importance for the subject's self-assurance or his reliance on the correctness of the answer than for the actual recollection of the syllable.

proceeds largely by analysis and the finding of parts and relations"
(112, p. 35).

The experiments of Frings (21) and Shepard and Fogelsonger (87)
shall here be briefly outlined in order to show how the principle of
grouping nonsense syllables, according to which the function of the same
principle varies with the group of which it forms a part, serves to explain
the experimental results. Köhler (45) has already called attention to the
fact that these experiments show the role of organization in learning nonsense syllables. One well established form of inhibition arises if a syllable
is connected successively with two different syllables. After learning both
a b and a c the presentation of a will have different results than it would
have if only a b had been learned. In the first case there will be a delay
in the reaction, or no reaction at all, or a number of incorrect reactions.
But this general rule seems to be contradicted by experiments in which
the subjects had to learn a series by accentuating every third syllable. In
such a series the following groups were included: x a b' and y a c'. After
several repetitions x a was presented and b reproduced without any delay.
In the same way the response c came without any indication of inhibition
after the presentation of y a.

Similar results were obtained in the following way. The subjects had
to learn nonsense syllables grouped either in pairs or in threes: a b / c d /
e f / g b and h i k / l m n / o p k. When testing the excitatory tendencies
of certain syllables, the quickest and most accurate responses were obtained by presenting c or l m. Certain signs of inhibition were found at
the presentation of h i or a, as one would infer from the general concept
of inhibitions; but the results were even less satisfactory when a g or h p
were presented together, although both a and g were associated with b
and both h and p with k.

The results described correspond to what we must expect according
to the principle formulated above. In the first experiment x a should reproduce the following b, and y a the following c without any sign of inhibition, because a has functions in group x a different from those in
group y a. In the second experiment, when both a b and g b are learned,
there is every reason to expect that a g will reproduce b after a delay,
because a g is a new group, in which the syllable a has a different function
from the one it had in the other often-repeated group a b. Likewise the
functions of syllable a differ when presented alone and when presented
in group x a.

Appendix 4

REMARKS CONCERNING THE HISTORY
OF THE TRACE CONCEPT

TO WRITE A HISTORY of the concept of traces would be of great interest. But in this place only certain important steps in the development of the concept will be pointed out—those which are connected with the differentiation between individual and structural traces and the hypotheses on the qualities of these traces presented in Chapter VIII. Special emphasis will therefore be placed on assumptions based on the gestalt theory which has exerted a great influence on the ideas on traces expressed by this writer.

According to the traditional trace theory individual ideas are stored in single cells of the brain, and these cells are connected with each other by association tracks. Among the manifold arguments advanced against this theory, those of greatest historical importance were made by von Kries (52) and Becher (8) in connection with the facts of transposition emphasized by von Ehrenfels. A person hears a melody in a key in which he has never before heard it; how is it possible that the new, changed stimuli communicate with the traces left by the former, different stimuli? Or: a strange green figure appears at the upper left of a visual field; nevertheless it is recognized if it is presented later at the lower right colored in red and much smaller. From such evidence Becher drew a negative conclusion: the structural qualities of our mental processes and the generally assumed qualities of the underlying physiological processes appeared to him so different as to make the formulation of a useful trace theory impracticable.

In the first experimental study on gestalt processes, in Wertheimer's paper on the phi-movement (apparent movement), it had been clearly stated what consequences the facts discovered have for our concepts in brain physiology. Wertheimer stressed the dynamic intercourse of the effects of two successively, as well as simultaneously, presented stimuli within a whole and stated: "Provided that the characteristic whole-qualities of a unitary physiological process are decisive for later effects—not the and-sum of the individual excitations—then various consequences would result; for example, in reproduction and recognition it would be essential to effect the former physiological pattern (*Gesamtform*) of the unitary process,—not to reproduce definite individual excitations" (102, p. 92n). Several years later Wertheimer made the following more definite statement: "The function of memory is bound mainly to whole-qualities and structural context" (104, p. 55).

Köhler first expressed the assumption that we may differentiate between memory effects attached to individual items and those attached to structural wholes. In reporting on his well-known experiments concerning absolute or relative choice by chickens, he offers a test which should determine whether one or the other memory effect deteriorates more rapidly after a lapse of time. "If the effect of memory is dependent on a function of structure, as well as on absolute color, then obviously by shortening the interval between training period and critical tests the effectiveness of the factor whose memory effects deteriorate more rapidly with time will appear the stronger" (43, p. 21). After discussing the results of his experiments Köhler concludes: "Recall which is dependent on absolute color suffers a strong decline through the effect of time" (p. 23); and again, "Learning which is dependent on definite data has the tendency to be forgotten easily," whereas true learning is closely bound to structure (p. 100).

Lashley's "reaction to ratio" is related to some extent to Köhler's assumption that the learning effect is dependent on the structure of a pair. When Lashley describes his ideas on the underlying physiological processes (54, pp. 157–76), he, too, refers to such phenomena as the recognition of a melody played in different keys and the performance by the left arm of a complicated movement which was learned by the right arm. He refutes the notion that individual ideas are stored in single cells of the brain. In training experiments "the response is, within wide limits, independent of the particular sensory cells stimulated" (55, p. 542). We have to explain "constant reaction to patterns, no matter in what part of a cortical field they occur" (54, p. 159). Lashley's positive characterization of the physiological processes begins therefore with the statement: "The problem of reaction to ratio seems to underly all phases of behavior" (54, p. 161). Reaction to ratio, or reaction to relations, is according to Lashley the essential problem of intelligent acts. We must assume a responsiveness of the neural field to ratios or a gradient of excitations, that is, we must assume "dynamic relations among the parts of the nervous system."

In extensive investigations which were made years later than the experiments on relative choice Köhler [1] has developed a theory of traces which was also accepted as the point of departure for Koffka's [2] discussion

---

[1] Köhler (44), Lauenstein (56), and Köhler (46).
[2] Koffka (50, pp. 439–70).

of traces. These studies, of which only a short account can be given here, already proved fruitful in numerous experimental investigations. Köhler discusses the concept of the trace in his investigation of successive comparison. He characterizes (44) successive comparison as a dynamic intercourse between the excited area and a trace. In his experiments the subjects listened to two taps, the second immediately succeeding the first, and had to state whether the second tap was louder, equal to, or softer than the first. It is assumed that the first tap left a trace behind; the comparison is then due to an organization embracing the trace of the first tap and the second tap. What is the nature of the traces that form the basis of comparison? We are able to compare rather exactly two closely succeeding sounds or two successive straight lines. Regular and therefore highly important deviations from the correct results occur, such as the "negative time error" due to which Köhler assumes that the trace of the first tap weakens in the first few seconds; yet in spite of these deviations the trace must represent its originator in a rather exact way. "The trace is a sufficiently adequate representative of the process by which it has been formed" (Köhler, 46, p. 267).

Köhler expressly assumes that the trace, which forms the basis of comparison, is the same trace which is later revived if someone remembers or recognizes the contents compared on an earlier occasion (44, pp. 170–74). "Nobody will assume that after an experience one trace is left which participates in successive comparison, while another trace of the same event makes facts of memory possible. The obvious view is, of course, that the same remnant operates in both cases" (46, p. 272).

It should not be inferred from this statement that the traces may not show different qualities immediately after their formation and when they are revived after a few hours, days, and weeks. In fact, Köhler himself investigated the changes of the traces occurring with the passage of time. The dynamic tendencies of the traces involve extensive transformations. In time the traces tend to assume a simpler and more regular organization (46, p. 256) [3] and to lose their individual characteristics (p. 259). The traces are dynamically active; in functional relationship with other traces larger trace systems are formed (Koffka, 50, p. 473).

Köhler has demonstrated various effects of organization in the realm of traces. The experiments of Köhler and Restorff on the different roles of accumulation and isolation, which we discussed in Chapter VII, could be transformed to prove that consecutively formed traces organize themselves in the same manner as perceptual processes. The same principles

[3] See also the reference to the experiments of Wulf and his followers on p. 206 above.

of organization were found to govern the persistence of items which followed each other without pause and others which were separated by intervals of about ten minutes (cf. Köhler, 46, pp. 261 ff.). On the basis of these experiments and many others, Köhler developed a theory of reproduction, that is, a theory of the conditions required for the revival of the traces, which we discuss at length in Chapter IX. The formation of a pair consisting of a trace and a new process was found to be the determining factor for memory effects, and pair formation is dependent on the organization of the components of the pair as influenced by the other components belonging to the same whole.

The concept of structural traces presented in Chapter VIII bears certain similarities to the theory of remembering developed by F. C. Bartlett (6). Therefore a full account of Bartlett's views will be given. We have already referred to some of his findings when we characterized reproduction as reconstruction. Bartlett summarized his theory as follows: "Remembering is not the re-excitation of innumerable fixed, lifeless, and fragmentary traces. It is an imaginative reconstruction, or construction, built out of the relation of our attitude toward the whole active mass of organized past reactions or experience, and to a little outstanding detail which commonly appears in image or in language form" (p. 213).

Bartlett's whole book constitutes an argument against the view "which treats recall as the re-excitement of fixed and changeless traces." Experiments with ink blots showed that perceiving is not a passive reception of stimuli and that remembering is not the simple duplication of the patterns formed by perceiving. Experiments in which the subject was asked to describe pictures seen once for ten seconds and to reproduce stories covering about half a printed page, which had been read twice, showed that remembering is rapidly affected by omissions, additions, and transformations: "Accurate recall is the exception and not the rule" (p. 61). In repeated reproduction of the stories the general form or scheme persisted; with frequent reproductions, remembering became stereotyped, and thereafter it suffered little change; whereas with infrequent reproductions the transformation of items appeared to go on almost indefinitely (p. 93).

"It looks as if the preservation of material, which is required in recognizing, is normally a preservation of schemes, of general settings, of order or form of arrangement; and as if the detailed re-instatement of individualized material is a special case" (p. 195). Therefore the theory that the brain is a storehouse of past impressions must be rejected, and Bartlett follows Sir Henry Head in using the term "schema" for the standard against which subsequent changes are measured. Determination by schemata is the most fundamental way in which we can be influenced by past reactions and experiences (p. 201).

"In a world of constantly changing environment, literal recall is extraordinarily unimportant" (p. 204), is Bartlett's explanation for the result of his experiments that "remembering appears to be far more decisively an affair of construction rather than one of mere reproduction." Construction is based largely on attitudes and is therefore influenced by feelings and affects. There is one apparent exception to the constructive process of remembering: the function of images, which is to pick items out of schemata (p. 209), to reinstate an old event "with much if not all of its individuality unimpaired" (p. 219). "Images are literally details picked out of schemes" (p. 303); the main conditions for their occurrence are found in their affective setting.

We used the term "individual trace" to indicate the bearer of fixed and specific recall, whereas according to Bartlett fixation of detail, if found in remembering, is due mainly to images. The identification of individual traces with images does not seem necessary. The main example of the formation of individual traces, the memorization of a series of unconnected items, results in a more-or-less automatic recitation, and introspection usually does not reveal any images. We have no reason to say that literal recall is due only to the persistence of images. Furthermore, the enduring basis of reconstructions must not be identified with attitudes and affective settings. Undoubtedly there are instances in which attitudes constitute the basis of recall, and memory is affectively determined. But memory is not always affective; in our experiments with rational learning processes integrated traces were formed which did not have an affective basis. In addition, the identification of structural traces with attitudes may imply that they are vague and indistinct—a notion which we had occasion to reject.

A more important point of disagreement with Bartlett concerns the stress which he places on everlasting fundamental changes in remembering, whereas in our experiments meaningful learning resulted in persistent application of principles. It is questionable whether the schemata of Bartlett are related to that which we called structure. Various parts of Bartlett's analysis appear to point to a theory different from our assumptions, which attribute stability and persistence to well-understood whole-qualities of a gestalt process. In Chapter IX we tried to clarify by experiment the crucial questions raised by contrasting Bartlett's assumptions with ours. There we investigate the question: what is learned and what is retained in meaningful learning?

The knowledge about traces, which is derived from studying the process of successive comparison, serves obviously only as an introduction to the theory of memory traces—not as its basis. Nevertheless, certain questions are raised in connection with the discussion of comparison which are of interest with regard to the qualities we attributed to the traces in Chapter VIII. It would be—so the author believes—a grave misunderstanding of Köhler's views on the formation of traces to assume that immediately after the occurrence of a process only "specific traces" are left, such as the trace of the first tap which is compared with a second tap. The quotations we gave above concerning Köhler's assumption that memory effects depend on structural wholes point in another direction, which we attempted to elaborate and to confirm by experiment when we discussed the qualities of the structural traces. We assumed that structural traces, left behind by relationships, whole-qualities, and principles which represent the well-understood center of perceptions and events, are formed as quickly as the other traces and are not conglomerations of former specific traces. In the qualities of such processes as reproduction and reconstruction we found justification for the assumption that there is a second type of trace, the individual trace. We characterized these traces, too, as different from exact representatives of the processes by which they originated. We assumed that one individual trace is formed by manifold processes, such as by one specific match task presented in four different positions and by the word "Chesterfield" perceived in many ways. We believe that one individual trace can be formed by a large and by a small, by a colored reproduction and by a gray reproduction, as well as by the original of a Raphael Madonna. If a person is shown a reproduction of a Raphael Madonna whose original he has seen a few months earlier, the new process will communicate with the older trace and will fuse with it and enrich it. The general assumption underlying our opinion on memory traces may therefore be stated in the following way: in studying the forms in which memory traces prove to be effective it does not seem to be necessary to assume the operation of an infinite number of traces, corresponding to the number of sensations or perceptions which we have had.[4]

The "comparison traces," to use that expression for the sake of brief-

[4] The question about the number of traces effective in memory functions is a very difficult one. To follow up our example about the Raphael Madonna: it may happen that I am able to differentiate in my memory between the original and the reproduction, which fact would imply the effectiveness of two separate traces. But usually I shall not be able to differentiate between the perceptions of the picture which I obtained when I saw the picture first from the left side and then from the right side.

ness, appear to have characteristics which are somewhat different from those just described. Therefore the following question arises: Under what circumstances may we assume the existence of a great number of immediate remnants which are exact representatives of the processes? Although the discussion of this question is only loosely connected with the trend of our main argument, we want to point briefly to the results of an earlier investigation by this author, according to which a representative and an exact aftereffect must be assumed only under certain special conditions of successive comparison. In that study a differentiation was made between direct perception of relations (*unmittelbare Relationswahrnehmung*) and indirect comparison. The former could be achieved only between two similar objects not separated by a third object and following each other closely.[5] If any of these conditions were not fulfilled, the exact comparison was disturbed. Then we usually resort to indirect comparison. "Absolute judgment" is one of the most frequent expedients. In this case there is no perceiving of a relation between two processes—but a trace derived from all previous processes of the same kind contributes to a new process, which therefore appears "big," "small," "loud," and so forth (Katona, 39, p. 86). Köhler asserts that in absolute judgments an average effect, derived from the aggregation of traces of many sounds, is operative (44, pp. 173 f.). He assumes that such a durable remnant, representing a certain medium level or standard, constitutes the intermediate link between "comparison traces" and "memory traces." Phenomena such as the absolute judgment do not necessarily imply the survival and the effectiveness of a great number of separate and exact traces. Thus the divergence between the qualities of the traces operative in comparison and in memory functions appears to be restricted to certain effects occurring within a very short time after the processes.

Let us suppose that we should be entitled to assume that the number of traces formed is not determined by the number of processes alone. In that case this question arises: Under what circumstances must we assume the formation of one unitary trace, and under what other circumstances the formation of two successive traces? Objective simultaneity of the stimuli cannot be considered the only circumstance bringing about a single individual trace.[6] Phenomenal simultaneity of impressions and even the occurrence of certain temporal units—for example, the hearing

---

[5] Katona, 39, p. 75; see also the experiments reported in Section 10 of that book.

[6] But that was the view of Semon, the author of an almost classical study on the nature of traces, who wrote in 1904: "All simultaneous excitations leave behind a connected engram-complex constituting a coherent unity" (86, p. 273). The word "engram" stands for trace.

of a word or a short sentence—must be assumed to play the same role. We can deduce the distinction between two successively formed traces, not from the objective time sequence, but only from experiential duality —the experience of a *duo* in contrast to an *unum*. The problem of *"unum and duo,"* extensively analyzed in Chapter III with respect to simultaneous perceptions, recurs in this context. As was shown before, it is a problem of organization according to gestalt principles. Hence the organization of the processes and the traces determines the number of separate traces formed, their mutual relationship, and their qualities.

Appendix 5

THE LEARNER AND HIS ATTITUDES

THE ROLE OF THE LEARNER in memorizing and in understanding constitutes a problem of great interest. The personality of the learner and his attitude toward the task of learning and the materials of learning are obviously factors influential in the learning process. But this study was undertaken from a different angle. Our interest was primarily in investigating the various forms in which the learning material can be organized in the processes of learning, remembering, and applying knowledge. Yet the emphasis on that approach to the problem of learning does not imply that we must assume a duality between the organized material of learning and the learner. The learner is without doubt an intrinsic part of the organization which results when a material is learned. He is not a foreign substance; he participates in the organization in some way. There may be instances in which that participation is the main factor in determining the form of organization. In other instances the forces of organization emanating from the material itself may be so strong that the learner appears to be drawn into the organization without having an active role. But in both cases there is an interrelation between learner and learning process.

It is because of an established technique of scientific research that we have not yet dealt with this problem. Science cannot attack the complexity of actual events without applying a principle of selection which restricts the scope of the investigation. Certain factors are taken as constant in order that the function of the other (variable) factors should be investigated and determined. Of course, the division between the constant and the variable factors must be made in accordance with the structure of the whole process concerned. In other words, it is unscientific to study isolated parts of a whole without regard to the whole to which they belong, but it is a scientific and also an advisable procedure to study one consistent whole (or sub-whole) by investigating it under circumstances in which the influence of the greater whole to which it belongs is constant. We have applied the latter method. The learning material, organized in a certain way, constituted in our investigation a consistent sub-whole of actual occurrences which was independent of its greater context inasmuch as it manifested different forms under the influence of a given constant attitude of the learner. Thus we studied the meaning and the lack of meaning in the materials and methods of learning uninfluenced by changes in the attitude of the learner—except by those changes that were determined by the organization of the material itself. Furthermore we attempted to determine the qualities and the laws of the learning process without taking the type of the learner into consideration. The selection of our subjects likewise brought about various constant factors, and we have yet to inquire whether or not the principles of learning established in the experiments are connected with a special type of learner.

The study of the dynamic relationship between the objects and the individual—whose relation to the learning material forms a special case in it—can hardly be undertaken within the limits of this work.[1] It would call for as much inquiry as was required for the investigation of the various forms of organizing the learning material which was the topic of this book. To arrive at an exhaustive quantitative answer to the questions just posed, new experiments would have to be performed. But in our experiments, which were undertaken in order to clarify a different problem, we have made certain observations which throw light on the learner's function, and especially on the question whether this function differs in meaningful and in senseless learning.

Remarks on the Dynamics of the Learning Situation

These are the main questions involved: Why do we learn? What is the role of the will to learn? Is it a necessary factor in all forms of learning? Let us make a brief survey of our experiments in order to gather the observations made with regard to these questions and to the differences in the dynamics of the learning situation in memorizing and in understanding.

We began the description of the card-trick experiment by stating that the subjects to whom the trick was shown wanted to learn how to perform it (p. 35). Curiosity about a performance—or, better still, interest in a matter—was sufficient incentive for undertaking the procedure that we called "learning by understanding." In some cases interest was such a strong incentive that we did not have to ask the subjects to "learn." Group Help in the match-task experiments was instructed to try to solve a problem and to understand the manipulations of the experimenter (the "helps")—with the result that the members of the group learned some-

---

[1] That problem has been attacked by Lewin (59), who speaks of the relation between the ego and the environmental forces; see also Koffka (50, p. 353).

thing. In the experiments with the "acceleration principle" we took great pains to avoid the formation of a situation in which the subjects try to learn with the intention to remember later what they learned: here the subjects acquired knowledge when their intention was to find the answer to a scientific question. We must contrast these cases with the situation in certain memorization experiments. In one group of experiments the subjects were told: "For the sake of an experiment on memory, please learn by heart the following series of numbers." Request to learn and compliance with that request because of kindness, coöperative attitude, or the group situation has here brought about the "will to learn." In other instances, not encountered in our experiments, expectation of reward may be the main motive of learning, and in drill situations the request to learn may take even the form of coercion. Lewin states on the basis of extensive research that "couplings created by habits are never, as such, the motor of a psychical event." Pressure of will or of a need creates the tensions which are the necessary conditions of such mental events as reproduction (Lewin, 59, p. 44). On the basis of our data we may say that pressure or tension arising from the situation (which embraces the learning material and the learner, for example, if it consists of curiosity about an unsolved task) are the drives which lead to the best learning process. Should such a tension be lacking, it may be created artificially. The will to learn is then the result of factors originally more or less external to the learning material; but during the learning process the expectation of a good mark or of some other reward may become a part of the learning situation.

Is there a correspondence between meaningful learning and tensions inherent in the situation, on the one hand, and senseless learning and externally created will to learn on the other hand? It is possible to cite a few instances in which the relationship between the attitudes and the kinds of learning resorted to appears to be less simple. Meaningful material with inherent tensions may in some cases not be learned in a meaningful way. If the material is not understood, for example, because of an organization inadequate to the structure, we cannot do otherwise than resort to memorization—which may also relieve the tension to some extent. Or, in the beginning we may not be interested in a problem; we want to learn something because we expect some profit from the acquisition of that knowledge—and, nevertheless, it may happen that in the course of the learning process we resort to meaningful organization and learn by understanding. The author would characterize such cases as exceptional, but he has no evidence to prove that point. It should therefore suffice to state that in many cases the quality and clarity of organization that result during the learning process are correlated with the interest in the matter, with the lack of coercion and of external motivations, and with the strength of conviction.

The distinction between activity and passivity of the learner is not connected in a simple way with the differences in the motives of learning. At the beginning of Chapter II we described the memorizers as those who learned actively, while the "understanders" appeared merely to listen passively to an explanation. But if we analyze later experiments with match tasks, we may arrive at a contrary view. Several times Group Mem. was shown the solution of a task: the memorizing process may be said to have consisted of passive apperception of recurring contents. Group Help, on the other hand, was given the active task of trying to solve a problem and to find the significance of the experimenter's assistance. Thus, irrespective of whether one is driven by interest in a matter or by a request to learn, a certain amount of activity may ensue. Whether a higher or lower degree of activity results, depends mainly on the material and method of learning.

Our reference to the activity of the learner who acquired understanding of the geometrical tasks by the method of help may be taken to indicate that a special attitude played a role in this case. Is the difference in the learning effects due to the fact that the memorizers were merely "learning," while the members of the other group worked on solving a problem? Discovery of the solution by a learner is one method which may bring about understanding. We introduced our description of the learning method applied by Class III to the number series by contrasting memorization to the discovery of a principle. But it was found that it was not necessary that the learner himself should actually make the discovery: in the case of the number series the results were the same when the subjects were informed of the principle instead of discovering it themselves (p. 13). Similarly, learning by examples yielded approximately the same results as learning by help in the case of the geometrical tasks. The problem-solving attitude, or the "constructive" attitude, may be of great help in arriving at essential whole-qualities, but it cannot be considered the indispensable prerequisite which produced the result in our experiments. Discovery without assistance, discovery due to certain cues and hints, development on the basis of examples, insight into the fact that a given principle or solution is appropriate—all may be forms of meaningful learning, yielding long retention and widely applicable knowledge. Real understanding is what is required to produce these effects, and it may be arrived at as a result of different ways of dealing with a task. In all these instances we must deal justly with the learning material, we must be concerned with its requirements, instead of taking a ready-made statement or solution as granted because it is given by the textbook, the teacher, or the experimenter (or, for that matter, by a newspaper, a political speaker, or the head of a government). The attitude with which we face the problem at the beginning is less important than the kind of learning arising through the organization of the material (understanding or memorizing), because the former may change in the course of the learning process.

Effort and strenuous work (in contrast to a leisurely and comfortable attitude) are not characteristic of only one kind of learning. In the card-trick experiments the greater effort could be attributed to those who learned by memorizing. But we could arrive at the opposite opinion if understanding the text of the "acceleration principle" were taken as an example of learning by dint of great effort. As compared to the difficulties of finding the substance and meaning of a complicated theory we may speak of "comfort" in learning by repetition. There are instances in which different examples, or a multitude of applications, increase the difficulties for the learner, while mechanical repetition produces the comforting feeling of knowing where one stands. It may be that the comfort in repetition, or the relief of tension by mechanical memorizing, is due only to the kind of education which most of us have had in school; it may be that the lack of that comfort in certain complicated, but meaningful, situations is caused only by a comparative lack of coherence in the presentation of the new material. In any case, comfort in repetition cannot be attributed to mechanical repetition alone; repeating in different forms and repeating the main points with the help of different examples can also bring it about.

The feeling of being successful, in contrast to the feeling of being at a loss or on the wrong track, undoubtedly assists in producing meaningful learning. Thorndike's law of effect, which states that success (a satisfying aftereffect) strengthens the connections, plays a role in the process of understanding. Koffka's following formulations should be quoted in this connection: "I am convinced that the law of effect is responsible for a great many reorganizations, i. e. for a great deal of learning, both in men and in animals" (50, p. 645). "Success transforms a process in such a way as to give it a new meaning, i. e. a new role in its goal-directed activity" (*ibid.*, p. 556). Perhaps we may add that in meaningful learning success is usually not something extraneous in origin, something that comes as a new additive element to the situation. It is our progress in gradually arriving at the appropriate organization which is accompanied by pleasure. That pleasure or success, as an inherent part of the learning process, may contribute to the stability and survival of knowledge.

The assumption that a special attitude is required for meaningful learning may have still another form. We said that when we learn by understanding the specific material of the learning period is often not learned as such: we do not learn the examples but learn by examples. Gelb and Goldstein (24; also Goldstein, 25, p. 30) differentiate between concrete and abstract (categorical) behavior, showing that persons with injured brains are often unable to act in any way other than according to their concrete immediate, experiences. They lose the capacity to deal with that which is not real. Professor Goldstein defined abstract behavior as the attitude toward the merely possible.[2] An attitude of that kind, implying a shifting from the immediate content of the examples to that which they exemplify, may be advantageous for achieving wide applicability. In most learning situations we are not conscious of that attitude. But investigations of pathological cases often serve to clarify general conditions of normal processes.

Remarks on the Dynamics of the Testing Situation

We shall begin our consideration of the dynamics of the testing situation by recalling the different forms of behavior manifested in our experiments. Reproduction may have the form of a quasi-automatic response to an appropriate stimulus. This behavior was most striking in the case of Group III in Experiment E: after having repeated the same tests several times, the subjects drew the design of their "solution" without actually solving a problem (p. 149). In the case of meaningful learning, on the other hand, reproduction took the form of reconstruction. Here the attitude of the subjects was about the same as it would have been in a novel problem-solving situation; they behaved in the tests as if they had been confronted with entirely new problems, except that they were aided in their endeavor by previously acquired knowledge. Memorizers also behaved as in a problem-solving situation when they were confronted with a new task, but their attitude was one of "reproducing" when they faced a well-learned task. The external form of the test and the instruction given by the experimenter were the same in both cases. Thus the different behavior and attitudes manifested by the memorizers and the understanders, respectively, in the test, was a consequence of the organization of the material.

In spite of such instances the role of *Einstellung,* or set, in determining the form and success of a test should not be neglected. Instruction, or *Einstellung,* often determines whether a process will or will not communicate with the organized traces.

Such a communication may be brought about by the situation, even

---

[2] Wertheimer pointed out that primitive thinking is in principle rooted in reality (*wirklichkeitsnahe*); it does not contain the potentiality of abstract-unreal (*wirklichkeitsabstrakt*) operations (101, p. 329 f.).

though it is not required. In one of our card-trick tests, described above, most subjects, a few minutes after they had learned a principle, applied it to an easy task that could have been solved in a much simpler way without use of the principle.[3] A situation formed by five successive similar tests prevented an unprejudiced scrutiny of the new task. Many similar cases of "automatism" caused by *Einstellung* are known in everyday life, just as are cases of the opposite type in which the situation prevents the use of knowledge belonging to another context. But it is questionable whether attitudes or feelings alone should be held responsible for such occurrences. The organization of the material, the belonging of a part to one or the other whole, is effective in all these cases.

Many well-known psychological experiments prove that the instruction, or a change in the nature of the instruction, may determine the recall—its speed as well as its nature.[4] One frequently-used experimental set-up is to keep the processes in the learning period constant and to determine how different instructions change the response, irrespective of the previously established associations. Bearing in mind that our results showed that organized traces formed by meaningful learning fuse easily with new similar processes, we must raise the following question: is the predominance of instruction or *Einstellung* perhaps restricted to senseless or ambiguous situations? It may be that the prevalence of the instruction is effective only in situations which offer a choice among many possibilities of action and recall.

In summarizing the factors determining what is retained, what is forgotten, and what is distorted in remembering, we must undoubtedly add to the functions of the material (and its organization) the functions of the learner (and his interrelations with the material). The learner's attitude toward the material and his personality may be the determining factors. The problems regarding the relative ease of remembering pleasant and unpleasant matters, or topics approved and topics rejected (see the discussion of the learner's attitudes toward the "acceleration principle" on p. 217), may serve as examples. Reference to the role of personality leads us to the topic of differential psychology.

Individual Differences

The study of individual differences is an important part of the psychology of learning. It was not part of the program of the present investigation, however. There are general qualities, principles, and laws of the

---

[3] That was the case with Task 6, discussed on p. 266; cf. the investigations quoted there.

[4] Cf. the experiments of the Wuerzburg School, of Ach (3), Lewin (58), also Helson (29).

learning process which can be studied without regard to the differences in the mental type of the learner or which are affected only in a secondary way by it.

In spite of the possibility and the advisability of a distinction between research in general psychology and in differential psychology, we must show briefly in what respect our experimental results were independent of the individual differences of the subjects, and in what respect they may have been affected by those differences. The individual differences may be classified first according to the differences in imagery: there were without doubt persons of visual, verbal, and kinesthetic types among our subjects. We have not noticed that such differences had any great influence with respect to our problems. For both memorizing and understanding may take place irrespective of the type of imagery of the subjects, determined only by the method of organization. Suppose a student who belongs to a repetition group in the match-task experiments is accustomed to use vivid visual images in learning. His process of memorizing will differ from that of another member of the same group who learns primarily by verbalizing. But our assertion is that if the same visual subject had belonged to an understanding group, he would have learned in a different manner. The fact of having visual images in both cases would not have determined his methods of organization, which would have been different in both cases. Similarly nonvisual persons were able to learn both by memorizing and by understanding. We have not made any observations which would suggest that persons subject to one special type of imagery were in an advantageous position to understand the match tasks. Organizing and grouping have general laws which hold true for both visual and nonvisual persons. The form of organization determines our images. We do not have visual and verbal images of, let us say, forty unconnected numerals, but we have images of groups of numbers, of artificial groups, as well as of groups corresponding to a principle.[5]

If we search for individual differences on a higher level, we may still repeat the statement that the method of learning determines the accomplishment to a much larger degree than differences in personality. Very intelligent subjects who memorized the solutions of the match tasks had a lower transfer effect than somewhat less intelligent subjects who

[5] These statements should not be understood to mean that the type of imagery has no influence at all on the reproduction. We only assert that even a very visual person needs longer to reproduce a number square in vertical than in forward order and to recite a long series of nonsense syllables in backward order than in backward groups (see pp. 178, 284). But in these extreme cases the difference in reproduction time will be usually (not always) smaller with a visual person than with a nonvisual person. Mueller (74, pp. 561–94) deals with the interrelation between types of imagery and grouping.

learned to understand the main point of the tasks.[6] Should the subjects be left alone with the tasks (in problem-solving experiments), then the form and speed of the solution depends on individual characteristics (not only on intelligence but also on many other qualities). But in our experimental set-up, when the application of a definite method of teaching restricted the choice of the subjects, individual differences have not affected our main result with regard to the different effects of understanding and memorizing. As a possible exception to this statement the rare transitions from one method of learning to another may be mentioned. We said above that there is no strict correspondence between the method of teaching and the method of learning, because some subjects may not have complied with the instructions. The subjects who in spite of having memorized the solution of the card trick tried to discover and to apply a principle, may have differed in type from the "pure memorizers."

If we assume that some persons usually proceed analytically and others in a more synthetic way, then some influence of individual differences on the methods of learning must be taken into account. In a few instances different types of subjects apparently reacted differently. For example, in the match-task experiments there were extensive individual differences in the results attained by the members of Group Arith. who were taught the arithmetical principle of the tasks. We may assume that for certain persons of an analytical type that learning method was more appropriate than for another type. The ability to give a written report on the principle of the tasks may be cited as a second instance, provided that we treat the verbal type of learner as related to the analytic type. Because of the nature of the tasks very few subjects were able to give a satisfactory verbal account. Some subjects, although they solved most of the tasks, found verbalization of the essential points extremely difficult. Different results were obtained with a few other subjects, who used a predominantly verbal type of learning because of their mental type and their learning habits. It is possible that a few extremely analytical subjects found it difficult to follow the instruction given to Group Help. It is possible that for these subjects another method of instruction would have resulted in a greater transfer effect. But the wide difference between the average results of the memorizing group and those of the understanding group permits us to treat such subjects as exceptions.

Beside the various mental types individual differences due to different past experiences of the subjects may play a role. Probably the college students, the subjects of the group experiments, were accustomed to use memorization in learning, at least were accustomed to use it to a greater

[6] Cf. Table 13, which shows that there were only three subjects with more than 100 percent transfer effect in all the memorizing groups.

extent than some of the older subjects with whom individual experiments were made. But in spite of the different learning habits of the subjects, the various learning methods could be applied successfully to most of them. Learning habits can be changed. Certain educational methods lead to emphasis on and perhaps even to preference for memorizing, but other "attitudes" may presumably result from changes in educational methods. Perhaps not only learning habits but also certain functions classified as "mental types" can be changed. Whether in a given instance we proceed analytically or synthetically may also depend on the task and the method of learning which we apply.

A related problem is evidenced by the fact that our subjects obviously constituted a selected group. We found that metropolitan college students were able to use different methods of learning. Can this result be generalized to all strata of the population—especially to people of lower intelligence? The different learning processes used by adults, children, psychopaths, primitives, and animals were not encompassed in our investigation. At this point we wish only to remark that it is not true that persons with low intelligence can do nothing else but memorize, whereas those with high intelligence can try to understand matters. The acquisition of experience as the effect of understanding inherent relations is a process most natural to human beings (and probably also to animals). It is questionable whether the same can be said also of mechanical memorizing. Schooling, that is, the creation of certain habits during several years, may be required to bring about the ability to memorize.

Long-Range Remembering

In 1913 Aall (1) discussed the possibility of the existence of two forms of memory, distinguished from each other according to the attitudes of the learner. In some of his experiments the subjects were asked to learn in order to prepare for examination on the following day, and in other experiments to prepare for examination on a later date. No test was given on the following day, however. When all the subjects were tested several weeks later, the recall of the second group, who had learned with the intention of recalling something at an indefinite future date, was better than that of the first group. Aall quotes evidence from everyday life supporting his data, but the question needs further clarification. We mentioned that several members of the groups which had memorized the number series became indignant when they were asked to recite the series at a later date (p. 10). "You should have told me that you would make a test after a long time" was the remark of one subject whose accomplishment showed a very high rate of forgetting. Remarks of a similar kind were also made by subjects who were asked to tell the substance of the "acceleration principle" four weeks after they had read about it (p. 216). They reproached the experimenter, saying that they were not told to learn and to retain the text. But when these subjects consented to give an account of the principle, the recollection proved to be rather satisfactory: most of them conveyed the meaning of the main points and also of a few specific facts.

Should we assume on the basis of these two examples that the distinction between the results of intention to learn in order to retain for a short time and for a long time may be applied only to memorizing, not to understanding? It would be consistent with our assumptions if it were to be found that memorizing, resulting usually in the temporary retention of specific items, may have somewhat more persistent effects because of a special attitude of the learner. But our material does not permit us to decide among the various possibilities to which belong also variations of such factors as the relationship between the learner's personality and the learning material. We must also recall that Aall used meaningful material in his experiments.[7] Therefore we can only raise the question: do the differences just discussed apply in the same way to memorizing and to understanding?

It seems that the effects of a conscious intention "to retain for a long time" may also be brought about by the circumstances of the learning situation. One may think in this connection of the persistence of individual traces which were formed by the contents of interrupted (unfinished) tasks.[8] Furthermore, affective or emotional factors may attribute such a salient role to one item of our experience that it will be fixated in memory for a long time to come. Such a case, the opposite of embeddedness of individual items, may also be due to the fact that the whole experience was concentrated on one point. Interaction between forces of the environment and forces of the ego (affects, personality) may thus result in persistent memory for specific facts, although there took place no memorizing and even no learning in the usual sense of the word. The organization responsible for such a result needs further investigation. Here we need only point out that there may occur enduring memory effects without learning, in the form of an effectiveness of both the structural and the individual traces over a long period of time. The psychology of learning is certainly the most important cue to our knowledge of memory, but there are memory phenomena which are not encompassed by an investigation of learning alone.

[7] Among other materials Aall used short stories, which were read once to boys and girls of high-school age. He tested retention by counting the number of omissions and falsifications made when the story was reproduced. This item-for-item test is, as emphasized before, not an appropriate test of meaningful learning.

[8] Cf. Zeigarnik (114); discussed also in Lewin (59).

BIBLIOGRAPHY

1. Aall, A. "Ein neues Gedaechtnisgesetz?" *Zeitschrift fuer Psychologie*, LXVI (1913), 1–50.
2. Abelson, H. H. The Art of Educational Research. Yonkers, 1933.
3. Ach, N. Ueber den Willensakt und das Temperament. Goettingen, 1910.
4. Adams, D. K. "A Restatement of the Problem of Learning," *British Journal of Psychology*, XXII (1931), 150–79.
5. Allport, G. W. Personality. New York, Henry Holt & Co., 1937.
6. Bartlett, F. C. Remembering; a Study in Experimental and Social Psychology. Cambridge, Cambridge University Press and Macmillan Co., 1932.
7. Bean, L. B. The Curve of Forgetting, *Archives of Psychology*, Vol. III (1912), No. 21.
8. Becher, E. Gehirn und Seele. Heidelberg, 1911.
9. Binet, A. Psychologie des grands calculateurs et joueurs d'échecs. Paris, 1894.
10. Bode, B. H. Conflicting Psychologies of Learning. Boston, New York, 1929.
11. Book, W. F. The Psychology of Skill. Chicago, 1925.
12. Bunch, M. E. "The Measurement of Reminiscence," *Psychological Review*, XLV (1938), 525–31.
13. Carr, H. A. Psychology; a Study of Mental Activity. Chicago, 1925.
14. Dashiell, J. F. "A Survey and Synthesis of Learning Theories," *Psychological Bulletin*, XXXII (1935), 261–75.
15. Duncker, K. "A Qualitative Study of Productive Thinking," *Pedagogical Seminar*, XXXIII (1926), 642–708.
16. ———— "Ueber induzierte Bewegung," *Psychologische Forschung*, XII (1929), 180–259.
17. Ebbinghaus, H. Memory. New York, 1913. The German original appeared in 1885.
18. Ellis, W. D. A Source Book of Gestalt Psychology. New York, 1938.
19. English, H. B., E. L. Wellborn, and C. D. Killian. "Studies in Substance Memorization," *Journal of General Psychology*, XI (1934), 233–60.
20. English, H. B., and A. L. Edwards. "Reminiscence, Substance

Learning and Initial Difficulty," *Psychological Review,* XLVI (1939), 253–64.

21. Frings, G. "Ueber den Einfluss der Komplexbildung auf die effektuelle und generative Hemmung," *Archiv für die gesamte Psychologie,* XXX (1914), 415–79.

22. Gelb, A. Die Farbenkonstanz der Sehdinge, in "Handbuch der normalen und pathologischen Physiologie," ed. by Bethe, 1929. XII (Part 1), 594–678.

23. Gelb, A., and K. Goldstein. Psychologische Analysen hirnpathologischer Faelle. Leipzig, 1920.

24. —— "Ueber Farbennamenamnesie," *Psychologische Forschung,* VI (1924), 127–86.

25. Goldstein, K. The Organism; a Holistic Approach to Biology. New York, American Book Co., 1939.

26. Gottschaldt, K. "Ueber den Einfluss der Erfahrung auf die Wahrnehmung von Figuren," *Psychologische Forschung,* VIII (1926), 261–317, and *Psychologische Forschung,* XII (1929), 1–87.

27. Guthrie, E. R. Psychology of Learning. New York, Harper & Brothers, 1935.

28. Harrower, M. R. "Organization in Higher Mental Processes," *Psychologische Forschung,* XVII (1932), 56–121.

29. Helson, H. "The Relation between Instructions and Past Experience in a Simple Observational Task," *Journal of Educational Psychology,* XXV (1934), 29–38.

30. Hollingworth, H. L. Psychology. New York, 1928.

31. Hull, C. L. "The Conflicting Psychologies of Learning—a Way Out," *Psychological Review,* XLII (1935), 491–516.

32. —— "Mind, Mechanism, and Adaptive Behavior," *Psychological Review,* XLIV (1937), 1–32.

33. Humphrey, G. The Nature of Learning. London, New York, 1933.

34. Hunter, W. S. "Experimental Studies of Learning," in Foundations of Experimental Psychology," ed. by C. Murchison. Worcester, Mass., 1929, pp. 564–627.

35. Jordan, A. M. Educational Psychology, rev. ed. New York, 1934.

36. Judd, C. H. "The Relation of Special Training to General Intelligence," *Educational Review,* XXXVI (1908), 28–42.

37. —— Psychology of Secondary Education. Boston, Ginn & Co., 1927.

38. —— Education as Cultivation of the Higher Mental Processes. New York, Macmillan Co., 1936.

39. Katona, G. Psychologie der Relationserfassung und des Vergleichens. Leipzig, 1924.

40. —— "Experimente ueber die Groessenkonstanz," *Zeitschrift fuer Psychologie*, XMVII (1925), 215–51.

41. —— "Zur Analyse der Helligkeitskonstanz," *Psychologische Forschung*, XII (1929), 94–126.

42. Kilpatrick, W. H. Foundations of Method. New York, Macmillan Co., 1925.

43. Köhler, W. Nachweis einfacher Strukturfunktionen beim Schimpansen und beim Haushuhn. Berlin, 1918. "Abhandlungen der preussischen Akademie der Wissenschaften," No. 2.

44. —— "Zur Theorie des Sukzessivvergleichs und der Zeitfehler," *Psychologische Forschung*, IV (1923), 115–75.

44a. —— "Komplextheorie und Gestalttheorie," *Psychologische Forschung*, VI (1925), 358–416, and "Bemerkungen zur Gestalttheorie," *Psychologische Forschung*, XI (1928), 188–234.

45. ——Gestalt Psychology. New York, Liveright, 1929.

46. —— The Place of Value in a World of Facts. New York, Liveright, 1938.

47. Köhler, W., and H. v. Restorff. "Analyse von Vorgaengen im Spurenfeld, Ueber die Wirkung von Bereichsbildungen im Spurenfeld," by H. v. Restorff, *Psychologische Forschung*, XVIII (1933), 299–342.

48. —— "Zur Theorie der Reproduktion," *Psychologische Forschung*, XXI (1935), 56–112.

49. Koffka, K. The Growth of the Mind. 2d ed. London, New York, Harcourt Brace & Co., 1928. German original published in 1921.

50. ——Principles of Gestalt Psychology. New York, Harcourt Brace & Co., 1935.

51. Kopfermann, H. "Psychologische Untersuchungen ueber die Wirkung zweidimensionaler Darstellungen koerperlicher Gebilde," *Psychologische Forschung*, XIII (1930), 293–364.

52. Kries, J. von. Ueber die materiellen Grundlagen der Bewusstseinserscheinungen. Tuebingen-Leipzig, 1901.

53. Krolik, W. "Ueber Erfahrungswirkungen beim Bewegungssehen," *Psychologische Forschung*, XX (1934), 47–102.

54. Lashley, K. S. Brain Mechanisms and Intelligence. Chicago, 1929.

55. —— Nervous Mechanisms in Learning, in "The Foundations of Experimental Psychology," ed. by C. Murchison. Worcester, Mass., 1929, pp. 524–63.

56. Lauenstein, O. "Ansatz zu einer physiologischen Theorie des Vergleichs und der Zeitfehler," *Psychologische Forschung*, XVII (1932), 130–77.

57. Leary, D. B. Educational Psychology. New York, 1932.

58. Lewin, K. "Das Problem der Willensmessung und der Assoziation." Part I, *Psychologische Forschung,* I (1922), 191–312; Part II, *Psychologische Forschung,* II (1922), 65–140.

59. —————— A Dynamic Theory of Personality. New York, 1935.

60. Luh, C. W. The Conditions of Retention, *Psychological Monographs,* Vol. XXXI (1922), No. 3.

61. McGeoch, G. O. "The Conditions of Reminiscence," *American Journal of Psychology,* XLVII (1935), 65–89.

62. McGeoch, J. A. "Experimental Studies of Memory," in Readings in General Psychology, ed. by Robinson and Robinson. Chicago, 1929, pp. 369–412.

63. —————— "Learning," in Psychology, ed. by Boring, Langfeld, Weld. New York, 1935, pp. 300–43.

64. McGeoch, J. A., and P. L. Whitely. "The Recall of Observed Material," *Journal of Educational Psychology,* XVII (1926), 419–25.

65. McGeoch, J. A., and A. W. Melton. "The Comparative Retention Values of Maze Habits and Nonsense Syllables," *Psychological Bulletin,* XXXVI (1929), 144.

66. Maier, N. R. F. "Reasoning in Humans," Part I, *Journal of Comparative Psychology,* X (1930), 115–43; Part II, *Journal of Comparative Psychology,* XII (1931), 181–94.

67. —————— "Reasoning and Learning," *Psychological Review,* XXXVIII (1931), 332–46.

68. Mann, C. R. The Teaching of Physics. New York, 1912.

69. Metzger, W. Gesetze des Sehens. Frankfurt a.M., 1936.

70. Mueller, G. E., and F. Schumann. "Experimentelle Beitraege zur Untersuchung des Gedaechtnisses," *Zeitschrift fuer Psychologie,* VI (1894), 81, 257.

71. Mueller, G. E., and A. Pilzecker. Experimentelle Beitraege zur Lehre vom Gedaechtnis, Ergaenzungs-Band 1, *Zeitschrift fuer Psychologie.* Leipzig, 1900.

72. Mueller, G. E. Zur Analyse der Gedaechtnistaetigkeit und des Vorstellungsverlaufs, Vol. I, Ergaenzungs-Band 5, *Zeitschrift fuer Psychologie.* Leipzig, 1911.

73. —————— Vol. III, Ergaenzungs-Band 8, *Zeitschrift fuer Psychologie.* Leipzig, 1913.

74. —————— Vol. II, Ergaenzungs-Band 9, *Zeitschrift fuer Psychologie.* Leipzig, 1917.

75. —————— Abriss der Psychologie. Goettingen, 1924.

76. Mursell, J. L. The Psychology of Secondary-School Teaching. Rev. ed. New York, W. W. Norton & Co., 1938.

77. Ogden, R. M. Psychology and Education. New York, 1926.

78. Orata, P. T. The Theory of Identical Elements. Columbus, 1928.
79. Radossawljewitsch, P. R. Das Behalten und Vergessen. Leipzig, 1907.
80. Raffel, G. "The Effect of Recall on Forgetting," *Journal of Experimental Psychology*, XVII (1934), 828–38.
81. Rubin, E. Visuell wahrgenommene Figuren. Kopenhagen, 1921.
82. Ruger, H. A. The Psychology of Efficiency, *Archives of Psychology*, Vol. II (1910), No. 15.
83. Ryan, J. J. "The Learning Process," in An Outline of Educational Psychology, ed. by S. Smith. New York, 1935.
84. Sandiford, P. Educational Psychology. London, New York, 1928.
85. Schultze, A. The Teaching of Mathematics in Secondary Schools. New York, 1924.
86. Semon, R. The Mneme. London, 1921. The German original appeared in 1904.
87. Shepard, G. F., and H. M. Fogelsonger. "Studies in Association and Inhibition," *Psychological Review*, XX (1913), 290–311.
88. Thorndike, E. L., and R. S. Woodworth. "Influence of Improvement in One Mental Function upon the Efficiency of Other Functions," *Psychological Review*, VIII (1901), 247, 384, 553.
89. Thorndike, E. L. The Psychology of Teaching. New York, 1906.
90. ———— The Psychology of Learning, Vol. II of Educational Psychology. New York, 1913.
91. ———— "The Effect of Changed Data upon Reasoning," *Journal of Experimental Psychology*, V (1922), 33–38.
92. ———— The Psychology of Algebra. New York, Macmillan Co., 1923.
93. ———— Human Learning. New York, Appleton-Century Co., 1931.
94. ———— The Fundamentals of Learning. New York, Teachers College, 1932.
95. ———— The Psychology of Wants, Interests and Attitudes. New York, Appleton-Century Co., 1935.
96. Tolman, E. C. Purposive Behavior in Animals and Men. New York, 1932.
97. ———— "The Acquisition of String-Pulling by Rats—Conditioned Response or Sign-Gestalt?" *Psychological Review*, XLIV (1937), 195–212.
98. Ward, L. B. "Reminiscence and Rote Learning," *Psychological Monographs*, Vol. XLIX (1937), No. 220.
99. Watson, J. B. Psychology from the Standpoint of the Behaviorist. Philadelphia, 1919.
100. ———— Behaviorism. New York, 1924.

101. Wertheimer, M. "Ueber das Denken der Naturvoelker," *Zeitschrift fuer Psychologie,* LX (1911), 321–79.

102. ———— "Experimentelle Studien ueber das Sehen von Bewegung," *Zeitschrift fuer Psychologie,* LXI (1912), 161–265.

103. ———— Ueber Schlussprozesse im produktiven Denken, 1920; reprinted in Drei Abhandlungen zur Gestalttheorie, Erlangen, 1925, pp. 164–84.

104. ———— "Untersuchungen zur Lehre von der Gestalt," Part I, *Psychologische Forschung,* I (1921), 47–59.

105. ———— "Untersuchungen zur Lehre von der Gestalt," Part II, *Psychologische Forschung,* IV (1923), 301–50.

106. ———— "Gestaltpsychologische Forschung," in Einfuehrung in die neuere Psychologie, ed. by E. Saupe, 2d ed., pp. 47–54.

107. ———— "Zu dem Problem der Unterscheidung von Einzelinhalt und Teil," *Zeitschrift fuer Psychologie,* MXXIX (1933), 353–57.

108. ———— "Some Problems in the Theory of Ethics," *Social Research,* II (1935), 353–68.

109. Wheeler, R. H. The Science of Psychology. New York, 1929.

110. Wheeler, R. H., and F. T. Perkins. Principles of Mental Development. New York, 1932.

111. Witasek, St. "Assoziation und Gestalteinpraegung," *Zeitschrift fuer Psychologie,* LXXIX (1918), 161–210.

112. Woodworth, R. S. Experimental Psychology. New York, Henry Holt & Co., 1938.

113. Wulf, F. "Ueber die Veraenderung von Vorstellungen," *Psychologische Forschung,* I (1922), 333–89.

114. Zeigarnik, B. "Ueber das Behalten von erledigten und unerledigten Handlungen," *Psychologische Forschung,* IX (1927), 1–85.

INDEX

Aall, A., 305, 306
Abelson, H. H., 274n
Absolute judgment, 294
Abstract-concrete forms of learning, 74, 124, 301
Accentuation, 166 ff., 174, 283, 285, 286
Accumulation, 184 ff., 290
Activity of learner, 36, 299, 300
Adams, D. K., quoted, 158
Affective factors, 230, 306
Allport, G. W., 26, 31n, 112n, 113, 127n, 133
Analytic type learner, 304
"And sums," 27, 72, 249, 258
Animal learning, 156, 158, 246, 251n, 274, 289, 305
Applicability, 8, 45, 48, 55, 155, 199, 239, 254
Applying, see Transfer of training
Arbitrariness, 15n, 27, 72, 232, 252
Articulation, of the material, 166 (see also Grouping); of the perception, 65, 66n, 69, 186, 197n, 245
Association, 3, 25, 164, 238, 242, 246, 249; backward, 283 f.; groups and members, 168 f., 283 f., 286; laws of, 22, 28, 29, 249; mediate, 170 ff.
Associationism, 21-26, 27, 158, 238
Attention, 23, 36, 166, 168n, 299
Attitudes, 118, 149, 292, 296 ff.; and transfer, 133 f.
Availability, of response, 24, 221; of traces, 221-29
Averages (and individual scores), 276 ff.

Bartlett, F. C., 43n, 291, 292
Bean, L. B., 140n
Becher, E., 288
Behaviorism, 21, 24-27, 115; purposive, 30
Belonging, 23, 24, 179, 182 ff.
Binet, A., 178, 217
Bode, B. H., 112
Book, W. F., 139
Brain physiology, 30, 288, 289
Breslich, E. R., 149n

Carr, H. A., 238n, 286
Carrying over, see Transfer of training
Children, learning by, 64, 91, 138, 158, 246
Comparison, 290, 293 f.
Concrete-abstract forms of learning, 26, 114, 124, 301
Conditioned response, 5, 21n, 24, 25, 26, 30, 126n, 246
Connections (bonds), 3-5, 22, 23, 24, 52, 175, 221, 232 ff., 242 f., 252; arbitrary, 16, 27, 232, 252; meaningful, 232 f., 247; senseless, 20, 232 ff., 235, 237 f., 246n, 247, 248
Constructive process of remembering (of reproduction), 15, 43, 118, 149, 162, 198, 213, 254, 291 f., 301
Contour, 65 f.

Dashiell, J. F., 21n
Detour (in learning and solving process), 52n, 72, 125, 244, 254
Differences in learning, 4; individual, 164, 269, 302-5; reliability of, 269-73
Direct practice, 108-11, 126, 128 ff., 174n, 259
Discovery, process of, 13, 50, 51, 53, 61, 75, 299; term defined, 50n
Drill, 5, 103, 150, 250n, 252, 298
Duncker, K., 51n, 244n, 267n
Duo, unum and, 65, 66n, 295

Ebbinghaus, H., 25, 137-44 passim, 162, 163, 165
Educational psychology, relation to educational practice, 255-60
Effect, law of, 300; satisfying aftereffects, 23, 24, 248
Ehrenfels, von, 288
Einstellung, 266, 301 f.
Elements, see Identical elements
Embeddedness, 224-29
English, H. B., quoted, 140-41
Examples, learning by, 58, 75, 82 ff., 88 ff., 116, 125, 132, 254